1st Workshop on Language + Molecules (Lang + Mol 2024)

Bangkok, Thailand
15 August 2024

ISBN: 979-8-3313-0167-5

Printed from e-media with permission by:

Curran Associates, Inc.
57 Morehouse Lane
Red Hook, NY 12571

CURRAN ASSOCIATES INC. proceedings.com

Some format issues inherent in the e-media version may also appear in this print version.

Printed with permission by Curran Associates, Inc. (2025)

Association for Computational Linguistics
209 N. Eighth Street
Stroudsburg, Pennsylvania 18360

Phone: 1-570-476-8006
Fax: 1-570-476-0860

acl@aclweb.org

Additional copies of this publication are available from:

Curran Associates, Inc.
57 Morehouse Lane
Red Hook, NY 12571 USA
Phone: 845-758-0400
Fax: 845-758-2633
Email: curran@proceedings.com
Web: www.proceedings.com

Lang + Mol 2024

The 1st Workshop on Language + Molecules

Proceedings of the Workshop

August 15, 2024

The Lang + Mol organizers gratefully acknowledge the support from the following sponsors.

Gold

Association for Computational Linguistics (ACL)
317 Sidney Baker St. S
Suite 400 - 134
Kerrville, TX 78028
USA
Tel: +1-855-225-1962
acl@aclweb.org

Introduction

Welcome to Language + Molecules, the inaugural workshop on integrating natural language with molecular structure! The workshop is scheduled to be held on August 15, 2024 in Bangkok, Thailand co-located with ACL 2024.

The world faces an enormous number of problems in the coming decades on scales of complexity never-before-seen, in areas such as climate change, healthcare, and pandemics. To address these issues, we need to discover inventive scientific solutions which are scalable, flexible, and inexpensive. Broadly speaking, many of these problems will require molecular solutions from the chemistry domain, such as developing new drugs, materials, and chemical processes. These solutions exist in extremely large search spaces, which makes AI tools a necessity. Excitingly, the chemistry field is posed to be substantially accelerated via multimodal models combining language with molecules and drug structures. Research in scientific NLP, integrating molecules with natural language, and multimodal AI for science/medicine has experienced significant attention and growth in recent months. This workshop was organized to help connect researchers working in this exciting nascent community.

A natural question to ask is why we want to integrate natural language with molecules. Combining these types of information has the possibility to accelerate scientific discovery: imagine a future where a doctor can write a few sentences describing a patient's symptoms and then receive the exact structure of the drugs necessary to treat that patient's ailment (taking into account the patient's genotype, phenotype, and medical history). Or, imagine a world where a researcher can specify the function they want a molecule to perform (e.g., antimalarial or a photovoltaic) rather than its low level properties (e.g., pyridine-containing). This high-level control of molecules requires a method of abstract description, and humans have already developed one for communication: language. The following key benefits of combining language and molecules were explored:

1. Generative Modeling: One of the largest problems in current LLMs—hallucination— becomes a strength for discovering molecules with high-level functions, abstract properties, and composition of many properties.

2. Bridging Modalities: Language can serve as a "bridge" between modalities (e.g., cellular pathways and drugs) when data is scarce.

3. Domain Understanding: Grounding language models into external real world knowledge can improve understanding of unseen molecules and advance many emerging tasks, such as experimental procedure planning and reasoning, which use LLMs as scientific agents.

4. Automation: Instruction-following, dialogue-capable, and tool-equipped models can guide automated discovery in silico and in robotic labs.

5. Democratization: Language enables scientists without computational expertise to leverage advances in scientific AI.

In particular, this year's workshop focused on the following themes:

- Going beyond language to incorporate molecular structure and interactions into LLMs.

- Addressing data scarcity and inconsistency: new training methodologies and methods for extracting data from scientific literature.

- Language-enabled solutions for discovering new drugs and molecules.

- Incorporating domain knowledge from human-constructed databases into LLMs.

- Instruction-following, dialogue-capable, and tool-equipped LLMs for molecules.
- Sequence representations for molecular structures, including organic molecules, proteins, DNA, and inorganic crystals.

The workshop had 27 total submissions, from which 11 papers and 7 shared task descriptions were accepted. Between these categories, 14 accepted submissions opted to be included in the archival proceedings. The shared task had two tracks: molecule generation and molecule captioning. For captioning, there were 28 participants who had a combined total of 188 submissions. For molecule generation, there were 19 participants and 88 submissions. Submissions achieved improvements over base models of up to 27% absolute metric increase for molecule captioning and 13 absolute for molecule generation. An overview of the shared task and submission results will be given at the workshop. This will include the release of the ensembled captioning results for the "mystery molecules".

The workshop will have 5 keynote speakers: Kyunghyun Cho, Elsa Olivetti, Marinka Zitnik, Huan Sun, and Lei Li. Additionally, a poster session, invited oral talks, and a panel discussion on future research directions will be held.

As a final note, we would like to thank the authors, invited speakers, committee members, and our scientific advisory board for helping make this workshop happen. We would like to thank the NSF Molecule Maker Lab Institute for supporting this initiative.

Organizing Committee

Program Chairs

Carl Edwards, University of Illinois Urbana-Champaign
Qingyun Wang, University of Illinois Urbana-Champaign
Manling Li, Northwestern University
Lawrence Zhao, Yale University
Tom Hope, Hebrew University of Jerusalem and Allen Institute for AI
Heng Ji, University of Illinois Urbana-Champaign

Program Committee

Area Chairs

Carl Edwards, University of Illinois Urbana-Champaign
Qingyun Wang, University of Illinois Urbana Champaign
Lijun Wu, ByteDance
Yaochen Xie, Amazon

Reviewers

Ralph Abboud
Chufan Gao
Giorgio Giannone
Zhihui Guo
Chi Han
Anna Hart
Jeonghwan Kim
Tuan Lai
Weijiang Li
Xuan Liu
Zequn Liu
Ziteng Liu
Ziqian Luo
Thao Nguyen
Siru Ouyang
Qizhi Pei
Brandon Philip Theodorou
Ziqi Wang
Azmine Toushik Wasi
Pengfei Yu

Invited Speakers

Kyunghyun Cho, New York University and Genentech
Elsa Olivetti, Massachusetts Institute of Technology
Marinka Zitnik, Harvard
Huan Sun, The Ohio State University
Lei Li, Carnegie Mellon University

Table of Contents

Program

Thursday, August 15, 2024

09:00 - 09:10	*Opening Remarks*
09:10 - 09:40	*Invited Talk 1*
09:40 - 10:10	*Invited Talk 2*
10:10 - 10:40	*Invited Talk 3*
10:40 - 11:00	*Coffee Break*
11:00 - 11:20	*Shared Task Overview*
11:30 - 12:30	*Oral Presentations*
12:30 - 13:30	*Lunch Break*
13:30 - 14:05	*Invited Talk 4*
14:05 - 14:40	*Invited Talk 5*
14:40 - 15:30	*Panel Discussion*
15:30 - 16:00	*Coffee Break*
16:00 - 17:15	*Poster Session*
17:15 - 17:30	*Closing Remarks*

L+M-24: Building a Dataset for Language+Molecules @ ACL 2024

Carl Edwards[1], **Qingyun Wang**[1], **Lawrence Zhao**[2] and **Heng Ji**[1]
[1]University of Illinois Urbana-Champaign [2]Yale University
{cne2, qingyun4, hengji}@illinois.edu, larry.zhao@yale.edu

Abstract

Language-molecule models have emerged as an exciting direction for molecular discovery and understanding. However, training these models is challenging due to the scarcity of molecule-language pair datasets. At this point, datasets have been released which are 1) small and scraped from existing databases, 2) large but noisy and constructed by performing entity linking on the scientific literature, and 3) built by converting property prediction datasets to natural language using templates. In this document, we detail the *L+M-24* dataset, which has been created for the Language + Molecules Workshop shared task at ACL 2024. In particular, *L+M-24* is designed to focus on three key benefits of natural language in molecule design: compositionality, functionality, and abstraction.[1]

1 Introduction

The world faces an enormous number of problems in the coming decades on scales of complexity never-before-seen, in areas such as climate change, healthcare, and pandemics. To address these issues, we need to discover inventive scientific solutions which are scalable, flexible, and inexpensive. Broadly speaking, many of these problems will require molecular solutions from the chemistry domain, such as developing new drugs (e.g. kinase inhibitors (Ferguson and Gray, 2018)), materials (e.g. organic photovoltaics (Kippelen and Brédas, 2009)), and chemical processes (Zhong et al., 2023). These solutions exist in extremely large search spaces, which makes AI tools a necessity.

Language-molecule models have emerged as an exciting direction for molecular discovery and understanding (Edwards et al., 2021; Zeng et al., 2022; Edwards et al., 2022; Su et al., 2022; Liu et al., 2022; Xu et al., 2023; Christofidellis et al., 2023; Liu et al., 2023b; Luo et al., 2023; Zhao et al., 2023c; Seidl et al., 2023). However, training these models is challenging due to the scarcity of molecule-language pair datasets. At this point, datasets have been released which are 1) small and scraped from existing databases (Edwards et al., 2021; Zeng et al., 2023; Liu et al., 2023a,c; Pei et al., 2023), 2) large but noisy and constructed by performing entity linking on the scientific literature (Zeng et al., 2022; Su et al., 2022), and 3) template-based built on prediction datasets (Zhao et al., 2023a; Fang et al., 2023). Approaches utilizing pseudo-data have also been attempted (Chen et al., 2023a). These approaches have helped remedy the problem of data scarcity in this domain; however, these approaches frequently ignore key benefits of natural language: 1) compositionality, 2) abstraction, and 3) functionality (Zhang et al., 2023). To this end, for the Language + Molecules Workshop at ACL 2024, we release *L+M-24*, which we construct to test these three goals, particularly compositionality, using recently released data sources (Zhao et al., 2023b; Kosonocky et al., 2023; Wishart et al., 2023). *L+M-24* is divided into four categories with important applications in the small-molecule domain: 1) Biomedical, 2) Light and Electricity, 3) Human Interaction and Organoleptics, and 4) Agriculture and Industry. Improving understanding of these applications can have important implications in problems such as drug discovery, climate issues, more efficient and green industrial processes, and improved food production.

2 Task Formulation

The dataset is primarily intended for language↔molecule translation, which consists of two tasks: generating 1) a caption given a molecule and 2) a molecule given a description.

[1]The dataset, finetuned baseline, and evaluation code are released publicly at github.com/language-plus-molecules/LPM-24-Dataset through HuggingFace.

Proceedings of the 1st Workshop on Language + Molecules (L+M 2024), pages 1–10
August 15, 2024 ©2024 Association for Computational Linguistics

2.1 Designing for Compositionality, Abstraction, and Function

Overall, we focused on four primary categories of importance: 1) Biomedical, 2) Light and Electricity, 3) Human Interaction and Organoleptics, and 4) Agriculture and Industry. These categories and three properties from each are displayed in Table 1. The biomedical category is focused on drug properties, functions, and interaction with proteins. Light and electricity is focused on the ability for a molecule to produce or absorb light or electricity. Human interaction and organoleptics focuses on the effect and experience molecules cause in humans. Agriculture and industry focuses on molecules used in industrial processes and food production.

Based on our data sources (below), the properties we have selected already encode a large degree of functionality, enhanced by our manual curation. Further, since these properties are generally short phrases indicating functionality, they are also abstract and apply to many molecules (e.g., "insecticide"). For compositionality, we explicitly select certain pairs of properties which we hold out of the dataset. For example, a molecule may share two properties which are desirable together (e.g., low toxicity and fungicidal). *L+M-24* will help to evaluate whether model's can generalize to unseen compositions of properties.

Biomedical	**Human Interaction**
anti neoplastic	pungent
glaucoma treatment	bitter
capillarigenic	nephrotoxic
Light and Electricity	**Agriculture and Industry**
photoelectric conversion	herbicide
photopolymerization	emulsifier
dielectric	carcinogen

Table 1: Example properties in the dataset. Antineoplastic drugs are used to treat cancer. Glaucoma is a group of eye diseases. Capillarigenic means producing or causing capillaries. Pungent means having a strong taste or smell. Nephrotoxic is toxicity in the kidneys. Photoelectric conversion is the conversion of light into electricity. Photopolymerization is the process through which monomers are linked together through a photochemical reaction. A dielectric is a poor conductor of electricity but can be polarized. A herbidicde is toxic to plants. An emulsifier stabilizes an emulsion. A carcinogen is an agent capable of causing cancer. The full property list and number of occurrences is available in the online data repository.

3 Data Sources

We constructed our dataset using three different databases. We will first describe the process we used to extract information from each, followed by our overall strategy for adding hierarchy into the dataset. We want to deeply thank the authors of these resources for making them publicly available for the community.

3.1 PubChem

We used properties extracted from PubChem (Kim et al., 2016, 2019) as described in (Zhao et al., 2023c). Properties from this approach include odor, taste, and decomposition. We note these properties consist of molecule-specific descriptions, which the other data sources do not provide.

3.2 Chemical Function (CheF)

Here, we used functional properties extracted from patent literature by Kosonocky et al. (2023). This allowed us to capture molecules from the patent literature in addition to the scientific literature. Here, we started with CheF prefinal_v3[2]. We created a set of properties from both CheF's property summarizations and from the ChatGPT summarization source. For the summarization source, we also applied the WordNet lemmatizer (Bird et al., 2009) for deduplication. After obtaining a list of properties, we removed properties pertaining to less than 100 molecules. We then kept properties falling into the categories of "X-icide", "anti-X", "X treatment", "X modulators", "X inhibitors", "X agonists", "X antagonists", "light", and "electricity." We manually removed uninformative labels which were too broad or didn't describe enough function. Further, we manually corrected errors in label naming and duplication.

3.3 ChemFOnt: the chemical functional ontology resource

In addition to CheF, we also take advantage of another new chemical function data resource: ChemFOnt (Wishart et al., 2023). From this datasource, we collect three categories: health effect relations, organoleptic effect relations, and role relations.

4 Dataset Details

To convert these properties to natural language, we follow a template-based procedure using GPT-4 (OpenAI, 2023) generated compositional templates.

[2]obtained via personal communication.

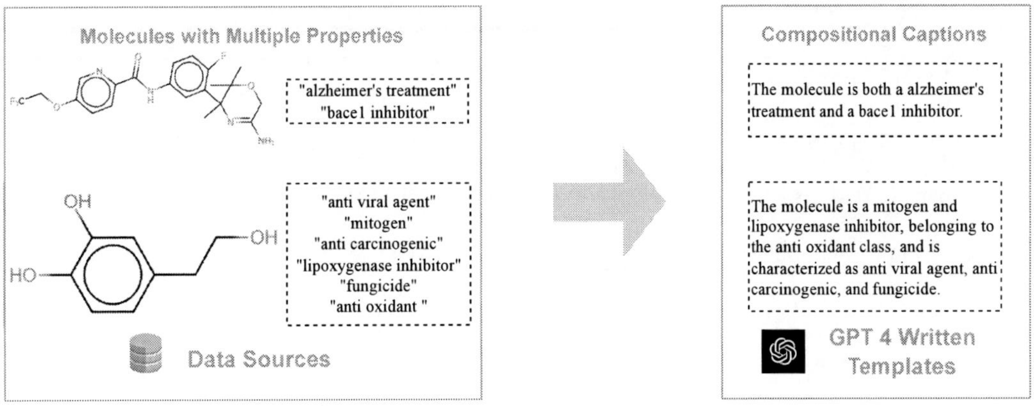

Figure 1: Example descriptions created for molecules from the training set.

4.1 Template Generation

We utilize GPT-4 (OpenAI, 2023) to generate specific templates for each combinations of molecular properties. Specifically, we manually write six templates: "*The molecule is a <0>.*"; "*It belongs to the <1> class of molecules.*"; "*It has an effect on <2>.*"; "*It impacts <3>.*"; "*The molecule is <4>.*"; and "*The molecule has a <5>.*". Subsequently, we use GPT-4 to generate a unique sentence template for each possible combination by rephrasing up to six combinations of the six initial templates as a single sentence. Ultimately, this process results in the generation of 917 distinct templates. The templates were manually checked and corrected to have a matching standard. The prompts and in-context examples for GPT-4 are given in the Appendix.

4.2 Converting Templates to Descriptions

For all properties in *L+M-24*, we first assigned them to possible templates based on their category or by individual consideration. Certain properties (e.g., polymerization, decomposition) were expressed in sentence format, so we did not use templates. Given a molecule with n properties, we first looked for a template that had the correct slots (e.g., <0>, <2>, and <2>) for its properties. When we found possible templates, we picked one at random and used it to generate a sentence for the molecule's properties. If there were no matching templates, we split the properties into two separate equal-sized groups and tried with each group. We return the concatenation of the two sentence templates as the molecule description. Note this process can repeat multiple times.

We note that we are also releasing a version of the dataset with 5 captions for each molecule. In this case, we split group sizes at random. Further, we split sentences apart 50% of the time (even when there were matching templates) to increase caption diversity.

4.3 Splitting

Duplicate molecules are merged using RDKit (Landrum, 2021) and molecules which cannot be processed are removed. We split the data by first examining property combinations. 20% of combinations are witheld into the evaluation set. From molecules in the remaining 80%, we keep 80% for training and put 20% in evaluation. The evaluation set is split into two tasks: molecule captioning and molecule generation. For each task, only one modality will be released prior to the shared task results.

The training set consists of 160,492 molecule-description pairs. For the evaluation set, both molecule generation and captioning contain 21,839 pairs. Further, special splits are released for the training set which allow for validation using the training data. They are constructed using the same procedure as the official evaluation dataset.

5 Evaluation Metrics

Overall, we adopt the evaluation metrics proposed by Edwards et al. (2022). However, we include invalid molecules in the calculations of FTS metrics (setting the score to zero for invalid molecules). We also add a uniqueness metric to the generated molecules for held-out combinations of properties (Polykovskiy et al., 2020). Further, we also look at property-specific precision, recall, and F-1 scores. These scores are calculated by matching tokenized names in the generated captions. These scores are

Model	BLEU-2	BLEU-4	ROUGE-1	ROUGE-2	ROUGE-L	METEOR	Text2Mol
Ground Truth							11.30
MolT5-Small	70.9	51.2	74.5	55.8	54.4	70.1	10.79
MolT5-Base	73.8	53.5	75.0	55.9	53.9	71.8	8.53
MolT5-Large	76.9	55.6	77.7	58.0	55.7	74.3	10.06
Meditron-7B	79.2	57.6	79.7	60.2	57.5	75.7	11.91

Table 2: Molecule captioning results on the validation split of *L+M-24*. Rouge scores are F1 values.

Model	Overall			Biomedical			Light+Electro			Human Interaction			Agr.+Industry			Held-out Combos		
	P	R	F-1	P	R	F-1	P	R	F-1	P	R	F-1	P	R	F-1	P	R	F-1
MolT5-Small	84.83	8.24	7.88	85.13	23.23	23.33	62.42	4.85	3.27	96.77	0.57	0.56	95.00	4.32	4.36	0.00	0.00	0.00
MolT5-Base	64.11	9.94	9.46	79.58	23.89	24.02	16.08	5.82	3.36	63.94	5.01	5.18	96.85	5.05	5.27	0.00	0.00	0.00
MolT5-Large	59.57	12.49	11.71	70.27	26.99	26.87	16.96	10.90	7.39	62.77	5.99	6.27	88.29	6.06	6.31	0.00	0.00	0.00
Meditron-7B	33.60	16.33	16.81	57.19	33.96	35.27	26.51	16.48	17.49	29.54	7.52	7.07	21.18	7.35	7.40	12.35	0.29	0.56

Table 3: Property-specific molecule captioning results on the validation split of *L+M-24*.

Model	P	R	F-1	P	R	F-1	P	R	F-1	P	R	F-1	P	R	F-1	P	R	F-1
	X-icides			**Toxins**			**Light**			**Electricity**			**X-inhibitors**			**anti-X**		
MolT5-Small	100.00	0.00	0.00	100.00	0.00	0.00	24.85	9.69	6.54	100.00	0.00	0.00	3.42	0.43	0.09	1.96	0.00	0.00
MolT5-Base	100.00	0.00	0.00	67.45	8.51	8.84	28.00	11.51	6.52	4.17	0.12	0.20	2.20	0.58	0.11	9.70	0.23	0.15
MolT5-Large	100.00	0.00	0.00	69.42	10.29	10.85	15.77	12.28	8.16	18.14	9.52	6.62	8.90	2.28	1.13	4.32	1.16	0.61
Meditron-7B	100.00	0.00	0.00	48.79	11.75	11.05	29.10	20.64	20.64	23.93	12.33	14.34	35.69	19.91	22.65	14.79	9.34	8.98
	X-modulator			**X-agonist**			**X-antagonist**			**X-treatment**			**X-disease**			**X cancer**		
MolT5-Small	100.00	0.00	0.00	100.00	0.00	0.00	100.00	0.00	0.00	55.49	1.99	1.70	87.44	50.08	49.94	71.86	21.03	24.27
MolT5-Base	100.00	0.00	0.00	100.00	0.00	0.00	100.00	0.00	0.00	58.90	2.25	1.80	94.61	55.16	59.18	45.06	25.49	24.54
MolT5-Large	21.30	0.58	0.88	5.91	1.96	1.23	14.30	0.58	0.42	14.27	2.67	2.22	97.18	81.07	81.86	65.76	52.06	51.56
Meditron-7B	42.43	21.24	24.98	39.19	23.23	26.35	34.22	18.98	21.15	28.75	11.35	15.13	97.34	81.11	82.02	79.80	68.65	72.62

Table 4: Selected subproperty group-specific molecule captioning results on the validation split of *L+M-24*.

Model	BLEU↑	Exact↑	Levenshtein↓	MACCS FTS↑	RDK FTS↑	Morgan FTS↑	FCD↓	Text2Mol↑	Validity↑
Ground Truth	100.0	100.0	0.00	100.0	100.0	100.0	0.00	11.26	100.0
MolT5-Small	56.56	0.00	56.34	64.22	58.10	37.44	NaN	0.49	80.52
MolT5-Base	68.38	0.00	44.79	76.03	65.23	47.46	NaN	7.06	100.0
MolT5-Large	56.42	0.00	55.40	75.70	65.01	39.51	17.52	7.69	99.44
Meditron-7B	69.40	0.01	46.49	77.16	69.34	50.07	2.46	7.80	99.63

Table 5: Molecule generation results on the validation split of *L+M-24*. The FCD and Text2mol metrics are computed using only syntactically valid molecules. We found FCD suffers from numerical instability for the small and base models.

Model	BLEU↑	Exact↑	Levenshtein↓	MACCS FTS↑	RDK FTS↑	Morgan FTS↑	FCD↓	Text2Mol↑	Uniqueness↑	Validity↑
Ground Truth	100.0	100.0	0.00	100.0	100.0	100.0	0.0	23.05	100.0	100.0
MolT5-Small	22.80	0.00	54.14	8.99	5.19	3.48	NaN	5.79	10.14	39.79
MolT5-Base	29.51	0.00	48.91	38.78	19.73	14.21	NaN	21.60	5.13	100.0
MolT5-Large	24.37	0.00	63.44	41.56	24.23	15.71	NaN	23.77	12.72	97.82
Meditron-7B	28.04	0.00	53.44	40.90	27.42	16.82	3.91	22.46	74.81	98.58

Table 6: Molecule generation results on the subset of held-out combinations from the validation split of *L+M-24* (2107 data points).

further aggregated across specific properties (e.g., inhibitors, X-icides, etc.) and the four broad categories. Aggregations are performed by averaging scores (i.e., macro-F1). We further compute these scores specifically for held-out combinations of properties.

6 Benchmarks

MolT5 models (Edwards et al., 2022) were finetuned for 20 epochs on the "split_train" data split and evaluated on the "split_valid", both of which are available online. Huggingface's transformers (Wolf et al., 2019) was used for finetuning with a learning rate of 2e-5 and weight decay of 0.01. A batch size of 128 was used for small and base models, and a batch size of 48 for large models. Further, Meditron-7B (Chen et al., 2023b) was finetuned for 5 epochs with a context length of 930, 2e-6 learning rate, and batch size of 8/16 (molecule/caption generation). Models are released online. Results for captioning are reported in Tables 2, 3 and 4. Tables 5, and 6 shows results for molecule generation.

Overall, the dataset proves to be fairly challenging for these naively finetuned models. On captioning, Meditron-7B achieves a maximum overall F-1 score of 16.81 for property identification (Table 3). However, overall it has a much higher precision than recall, indicating the model only labels

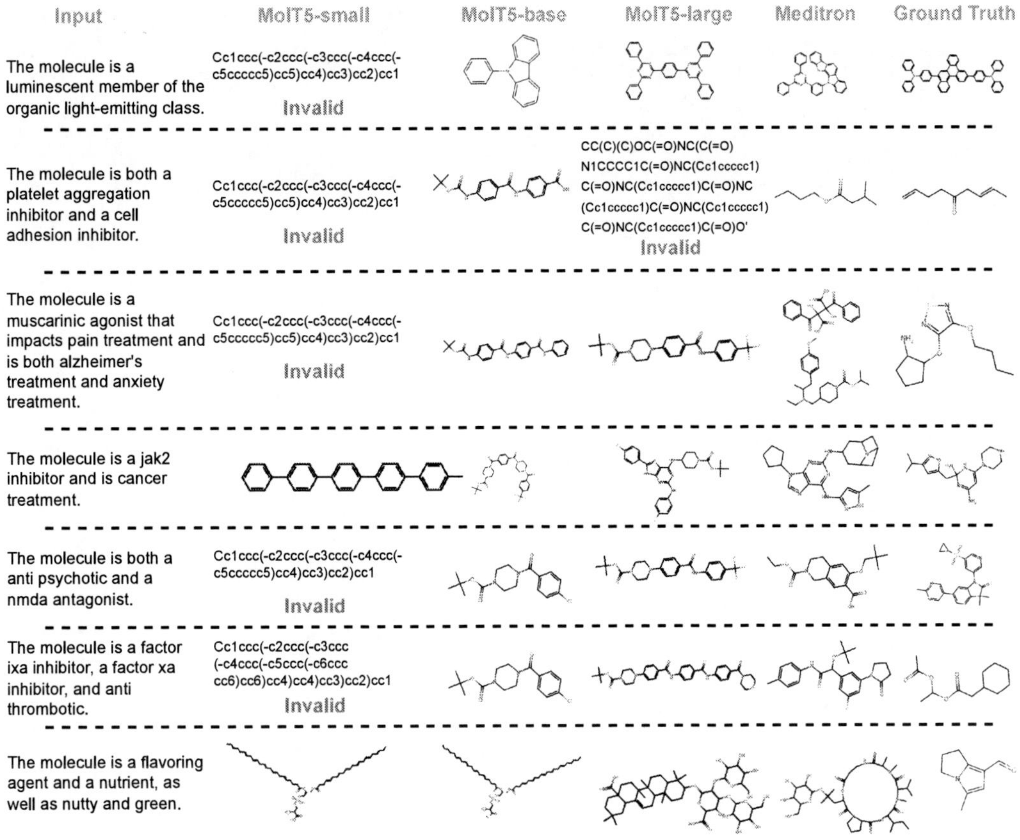

Figure 2: Examples of molecules generated by different models for never-before-seen property combinations.

a molecule with a certain property when having higher confidence. Certain classes of molecules, such as X-icides, are never identified (Table 4). Other classes, such as toxins or electricity, show emergent behavior as model size scales. Interestingly, the models appear to be fairly capable at linking molecules to certain diseases or cancers. We find that, likely due to poor performance on individual properties, only the largest model succeeds on predicting held-out combos, and with poor results. Additionally, we find that the Text2Mol metric, as trained on ChEBI-20, shows poor domain transfer to *L+M-24*.

The models are able to capture a number of useful properties, such as electroluminescence, diabetes treatment, non-alcoholic fatty liver disease, and emulsifiers. In some cases, the model captures important characteristics about the molecule but uses differing language. This poses a challenge for our evaluation metrics. For example, a molecule identified in the ground truth as an anti tumor agent is identified as being a cancer treatment by the model. In particular, the models appear to struggle with rarer properties, which are common in our dataset formulation and in the chemical domain as a whole. They also struggle with identifying molecule-protein interactions (e.g., "monoamine reuptake inhibitor"), although Meditron shows a large performance jump.

For the molecule generation task, we also find the dataset to be challenging. We show results generated by different models on never-before-seen property combinations in Figures 2 and 3. We believe the difficulty is for two reasons. First, common property combinations may have structurally very different molecules which exhibit those properties, making evaluation difficult. Second, the model may not grasp rare properties well. Overall, this results in the naively finetuned models producing similar outputs to many different prompts. Further, as expected, performance falls on unseen property combinations and larger models prove

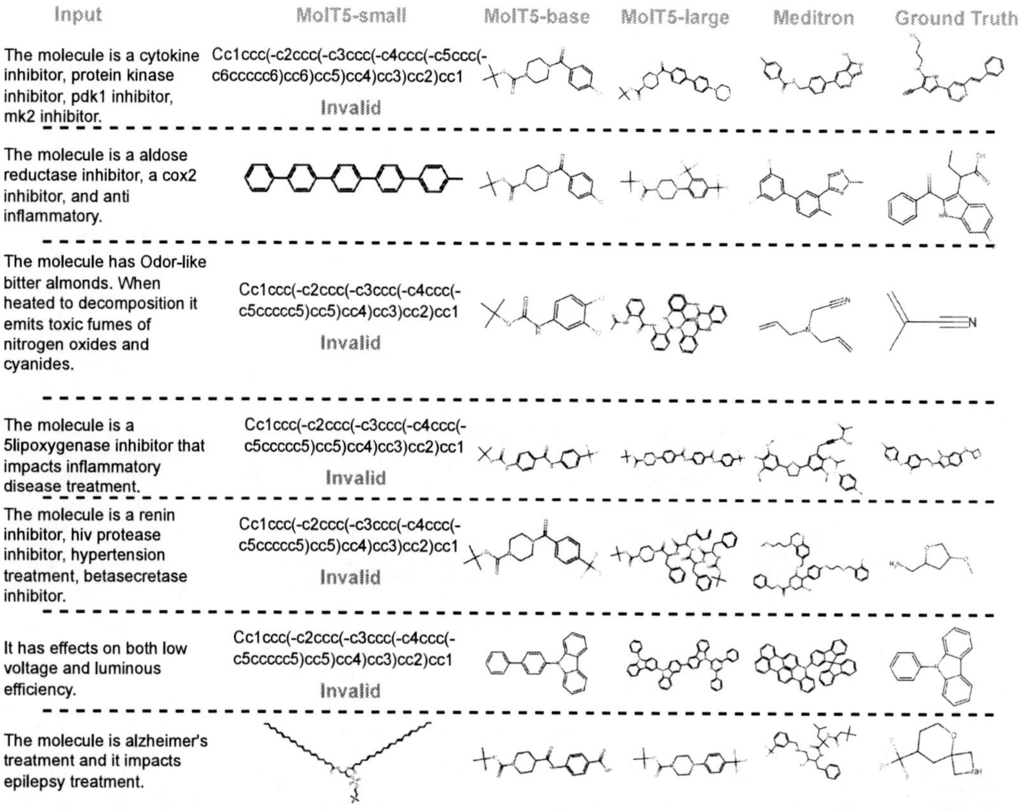

Figure 3: Examples of molecules generated by different models for never-before-seen property combinations.

more effective (Table 6).

7 Future Directions

Overall, this dataset proves to be quite challenging. We find that some specific properties in particular are challenging for the model. This may be because the model understands these properties, but is unwilling to use them in its descriptions due to the training procedure. This limitation may be addressed with more sophisticated decoding algorithms or by better finetuning methods. Future work will also likely benefit from incorporating other modalities, such as proteins, to provide better understanding to the model for some property types. Notably, certain properties display what may be emergent behavior; scaling training data or model size may yield non-linear improvements.

In this dataset, we focus on composition, abstraction, and function. Future work may also wish to integrate other recent trends: instruction-following and dialogue (Fang et al., 2023; Cao et al., 2023; Zeng et al., 2023; Zhao et al., 2024; Zhang et al., 2024; Yu et al., 2024), tool use (Boiko et al., 2023; Bran et al., 2023), additional molecule representations (e.g., 3D (Tang et al., 2023)), additional modalities (Xu et al., 2023), or molecule editing (Su et al., 2022). Further, we note the need for improved evaluation metrics, especially in the case of molecule generation for function where there may be many possible outputs. Specific methods for improving compositionality may be another fruitful avenue for research (Yellinek et al., 2023). It may also be interesting to use molecule-language instruction-following models within larger search frameworks, such as ChemReasoner (Sprueill et al., 2023, 2024).

8 Conclusion

In this manuscript, we describe the process for creating the *L+M-24* dataset. *L+M-24* is designed to focus on three key benefits of natural language in molecule design: compositionality, functionality, and abstraction. It is the featured shared task at the First Language + Molecules Workshop at ACL 2024.

Acknowledgements

We would like to thank the authors and creators of our data sources for freely allowing the use of their work. We would like to acknowledge NVIDIA Corporation's contributions to this work through a grant of NVIDIA A100 Tensor Core GPUs. This work is supported by the Molecule Maker Lab Institute: an AI research institute program supported by NSF under award No. 2019897, by DOE Center for Advanced Bioenergy and Bioproducts Innovation U.S. Department of Energy, Office of Science, Office of Biological and Environmental Research under Award Number DESC0018420, and by AI Algriculture: the Agriculture and Food Research Initiative (AFRI) grant no. 2020-67021- 32799/project accession no.1024178 from the USDA National Institute of Food and Agriculture. The views and conclusions contained herein are those of the authors and should not be interpreted as necessarily representing the official policies, either expressed or implied of, the National Science Foundation, the U.S. Department of Energy, and the U.S. Government. The U.S. Government is authorized to reproduce and distribute reprints for governmental purposes notwithstanding any copyright annotation therein.

References

Steven Bird, Ewan Klein, and Edward Loper. 2009. *Natural language processing with Python: analyzing text with the natural language toolkit.* " O'Reilly Media, Inc.".

Daniil A Boiko, Robert MacKnight, and Gabe Gomes. 2023. Emergent autonomous scientific research capabilities of large language models. *ArXiv preprint*, abs/2304.05332.

Andres M Bran, Sam Cox, Andrew D White, and Philippe Schwaller. 2023. Chemcrow: Augmenting large-language models with chemistry tools. *arXiv preprint arXiv:2304.05376*.

He Cao, Zijing Liu, Xingyu Lu, Yuan Yao, and Yu Li. 2023. Instructmol: Multi-modal integration for building a versatile and reliable molecular assistant in drug discovery. *arXiv preprint arXiv:2311.16208*.

Yuhan Chen, Nuwa Xi, Yanrui Du, Haochun Wang, Chen Jianyu, Sendong Zhao, and Bing Qin. 2023a. From artificially real to real: Leveraging pseudo data from large language models for low-resource molecule discovery. *arXiv preprint arXiv:2309.05203*.

Zeming Chen, Alejandro Hernández Cano, Angelika Romanou, Antoine Bonnet, Kyle Matoba, Francesco Salvi, Matteo Pagliardini, Simin Fan, Andreas Köpf, Amirkeivan Mohtashami, et al. 2023b. Meditron-70b: Scaling medical pretraining for large language models. *arXiv preprint arXiv:2311.16079*.

Dimitrios Christofidellis, Giorgio Giannone, Jannis Born, Ole Winther, Teodoro Laino, and Matteo Manica. 2023. Unifying molecular and textual representations via multi-task language modelling. *arXiv preprint arXiv:2301.12586*.

Carl Edwards, Tuan Lai, Kevin Ros, Garrett Honke, Kyunghyun Cho, and Heng Ji. 2022. Translation between molecules and natural language. In *Proceedings of the 2022 Conference on Empirical Methods in Natural Language Processing*, pages 375–413, Abu Dhabi, United Arab Emirates. Association for Computational Linguistics.

Carl Edwards, ChengXiang Zhai, and Heng Ji. 2021. Text2Mol: Cross-modal molecule retrieval with natural language queries. In *Proceedings of the 2021 Conference on Empirical Methods in Natural Language Processing*, pages 595–607, Online and Punta Cana, Dominican Republic. Association for Computational Linguistics.

Yin Fang, Xiaozhuan Liang, Ningyu Zhang, Kangwei Liu, Rui Huang, Zhuo Chen, Xiaohui Fan, and Huajun Chen. 2023. Mol-instructions: A large-scale biomolecular instruction dataset for large language models. *arXiv preprint arXiv:2306.08018*.

Fleur M Ferguson and Nathanael S Gray. 2018. Kinase inhibitors: the road ahead. *Nature reviews Drug discovery*, 17(5):353–377.

Sunghwan Kim, Jie Chen, Tiejun Cheng, Asta Gindulyte, Jia He, Siqian He, Qingliang Li, Benjamin A. Shoemaker, Paul A. Thiessen, Bo Yu, et al. 2019. Pubchem 2019 update: improved access to chemical data. *Nucleic acids research*, 47(D1):D1102–D1109.

Sunghwan Kim, Paul A. Thiessen, Evan E. Bolton, Jie Chen, Gang Fu, Asta Gindulyte, Lianyi Han, Jane He, Siqian He, Benjamin A. Shoemaker, et al. 2016. Pubchem substance and compound databases. *Nucleic acids research*, 44(D1):D1202–D1213.

Bernard Kippelen and Jean-Luc Brédas. 2009. Organic photovoltaics. *Energy & Environmental Science*, 2(3):251–261.

Clayton W Kosonocky, Claus O Wilke, Edward M Marcotte, and Andrew D Ellington. 2023. Mining patents with large language models demonstrates congruence of functional labels and chemical structures. *arXiv preprint arXiv:2309.08765*.

Greg Landrum. 2021. Rdkit: Open-source cheminformatics software.

Pengfei Liu, Yiming Ren, and Zhixiang Ren. 2023a. Git-mol: A multi-modal large language model for molecular science with graph, image, and text. *arXiv preprint arXiv:2308.06911*.

Shengchao Liu, Weili Nie, Chengpeng Wang, Jiarui Lu, Zhuoran Qiao, Ling Liu, Jian Tang, Chaowei Xiao, and Anima Anandkumar. 2022. Multi-modal molecule structure-text model for text-based retrieval and editing. *arXiv preprint arXiv:2212.10789*.

Zequn Liu, Wei Zhang, Yingce Xia, Lijun Wu, Shufang Xie, Tao Qin, Ming Zhang, and Tie-Yan Liu. 2023b. Molxpt: Wrapping molecules with text for generative pre-training. *arXiv preprint arXiv:2305.10688*.

Zhiyuan Liu, Sihang Li, Yanchen Luo, Hao Fei, Yixin Cao, Kenji Kawaguchi, Xiang Wang, and Tat-Seng Chua. 2023c. Molca: Molecular graph-language modeling with cross-modal projector and uni-modal adapter. *arXiv preprint arXiv:2310.12798*.

Yizhen Luo, Kai Yang, Massimo Hong, Xingyi Liu, and Zaiqing Nie. 2023. Molfm: A multimodal molecular foundation model. *arXiv preprint arXiv:2307.09484*.

OpenAI. 2023. Gpt-4 technical report. *ArXiv preprint*, abs/2303.08774.

Qizhi Pei, Wei Zhang, Jinhua Zhu, Kehan Wu, Kaiyuan Gao, Lijun Wu, Yingce Xia, and Rui Yan. 2023. Biot5: Enriching cross-modal integration in biology with chemical knowledge and natural language associations. *arXiv preprint arXiv:2310.07276*.

Daniil Polykovskiy, Alexander Zhebrak, Benjamin Sanchez-Lengeling, Sergey Golovanov, Oktai Tatanov, Stanislav Belyaev, Rauf Kurbanov, Aleksey Artamonov, Vladimir Aladinskiy, Mark Veselov, et al. 2020. Molecular sets (moses): a benchmarking platform for molecular generation models. *Frontiers in pharmacology*, 11:1931.

Philipp Seidl, Andreu Vall, Sepp Hochreiter, and Günter Klambauer. 2023. Enhancing activity prediction models in drug discovery with the ability to understand human language. *ArXiv preprint*, abs/2303.03363.

Henry W Sprueill, Carl Edwards, Khushbu Agarwal, Mariefel V Olarte, Udishnu Sanyal, Conrad Johnston, Hongbin Liu, Heng Ji, and Sutanay Choudhury. 2024. Chemreasoner: Heuristic search over a large language model's knowledge space using quantum-chemical feedback. *arXiv preprint arXiv:2402.10980*.

Henry W Sprueill, Carl Edwards, Mariefel V Olarte, Udishnu Sanyal, Heng Ji, and Sutanay Choudhury. 2023. Monte carlo thought search: Large language model querying for complex scientific reasoning in catalyst design. *arXiv preprint arXiv:2310.14420*.

Bing Su, Dazhao Du, Zhao Yang, Yujie Zhou, Jiangmeng Li, Anyi Rao, Hao Sun, Zhiwu Lu, and Ji-Rong Wen. 2022. A molecular multimodal foundation model associating molecule graphs with natural language. *ArXiv preprint*, abs/2209.05481.

Xiangru Tang, Andrew Tran, Jeffrey Tan, and Mark B Gerstein. 2023. Mollm: A unified language model to integrate biomedical text with 2d and 3d molecular representations. *bioRxiv*, pages 2023–11.

David S Wishart, Sagan Girod, Harrison Peters, Eponine Oler, Juan Jovel, Zachary Budinski, Ralph Milford, Vicki W Lui, Zinat Sayeeda, Robert Mah, et al. 2023. Chemfont: the chemical functional ontology resource. *Nucleic Acids Research*, 51(D1):D1220–D1229.

Thomas Wolf, Lysandre Debut, Victor Sanh, Julien Chaumond, Clement Delangue, Anthony Moi, Pierric Cistac, Tim Rault, Rémi Louf, Morgan Funtowicz, et al. 2019. Huggingface's transformers: State-of-the-art natural language processing. *arXiv preprint arXiv:1910.03771*.

Hanwen Xu, Addie Woicik, Hoifung Poon, Russ B Altman, and Sheng Wang. 2023. Multilingual translation for zero-shot biomedical classification using biotranslator. *Nature Communications*, 14(1):738.

Nir Yellinek, Leonid Karlinsky, and Raja Giryes. 2023. 3vl: using trees to teach vision & language models compositional concepts. *arXiv preprint arXiv:2312.17345*.

Botao Yu, Frazier N Baker, Ziqi Chen, Xia Ning, and Huan Sun. 2024. Llasmol: Advancing large language models for chemistry with a large-scale, comprehensive, high-quality instruction tuning dataset. *arXiv preprint arXiv:2402.09391*.

Zheni Zeng, Bangchen Yin, Shipeng Wang, Jiarui Liu, Cheng Yang, Haishen Yao, Xingzhi Sun, Maosong Sun, Guotong Xie, and Zhiyuan Liu. 2023. Interactive molecular discovery with natural language. *arXiv preprint arXiv:2306.11976*.

Zijie Zeng, Xinyu Li, Dragan Gasevic, and Guanliang Chen. 2022. Do deep neural nets display human-like attention in short answer scoring? In *Proceedings of the 2022 Conference of the North American Chapter of the Association for Computational Linguistics: Human Language Technologies*, pages 191–205, Seattle, United States. Association for Computational Linguistics.

Di Zhang, Wei Liu, Qian Tan, Jingdan Chen, Hang Yan, Yuliang Yan, Jiatong Li, Weiran Huang, Xiangyu Yue, Dongzhan Zhou, et al. 2024. Chemllm: A chemical large language model. *arXiv preprint arXiv:2402.06852*.

Xuan Zhang, Limei Wang, Jacob Helwig, Youzhi Luo, Cong Fu, Yaochen Xie, Meng Liu, Yuchao Lin, Zhao Xu, Keqiang Yan, et al. 2023. Artificial intelligence for science in quantum, atomistic, and continuum systems. *arXiv preprint arXiv:2307.08423*.

Haiteng Zhao, Shengchao Liu, Chang Ma, Hannan Xu, Jie Fu, Zhi-Hong Deng, Lingpeng Kong, and Qi Liu. 2023a. Gimlet: A unified graph-text model for instruction-based molecule zero-shot learning. *bioRxiv*, pages 2023–05.

Lawrence Zhao, Carl Edwards, and Heng Ji. 2023b. What a scientific language model knows and doesn't know about chemistry. In *NeurIPS 2023 AI for Science Workshop*.

Wenyu Zhao, Dong Zhou, Buqing Cao, Kai Zhang, and Jinjun Chen. 2023c. Adversarial modality alignment network for cross-modal molecule retrieval. *IEEE Transactions on Artificial Intelligence*.

Zihan Zhao, Da Ma, Lu Chen, Liangtai Sun, Zihao Li, Hongshen Xu, Zichen Zhu, Su Zhu, Shuai Fan, Guodong Shen, et al. 2024. Chemdfm: Dialogue foundation model for chemistry. *arXiv preprint arXiv:2401.14818*.

Ming Zhong, Siru Ouyang, Yizhu Jiao, Priyanka Kargupta, Leo Luo, Yanzhen Shen, Bobby Zhou, Xianrui Zhong, Xuan Liu, Hongxiang Li, Jinfeng Xiao, Minhao Jiang, Vivian Hu, Xuan Wang, Heng Ji, Martin Burke, Huimin Zhao, and Jiawei Han. 2023. Reaction miner: An integrated system for chemical reaction extraction from textual data. In *Proc. The 2023 Conference on Empirical Methods in Natural Language Processing (EMNLP2023) Demo Track*.

A Prompts and examples for GPT4

- Prompts: You are an expert in the chemical domain whose task is to create templates to describe the properties of molecules. You will be challenged with a list of different cases. Each case willl have a list of **templates**, and a **question**. Each template will describe certain properties. Your goal is to generate a new template in a sentence based on all the previous templates.
- Case 1: Templates: - The molecule is a <0>. - It belongs to the <1> class of molecules. Answer: The molecule, characterized as a <0>, falls under the <1> category of chemical compounds.
- Case 2: Templates: - It has an effect on <2>. - It impacts <3>. Answer: It impacts <2> and has an effect on <3>.
- Case 3: Templates: - The molecule is <4>. - The molecule has a <5>. Answer: The molecule is <4>. and has a <5>.
- Case 4: Templates: - The molecule is a <0_1>. - The molecule is a <0_2>. Answer: The molecule is a <0_1> and exhibits <0_2> properties.
- Case 5: Templates: - It belongs to the <1_1> class of molecules. - It belongs to the <1_2> class of molecules. Answer: The molecule is in the <1_1> class of compounds, characterizing it as a member of the <1_2> family.

B Additional Dataset Statistics

Here, we give a brief description of properties in the dataset. Table 7 shows the number of property-molecule pairs for different property classes. Figure 4 breaks the dataset down into different property classes. More details can be found in the dataset repository.

Group	Property-Molecule Pair Count
Total	1512865
Biomedical	776712
anti-X	24884
Modulators	2787
Inhibitors	23257
Agonists	1161
Antagonists	3172
Treatments	53070
Disease	316380
Cancer	41456
Inducers	31
Preventive	0
Blocker	47
Drug	260
X-genic	172
X-tropic	17
X-lytic	84
Relaxant	40
Binder	4
Stimulant	60
Depressant	52
health_effect_relations	309532
Light and Electricity	14077
Light	11069
Electricity	3008
Human Interaction	27457
Toxins	1070
organoleptic_effect_relations	20501
Agric. and Industry	694619
X-icides	809
role_relation	693648

Table 7: Number of property-molecule pairs for different property groups.

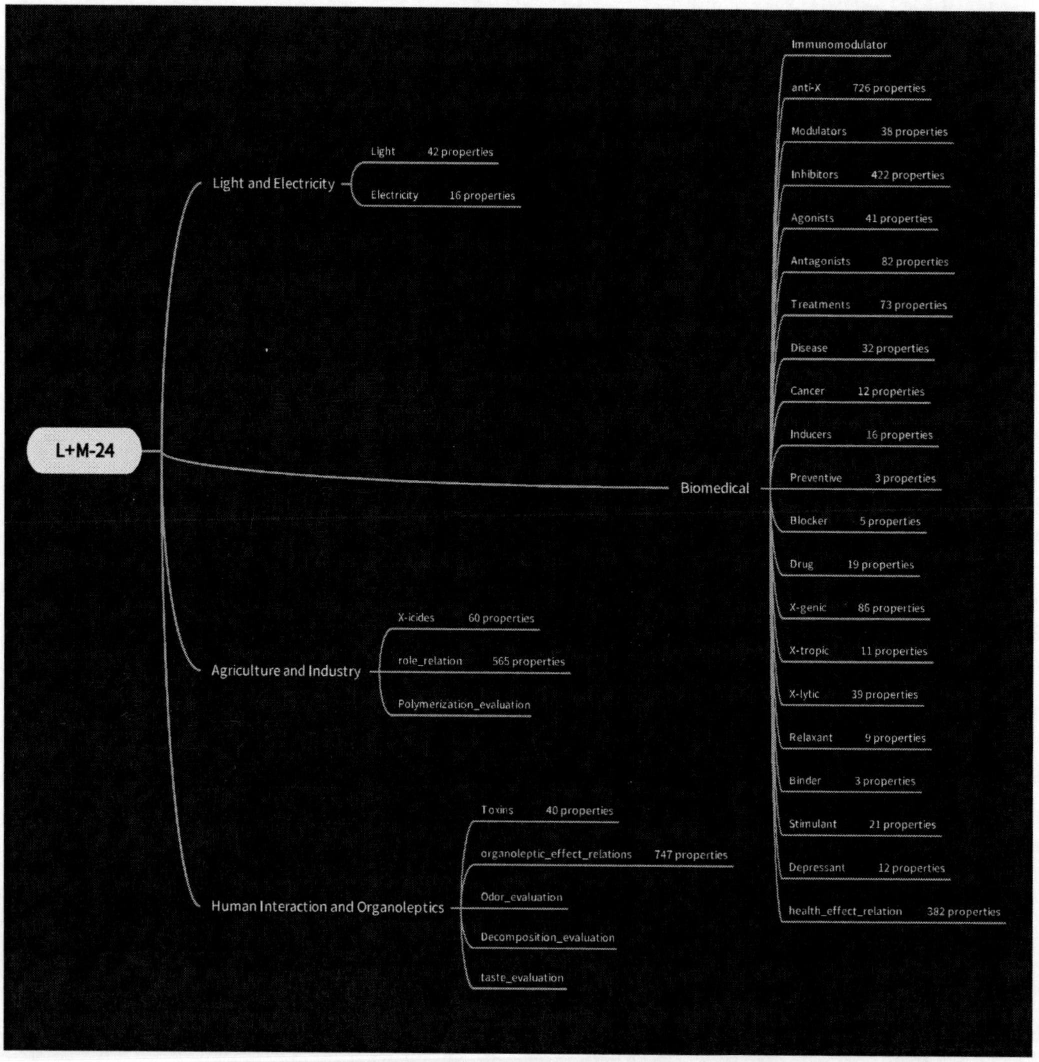

Figure 4: Breakdown of different property classes in *L+M-24*.

Could Chemical Language Models benefit from Message Passing

Jiaqing Xie, Ziheng Chi
Department of Computer Science
ETH Zurich
{jiaxie, zihchi}@student.ethz.ch

Abstract

Pretrained language models (LMs) showcase significant capabilities in processing molecular text, while concurrently, message passing neural networks (MPNNs) demonstrate resilience and versatility in the domain of molecular science. Despite these advancements, we find there are limited studies investigating the relationship between molecular structures and their corresponding textual representations. Therefore, in this paper, we propose two strategies to evaluate whether an information integration can enhance the performance: contrast learning, which involves utilizing an MPNN to supervise the training of the LM, and fusion, which exploits information from both models. Our empirical analysis reveals that the integration approaches exhibit superior performance compared to baselines when applied to smaller molecular graphs, while these integration approaches do not yield performance enhancements on large scale graphs. Furthermore, we conduct experiments to assess the impact of dataset splitting strategies and random seeds on the overall performance.

1 Introduction

The success of attention mechanisms on sequential data has introduced a massive family of large language models based on Transformer architecture (Vaswani et al., 2017). It is evident that these large language models are useful for encoding sequential objects such as text (Liu et al., 2019), molecules (Honda et al., 2019), speech (Huang et al., 2021), and forecasting data (Giuliari et al., 2021). It has been demonstrated that pretrained molecule language models are capable of encoding chemical elements semantically without learning structures (Honda et al., 2019; Xia et al., 2022; Chithrananda et al., 2020; Wang et al., 2019a). Especially for proteins which function as natural components of the human body and a representative of molecule family, they could be efficiently encoded by transformer (Rao et al., 2019; Elnaggar et al., 2021; Rives et al., 2021; He et al., 2021) which acts as masked language modelers.

In contrast to text, molecules contain inherent relationships between their elements, indicating that structural encoding is necessary in addition to word embeddings. Message passing neural network (MPNN), emerging as a prominent method for encoding structural information in recent years, has demonstrated its robustness and versatility within the field of molecular sciences. By leveraging the 2-dimensional topological and 3-dimensional geometrical information as augmented features (Liu et al., 2021; Stärk et al., 2022), it is possible to learn molecular embeddings from structures without sequentially encoding traditional SMILES expressions.

The advent of MPNNs has promoted the exploration of graph-based learning methods for molecular science. Graph contrastive learning captures potential different structural distributions to finetune self-learned representations, where both local and global features are enhanced with chemical domain expertise (Stärk et al., 2022; You et al., 2021; Wang et al., 2022). Besides, the success of GPT (Radford et al., 2018) in traditional natural language processing tasks also motivates the research on graph transformers and graph GPT tailored for the molecule domain (Hu et al., 2020b; Bagal et al., 2021; Rong et al., 2020; Ying et al., 2021; Zhu et al., 2022). Few studies has been investigated to appropriately merge text embeddings and graph embeddings for learning molecule representation better. There has been one study which demonstrated such relationship but with additional prompting with GPT model (Chen et al., 2024), which is out of our scope. In this paper, we aim to explore the interplay between molecular graph embeddings and SMILE token embeddings. We propose two categories of techniques for integrating information: contrast learning and fusion. In contrast learning-based methods, we incorporate

Proceedings of the 1st Workshop on Language + Molecules (L+M 2024), pages 11–21
August 15, 2024 ©2024 Association for Computational Linguistics

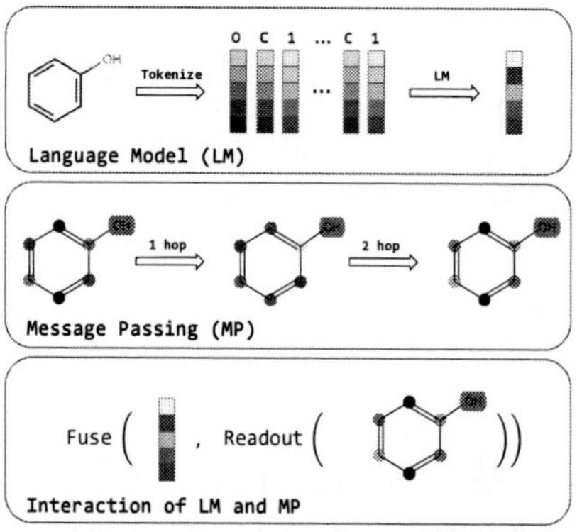

Figure 1: Baseline model: language model (LM) and message passing networks (MPNN). An interaction of LM and MPNN is investigated in this research.

an MPNN as an auxiliary model to supervise the training of the language model, operating at node or graph levels, while we only utilize the language model for downstream tasks. In fusion-based methods, we exploit information from both models to generate outputs for downstream tasks. This is achieved either by merging the output embeddings from both models or by integrating the output embeddings from one model with the input embeddings of the other.

Our main contributions are to as follows:

1. Explore various information integration approaches to assess the necessity of incorporating supplementary structural features in molecular LLMs research, instead of pursuing state-of-the-art performance.

2. Benchmark a series of combination of sequential-based methods (LM) and structural-based methods (MPNN) as baselines for further research.

2 Related Work

2.1 Molecule Representation Learning

The Simplified Molecular Input Line Entry System (SMILES) has become a cornerstone in cheminformatics, providing a compact and standardized representation for chemical structures. Conserving molecular structural information and atom orderings, the SMILES descriptor converts a molecule from its structural representation into a condensed 1-dimensional textual sequence. For example, a phenol molecule (C_6H_5OH) is represented as `C1=CC=C(C=C1)O`. Similar to the tokenization in natural language settings, a molecule is expressed as a sentence and atoms are expressed as words. This allows efficient utilization of large language models in chemical research.

2.2 Pretrained Large Language Models

The advent of the transformer architecture (Vaswani et al., 2023) represents a breakthrough in the field of natural language processing. Over the past few years, many excellent pretraining strategies have been proposed, such as BERT (Devlin et al., 2019) and RoBERTa (Liu et al., 2019), significantly improving the capabilities of the large language models. As SMILES allows converting molecular structures into textual sentences, it is possible to apply language models for molecular machine learning, which facilitates the research on pretraining molecular language models.

Based on the implementation of RoBERTa, ChemBERTa (Chithrananda et al., 2020) employs chemistry oriented masked-language modelling as its pretraining strategy, while the improved version ChemBERTa-2 (Ahmad et al., 2022) adopts multi-task regression as another pretraining task and uses larger training datasets. There are also other BERT-like transformer models, such as MolBERT (Fabian et al., 2020) and SMILES-BERT (Wang et al., 2019b), which are pretrained with different objectives on different molecule datasets.

2.3 Contrastive Learning

Contrastive learning has emerged as a powerful paradigm in self-supervised learning. Unlike traditional methods that rely solely on labeled data, this approach leverages the differences between data to learn representations. Based on the assumption that similar instances should be closer in the embedding space, the objective is to maximize the similarity between positive data pairs while minimizing the similarity between negative data pairs. So far, contrastive learning has demonstrated efficacy across diverse domains. A common practice of this approach is based on data augmentation (You et al., 2021), where the utilization of unlabeled data enhances model generalizability and robustness. Furthermore, this approach is also widely adopted in the field of multimodality (Radford et al., 2021), where the availability of different data forms allows leveraging one representation to supervise the other.

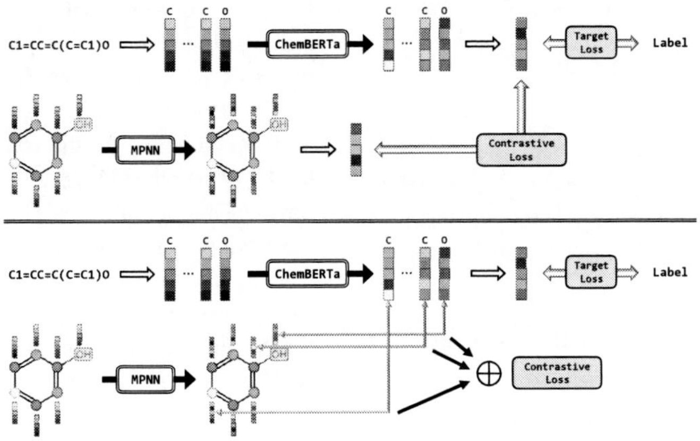

Figure 2: Contrastive Learning. Above: Node level contrastive learning. Below: Graph level contrastive learning.

3 Methods

We investigate two kinds of information merging methods: contrast learning-based methods and fusion-based methods. In contrast learning-based methods, we use GNN as an auxiliary model to supervise the training of the language model, while we only use the language model for downstream tasks. In fusion-based methods, we make use of information from both models to generate the output for downstream tasks. For each kind of method, we consider different model architectures. In this section, we will first briefly review the two baseline models ChemBERTa (Chithrananda et al., 2020) and NNConv (Gilmer et al., 2017), and then describe the contrast learning-based methods and the fusion-based methods.

3.1 Baseline (Fig. 1)

Language Models. We choose ChemBERTa (Chithrananda et al., 2020) as our baseline model. The architecture of ChemBERTa is similar to BERT (Devlin et al., 2019), consisting of an embedding layer and several encoder layers. A molecule is first converted into the textual format through SMILES, and then a SMILES tokenizer is applied to convert the words into input tokens. After embedding lookup, each token is assigned with an embedding. Then the encoder layers which consist of a multi-head self-attention layer and a feed-forward layer transform the input token embeddings to hidden state representations. Finally, the task-specific output layer (classifier or regressor) predicts the result.

We ask the ChemBERTa model to produce three-level information for a molecule. First, node embeddings are extracted from the final hidden state representations. Since the SMILES transformation preserves atom orderings, each atom in the original molecule corresponds to a specific output token embedding. Second, the graph embedding is extracted from the special token at the beginning of the sequence. Third, the property prediction result is the final output.

The entire process can be depicted as follows:

$$\begin{aligned}
\texttt{Tokens} &= \texttt{Tokenizer}(\texttt{Sequence}) \\
E_{\text{in}} &= \texttt{Embedding}(\texttt{Tokens}) \\
E_{\text{out}} &= \texttt{Encoder}(E_{\text{in}}) \\
N &= E_{\text{out}}[\texttt{Node_Indices}] \\
G &= E_{\text{out}}[0] \\
P &= \texttt{Predictor}(G)
\end{aligned} \tag{1}$$

where E_{in} and E_{out} represent the input token embeddings and final hidden state representations; N, G, and P represent the node embeddings, graph embedding, and property prediction result.

Message Passing Neural Networks. There are different types of graph neural networks, which include graph convolution, graph attention and neural message passing networks (MPNN). Edge attributes or edge features are important in message passing mechanisms (Johannes et al., 2020; Gilmer et al., 2017). For the baseline model, we follow the model setting in the first paper of MPNN for Quantum Chemistry dataset QM9 (Gilmer et al., 2017), which iteratively updates the message m_v^t

and the hidden state h_v^t for each node v:

$$m_v^{(t+1)} = \sum_{u \in \mathcal{N}(v)} \mathtt{Aggr}[h_v^{(t)}, h_u^{(t)}, e_{uv}] \quad (2)$$

$$h_v^{(t+1)} = \mathcal{U}(h_v^{(t)}, m_v^{(t+1)}) \quad (3)$$

$\mathtt{Aggr}[\cdot]$ is the function that aggregates neighbor node u's information as well as the attributes e_{uv} of the shared edge with u. $\mathcal{U}(\cdot,\cdot)$ updates hidden states for v.

3.2 Integration 1: Contrastive Learning (Fig. 2)

Node Level Contrastive Learning In order to compute the constrastive loss, we need a triple $\langle$**anchor, positive, negative**$\rangle$. Anchor and positive node embeddings are sampled from language models and message passing networks respectively. Negative samples are randomly generated from graphs with a different permutation. For an example node triple $t = \langle a, p, n \rangle$, its corresponding contrastive learning loss triplet loss is given by:

$$L(t) = \max\{d(a,p) - d(a,n) + \text{margin}, 0\} \quad (4)$$

where margin is 1.0 and distance measurement $d(i,j)$ is defined as L_p-norm : $d(i,j) = \|i - j\|_p$. p is often set to 2 as an Euclidean distance metric. In a $\mathcal{M}$ mini-batch of training graphs (number of $\mathcal{N}$ nodes) with $\mathcal{K}$ triples, the triplet loss is given by:

$$\text{L} = \sum_{m=1}^{\mathcal{M}} \sum_{i=0}^{\lceil \frac{\mathcal{N}}{\mathcal{K}} \rceil - 1} \sum_{j=1}^{\mathcal{K}} \max\{d(a_k^m, p_k^m) - d(a_k^m, n_k^m) + \text{margin}, 0\} \quad (5)$$

where $k = |\mathcal{K}|i + j$. Consider a binary classification problem, as mentioned we need to perform $\mathtt{Readout}$ function to obtain the global information of a graph. If it is an average function, the total loss is given by a prediction loss such as negative log likelihood (NLL) loss, and a regularized triplet contrastive loss which has been defined above:

$$\text{L} = \sum_{m=1}^{\mathcal{M}} \text{NLL}\left(\text{MLP}\left(\frac{1}{\mathcal{N}} \sum_{i=0}^{\lceil \frac{\mathcal{N}}{\mathcal{K}} \rceil - 1} \sum_{j=1}^{\mathcal{K}} a_k^m\right), y^m\right) + \alpha \cdot \sum_{m=1}^{\mathcal{M}} \sum_{i=0}^{\lceil \frac{\mathcal{N}}{\mathcal{K}} \rceil - 1} \sum_{j=1}^{\mathcal{K}} \max\{d(a_k^m, p_k^m) - d(a_k^m, n_k^m) + \text{margin}, 0\} \quad (6)$$

where $k = |\mathcal{K}|i + j$ likewise and α is a regularization term.

Graph Level Contrastive Learning. Apart from establishing negative samples between each pair of nodes at a fine grained level, we estimate contrastive learning at a coarse grained level which aims at computing the difference between language model graph embeddings and MPNN graph embeddings. This could potentially avoid the situation that individual nodes with large difference contribute more to the difference of the molecule property. Moreover, the complexity is pretty lower than the complexity of node level comparison, which will be discussed in part 3.4. Similar to the node level training loss in (6), the graph level training loss is defined as:

$$\text{L} = \sum_{m=1}^{\mathcal{M}} \text{NLL}\left(\text{MLP}\left(a^m\right), y^m\right) + \alpha' \cdot \sum_{m=1}^{\mathcal{M}} \max\{d(a^m, p^m) - d(a^m, n^m) + \text{margin}, 0\} \quad (7)$$

where α' is a regularization term. Note that different molecules could have a similar graph embedding which could lead to a similar quantum property, for example isomers. And also note that we use message passing network outputs to self-supervise (or fine-tune) language model outputs either in node level and graph level settings. It means that we do not directly use MPNN outputs to perform predictions. This is because we want to see if injecting geometry information of molecules is beneficial to the end-to-end training of **language models**. It is different from the collaborative training (fusion) which would be introduced in the following parts.

3.3 Integration 2: Fusion (Fig. 3)

Late Fusion Different from self-supervised learning settings in part 3.2, we introduce another important interaction between LM embeddings and MPNN embeddings: late fusion (Sachan et al., 2021). It is called late fusion since the interaction happens after their corresponding embeddings h_{LM} and h_{MPNN} are extracted. The interaction is given by the notation $\bigoplus$, and the prediction is then given as:

$$y_{\text{pred}} = \text{MLP}\left(h_{\text{LM}} \bigoplus h_{\text{MPNN}}\right) \quad (8)$$

$$\bigoplus = \{+, \max, \|, \odot\} \quad (9)$$

$$L = \sum_{i=1}^{\mathcal{M}} \text{NLL}(y_{\text{pred}}^i, y^i) \quad (10)$$

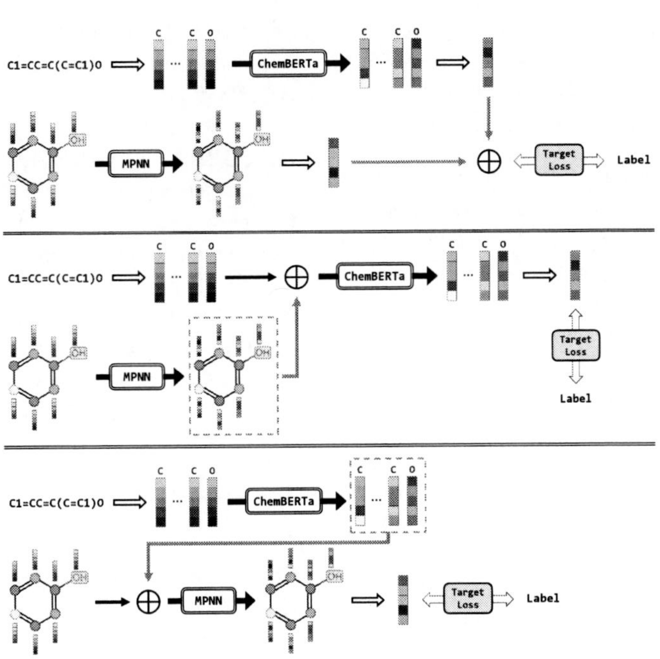

Figure 3: Fusion. Top: Late Fusion. Middle: MPNN2LM Joint Fusion. Bottom: LM2MPNN Joint Fusion.

where the interaction contains element-wise addition, maximization, concatenation and gate function which is used for building highway layers.

Joint Fusion. Based on the late fusion, we consider two situations: 1) MPNN2LM: fuse initial graph embeddings and LM outputs $\Rightarrow$ perform MPNN downstream tasks, and 2) LM2MPNN: fuse initial token embeddings and MPNN outputs $\Rightarrow$ finetune LM downsteam tasks.

MPNN2LM We initialized the word embedding for language model: $h_{\text{LM}}^{(0)}$. MPNN embedding is given by h_{MPNN}. Then the fused embedding is $h_{\text{LM}}^{(0)} \bigoplus h_{\text{MPNN}}$, which would be the input embedding for the pretrained language model. The node mask is also considered since in part 3.1 we mentioned that paddings are added to ensure the same length of input. After fine-tuning pretrained **LM**, we readout the global information h' to perform downstream tasks. Overall, the graph embedding prepared for MLP is:

$$h' = \texttt{Readout}\left(\textbf{LM}\left(h_{\text{LM}}^{(0)} \bigoplus h_{\text{MPNN}}, \textbf{mask}\right)\right) \tag{11}$$

LM2MPNN Revisiting how MPNN works by (1) and (2), the node embedding for v are fused with the LM output for mask index v: $h_v^{(t)} \bigoplus h_{\text{LMM}(v)}$. Similar to the neighbor node u, they are fused with the LM output for mask index u: $h_u^{(t)} \bigoplus h_{\text{LMM}(u)}$. Then the message is aggregated by:

$$m_v^{(t+1)} = \sum_{u \in \mathcal{N}(v)} \texttt{Aggr}\left(h_v^{(t)} \bigoplus h_{\text{LMM}(v)}, h_u^{(t)} \bigoplus h_{\text{LMM}(u)}, e_{uv}\right) \tag{12}$$

For the update function $\mathcal{U}(\cdot,\cdot)$, the new update rule:

$$h_v^{(t+1)} = \mathcal{U}\left(h_v^{(t)} \bigoplus h_{\text{LMM}(v)}, m_v^{(t+1)}\right) \tag{13}$$

3.4 Complexity Analysis

Baseline Models. The time complexity for baseline models are mainly dominated by their corresponding model architecture. Assume the input size $\in \mathbb{R}^{N \times d}$ For the pretrained transformer model, the self-attention module is the bottleneck, which is bounded by $O(N^2 \cdot d)$. Assume that there are L self-attention layers, then it will increase to $O(N^2 \cdot d \cdot L)$. The complexity for feed forward layers is $O(N \cdot d^2 \cdot L)$. The overall complexity for baseline LM is then $O(N^2 \cdot d \cdot L + N \cdot d^2 \cdot L)$. For MPNN, computing each message has a complexity of $O(d)$. The total complexity for the message passing step is then $O(E \cdot d)$. Updating nodes will be $O(N \cdot d^2)$. L layers lead to $O(L \cdot E \cdot d + L \cdot N \cdot d^2)$.

So it depends on whether the graph is sparse or not. If graph is sparse, $N^2 \gg E$, then the complexity of LM is greater than the complexity of MPNN. This situation often occurs in real world applications.

Contrastive Learning. For contrastive learning, apart from the basic complexity for LM and MPNN, it also includes the complexity for computing contrastive loss. Take triplet loss as an example, in equation (5), the complexity is dominated by the last term. Assume that computing max only requires O(1). Computing $d(\cdot,\cdot)$ requires $O(d)$ if the dimension of inputs is d. Then the overall complexity is $O(d \cdot N)$ where N is the number of nodes in the graph. A node level contrastive learning then requires $O(N^2 \cdot d \cdot L + 2 \cdot N \cdot d^2 \cdot L + d \cdot N + L \cdot d \cdot E)$. For graph level contrastive learning we find that only complexity of model terms dominates, which leads to $O(N^2 \cdot d \cdot L + 2 \cdot N \cdot d^2 \cdot L + L \cdot d \cdot E + d)$, which is faster than that of node level.

Fusion We simply investigate $\bigoplus$ by choosing max which requires $O(1)$. The element wise maximization requires $O(N \cdot d)$ since input size is $N \times d$. Then the time complexity of late fusion would be the same as the complexity of nodel level contrastive learning, which is $O(N^2 \cdot d \cdot L + 2 \cdot N \cdot d^2 \cdot L + L \cdot d \cdot (N + E))$. MPNN2LM has the same complexity while LM2MPNN is much more complex since $\bigoplus$ directly affects the complexity of message passing operation. We already know that the complexity of MPNN is $O(E \cdot d)$. We assume that the average number of nodes is $\frac{2E}{N}$. Then the additional element wise addition contributions additional $O(E \cdot d)$, which leads to the overall complexity for LM2MPNN: $O(N^2 \cdot d \cdot L + 2 \cdot N \cdot d^2 \cdot L + L \cdot d \cdot (N + 2E))$.

4 Experiment settings

4.1 Dataset

We follow the following paradigm (Luo et al., 2022) for prediction on quantum chemistry based datasets: first we perform tests on small scale and classifical benchmark molecule datasets. In our future works, we want to test its robustness on large scale and recently proposed benchmarks such as PCQM4Mv2 (Hu et al., 2020a). For small datasets we choose from MoleculeNet dataset (Wu et al., 2018) which collects data from physical chemistry, biophysics and physiology field. It has provided plenty of molecule datasets to play with (Wu et al., 2018). For large datasets, we choose **QM9** (Gilmer et al., 2017) as tested in MPNN. The task is to predict property for each molecule using models in part 3. Selected datasets are **HIV**, **BACE**, **ESOL** and **BBBP** (Wu et al., 2018). A simple description of chosen dataset and task type is listed in table 3. **HIV**, **BBBP**, and **BACE** are used for binary classification settings, while **ESOL** and **QM9** are used for regression settings. For simplicity, we only choose the first target from all 19 classes, which is the Dipole moment μ. For the regression problem, the performance is measured by mean absolute error (mae). As for the classification, it is measured by the mean accuracy (acc). Specifically, the pretrained ChemBERTa is time-consuming on QM9 and HIV dataset.

4.2 Hyper-parameter settings

There are two pretrained model to choose from: ChemBERTa and its improved version ChemBERTa-2. We choose Adam optimizer for optimizing model parameters with default learning rate 0.001 when running with pretrained ChemBERTa-2 (<4G). The initial learning rate is tuned to 0.0002 when running with ChemBERTa since the model size is large (>16G) which requires a small learning rate. We follow a 8:1:1 train-valid-test ratio for MoleculeNet dataset, and follow an approximate 21:2:2 train-valid-test ratio for **QM9** dataset. Hidden dimension is set to 64. The default choice for $\bigoplus$ is sum (addition). Five fixed seeds are 0, 7, 42, 100, 2024 for result reproduction.

4.3 Scalability

A single NVIDIA A100 GPU could satisfy all our experiments. In other words, it is scalable for training all datasets including large scaled ones. The maximum usage is observed when running pretrained ChemBERTa on HIV dataset. For other datasets it's also possible to train on a GeForce RTX 3090 GPU.

5 Results

Observation 0: Protein language models are more preferred. A fundamental observation from experimenting on MoleculeNet is that purely using message passing neural networks are inferior to language models in molecule property prediction. This phenomenon is also mentioned in the previous research work (Xu et al., 2022). This has indicated some works to include the geometric properties such as 3D information and rotation invariant parameters in message passing

Model	HIV (**acc.**) ↑	BACE (**acc.**) ↑	BBBP (**acc.**) ↑	ESOL (**mae.**) ↓
ChemBERTa	0.9776 ± 0.0021	0.8280 ± 0.0319	0.9105 ± 0.0153	0.5529 ± 0.0332
MPNN	0.9774 ± 0.0022	0.8080 ± 0.0256	0.8737 ± 0.0140	0.6252 ± 0.0072
ChemBERTa contra. MPNN (node)	$\mathbf{0.9782 \pm 0.0035}$	0.8280 ± 0.0271	0.9118 ± 0.0245	0.5326 ± 0.0534
ChemBERTa contra. MPNN (graph)	0.9774 ± 0.0022	0.8300 ± 0.0352	0.9131 ± 0.0307	0.5404 ± 0.0495
ChemBERTa + MPNN (graph)	0.9778 ± 0.0020	0.8320 ± 0.0331	0.9065 ± 0.0147	0.5002 ± 0.0339
ChemBERTa ← MPNN	0.9773 ± 0.0022	0.8060 ± 0.0422	0.9053 ± 0.0099	$\mathbf{0.4819 \pm 0.0325}$
ChemBERTa → MPNN	0.9773 ± 0.0022	$\mathbf{0.8380 \pm 0.0366}$	$\mathbf{0.9184 \pm 0.0189}$	0.5561 ± 0.0461

Table 1: Performance of pretrained ChemBERTa on MoleculeNet datasets.

Model	HIV (**acc.**) ↑	BACE (**acc.**) ↑	BBBP (**acc.**) ↑	ESOL (**mae.**) ↓
ChemBERTa-2	0.9792 ± 0.0018	0.8560 ± 0.0206	0.9171 ± 0.0136	0.4738 ± 0.0330
MPNN	0.9774 ± 0.0022	0.8010 ± 0.0392	0.8737 ± 0.0140	0.6252 ± 0.0072
ChemBERTa-2 contra. MPNN (node)	0.9791 ± 0.0011	0.8620 ± 0.0256	$\mathbf{0.9290 \pm 0.0128}$	$\mathbf{0.4393 \pm 0.0338}$
ChemBERTa-2 contra. MPNN (graph)	$\mathbf{0.9800 \pm 0.0017}$	0.8540 ± 0.0258	0.9197 ± 0.0163	0.4643 ± 0.0354
ChemBERTa-2 + MPNN (graph)	0.9791 ± 0.0012	$\mathbf{0.8680 \pm 0.0293}$	0.9263 ± 0.0113	0.4493 ± 0.0328
ChemBERTa-2 ← MPNN	0.9772 ± 0.0016	0.8400 ± 0.0374	0.8974 ± 0.0098	0.5012 ± 0.0335
ChemBERTa-2 → MPNN	0.9789 ± 0.0012	0.8480 ± 0.0204	0.9224 ± 0.0141	0.4516 ± 0.0264

Table 2: Performance of improved pretrained ChemBERTa-2 on MoleculeNet datasets.

Name	#graphs	#nodes	#features	#classes
HIV	41,127	~25.5	9	1
BBBP	2,050	~23.9	9	1
BACE	1,513	~34.1	9	1
ESOL	1,128	~13.3	9	1
QM9	130,831	~18.0	11	19

Table 3: Descriptions of selected datasets from MoleculeNet

networks to reinforce its prediction and expressive power. The explanation of this phenomenon would be that 1) model size of either ChemBERTa-1 or ChemBERTA-2 model is larger than the size of message passing networks and 2) either ChemBERTa-1 or ChemBERTA-2 model has been pretrained on some more larger datasets for example ZINC dataset, while message passing networks do not follow the pretraining scheme of large language models.

Observation 1: Integration on relatively small graphs are more preferred. Using the pretraind ChemBERTa-2, we found that both contrastive learning and fusion methods outperform baseline models in **ESOL**, **BACE**, and **BBBP** where they are relatively small compared with **QM9** and **HIV** datasets. Especially, node level contrastive learning performs the best and it seems to be robust among all tasks, followed by late fusion methods and joint fusion methods when injecting LLM to MPNNs. In large dataset, the tuning strategy might influence the potential performance, where it splits the dataset in a better way therefore we perform one ablation regarding train test split (in section 6) to avoid the difference that brought by dataset itself.

Observation 2: Integration w.r.t both regression and classification are useful. In terms of training convergence, we observe that the accuracy or mean absolute error converges quickly to a high or low score respectively. For small graph datasets **BACE** and **BBBP** on graph classification problem, an improvement of $\approx$**1%** on average accuracy is observed with method `MPNN2LM` for pretrained ChemBERTa. For version 2, 1.4% improvement is observed with late fusion on **BACE** and 1.3% improvement is observed with node contrastive learning on **BBBP** . For small graph dataset **ESOL** on regression problem, a great improvement is observed where 12.8% improvement on mae with MPNN2LM method with pretrained ChemBERTa, and 7.3% improvement on mae with MPNN2LM method with pretrained ChemBERTa-2. For **HIV**, we observe a little improvement with node level contrastive learning. Using a combination of LLM representation and graph representation during the training would make the prediction worse. For **QM9**, most of the injection / fusion methods would potentially improve the performance except for MPNN2LM fusion. Using LM2MPNN would potentially improve 8.6 %. We found that pure MPNN's performance is better than the performance of a chemical LLM (table 4).

Observation 3: Pretrained language models are important for downstream predictions. In comparison to ChemBERTa-2, ChemBERTa performs worse when comparing each entry in table 1 and table 2. Although we could always try to improve those two baselines with different injection or fusion methods, the best of them are not the same. For example, contrastive learning is much more preferred to ChemBERTa-2 while fusion methods are much more preferred to ChemBERTa model. When it comes with a new pretrained large language model, using our proposed method could tell the similarity between tasks and the model's pretraining strategy. As there is no general conclusion about how a chemical LLM and a MPNN could be combined to predict the best, it is still a pioneering area that requires more pretrained models to test its robustness. To select the most appropriate pretrained language model for further training, researchers should first integrate a list of pretrained models, followed by an investigation with different fusion / injection methods.

Observation 4: Joint Fusion to some extent helps learn MPNN better but learn original Chemical LLM worse. We also focus on if such multimodal module (Fig. 2, Fig. 3) helps learn individual module (Fig. 1) better. It improves a lot for single MPNN baseline if we consider its language level information as augmented features. For example, for **BACE** dataset, MPNN has an average accuracy of 0.808 with ChemBERTa. With injecting pretrained language information, an improvement of 3.7% is observed (LM2MPNN). However, it might not work very well on the opposite when we inject information from MPNN to LLM. For simplicity we just examined with pretrained ChemBERTa-2. For ESOL dataset, it decreased from 0.4738 to 0.5012 (5.78%). For BBBP dataet, it decreased from 0.9171 to 0.8974 (2.15%). We further suggest that the researchers should not directly use the structural information from graphs as additional input when they want to modify their LLM models, but trying to leverage them as auxiliary ground-truth to finetune the token embeddings.

Model	QM9 (target = 0)
ChemBERTa-2 baseline	0.4825 ± 0.0113
MPNN baseline	0.4669 ± 0.0065
ChemBERTa-2 contra. MPNN (node)	0.4613 ± 0.0065
ChemBERTa-2 contra. MPNN (graph)	0.4662 ± 0.0046
ChemBERTa-2 + MPNN (graph)	0.4596 ± 0.0078
ChemBERTa-2 ← MPNN	0.5231 ± 0.0083
ChemBERTa-2 → MPNN	$\mathbf{0.4409 \pm 0.0048}$

Table 4: Performance of improved pretrained ChemBERTa-2 on QM9 dataset.

6 Ablation Study

Effects of datasets. We choose another dataset in MoleculeNet to certify that the proposed models are still robust on this dataset. Take **FreeSolv** as an example, we figure out that none of the injection or contrastive learning methods is still robust on this regression task. Even if late fusion performs the best which has an average mae of 0.6568, which is close to the result of pure chemical LLM training (0.6420), there's still a 2.3% decrease in performance. Both LM2MPNN and MPNN2LM did not work well, but it still commits to our fourth main observation, which is that injecting token embeddings into message passing layers would still improve the performance, but injecting structural information into word embeddings would be a bad idea. A potential reason is that **FreeSolv** is too small. We suggest that researchers should be careful when fine-tuning the individual language model with additional structural features.

Model	FreeSolv (**mae.**) ↓
ChemBERTa-2 baseline	0.6420 ± 0.0814
MPNN baseline	0.9904 ± 0.1375
ChemBERTa-2 contra. MPNN (node)	0.6642 ± 0.0600
ChemBERTa-2 contra. MPNN (graph)	0.6745 ± 0.0995
ChemBERTa-2 + MPNN (graph)	0.6568 ± 0.0658
ChemBERTa-2 ← MPNN	0.9188 ± 0.0686
ChemBERTa-2 → MPNN	0.7475 ± 0.0805

Table 5: Performance of improved pretrained ChemBERTa-2 on FreeSolv dataset

Effects of dataset split. We want to figure out if different splits of training, validation and test datasets lead to different performance. We run on **BBBP** (classification) and **ESOL** (regression). Four ratios are considered: 9:0.5:0.5, 8:1:1, 7:2:1, and 6:2:2. Model prediction power is highest at a ratio of 8:1:1 for **ESOL** while the prediction power is reducing for **BBBP** when ratio of training sets is decreasing.

Train test split	BBBP (**acc.**) ↑	ESOL (**mae.**) ↓
9: 0.5 : 0.5	$\mathbf{0.9500 \pm 0.0174}$	0.4672 ± 0.0338
8 : 1 : 1	0.9290 ± 0.0128	$\mathbf{0.4393 \pm 0.0338}$
7 : 2 : 1	0.9211 ± 0.0110	0.4837 ± 0.0447
6 : 2 : 2	0.9152 ± 0.0032	0.4947 ± 0.0060

Table 6: Model (node level contrast.)

Effects of different fusion operations $\bigoplus$ We first follow the default train valid test split of 8:1:1. As mentioned, there are four fusion operations $\bigoplus$, which are max, sum, concatenation and gate function. Our default fusion operation is sum function. Surprisingly we found that concatenation and max function are better fusion choice for both **BBBP** and **ESOL**. We suggest that researchers could simply concatenate token embeddings and graph embeddings together.

Fusion Operation	BBBP (**acc.**) ↑	ESOL (**mae.**) ↓
sum	0.9263 ± 0.0113	0.4493 ± 0.0328
max	0.9289 ± 0.0146	0.4281 ± 0.0339
concate	$\mathbf{0.9289 \pm 0.0241}$	$\mathbf{0.4255 \pm 0.0335}$
gate	0.9224 ± 0.0197	0.4363 ± 0.0354

Table 7: Model: Late Fusion

Effects of different graph neural networks As mentioned in section 3, there are three types of graph neural networks in mainstream GNN research, which are graph convolution (GraphConv), message passing neural networks (MPNN), and graph attention networks. We substitute MPNN with with a two-layer GraphConv model to see if MPNN is much better than other types of GNN for baselines. The results show that MPNN is more preferred to **BBBP** but GraphConv is more preferred to **ESOL**. Overall the difference would not be too large for a graph convolution network and a neural message passing layer therefore we suggest researchers try out both ways to improve the results.

Fusion Operation	BBBP (**acc.**) ↑	ESOL (**mae.**) ↓
MPNN	$\mathbf{0.9289 \pm 0.0146}$	0.4281 ± 0.0339
GraphConv	0.9237 ± 0.0148	$\mathbf{0.4144 \pm 0.0252}$

Table 8: Model: Late Fusion

7 Conclusion

In this paper, we delved into various information integration approaches to assess whether the collaborative utilization of chemical large language models (chemical LLMs) and message passing neural networks (MPNNs) surpasses the individual efficacy of these models. We evaluated the integration approaches over different graph scales on both classification and regression tasks. Our empirical analysis has demonstrated that the integration approaches outperform the baselines on small-scale graphs but do not yield improvements on datasets of larger scales. Furthermore, we have found that differences in dataset splitting strategies, and aggregation choices in fusion have an impact on the overall performance. We wish to extend our proposed methods on large scale benchmark datasets such as PCQM4Mv2 (Hu et al., 2020a).

References

Walid Ahmad, Elana Simon, Seyone Chithrananda, Gabriel Grand, and Bharath Ramsundar. 2022. Chemberta-2: Towards chemical foundation models.

Viraj Bagal, Rishal Aggarwal, PK Vinod, and U Deva Priyakumar. 2021. Molgpt: molecular generation using a transformer-decoder model. *Journal of Chemical Information and Modeling*, 62(9):2064–2076.

Zhikai Chen, Haitao Mao, Hang Li, Wei Jin, Hongzhi Wen, Xiaochi Wei, Shuaiqiang Wang, Dawei Yin, Wenqi Fan, Hui Liu, et al. 2024. Exploring the potential of large language models (llms) in learning on graphs. *ACM SIGKDD Explorations Newsletter*, 25(2):42–61.

Seyone Chithrananda, Gabriel Grand, and Bharath Ramsundar. 2020. Chemberta: large-scale self-supervised pretraining for molecular property prediction. *arXiv preprint arXiv:2010.09885*.

Jacob Devlin, Ming-Wei Chang, Kenton Lee, and Kristina Toutanova. 2019. Bert: Pre-training of deep bidirectional transformers for language understanding.

Ahmed Elnaggar, Michael Heinzinger, Christian Dallago, Ghalia Rehawi, Yu Wang, Llion Jones, Tom Gibbs, Tamas Feher, Christoph Angerer, Martin Steinegger, et al. 2021. Prottrans: Toward understanding the language of life through self-supervised learning. *IEEE transactions on pattern analysis and machine intelligence*, 44(10):7112–7127.

Benedek Fabian, Thomas Edlich, Héléna Gaspar, Marwin Segler, Joshua Meyers, Marco Fiscato, and Mohamed Ahmed. 2020. Molecular representation learning with language models and domain-relevant auxiliary tasks.

Justin Gilmer, Samuel S Schoenholz, Patrick F Riley, Oriol Vinyals, and George E Dahl. 2017. Neural message passing for quantum chemistry. In *International conference on machine learning*, pages 1263–1272. PMLR.

Francesco Giuliari, Irtiza Hasan, Marco Cristani, and Fabio Galasso. 2021. Transformer networks for trajectory forecasting. In *2020 25th international conference on pattern recognition (ICPR)*, pages 10335–10342. IEEE.

Liang He, Shizhuo Zhang, Lijun Wu, Huanhuan Xia, Fusong Ju, He Zhang, Siyuan Liu, Yingce Xia, Jianwei Zhu, Pan Deng, et al. 2021. Pre-training co-evolutionary protein representation via a pairwise masked language model. *arXiv preprint arXiv:2110.15527*.

Shion Honda, Shoi Shi, and Hiroki R Ueda. 2019. Smiles transformer: Pre-trained molecular fingerprint for low data drug discovery. *arXiv preprint arXiv:1911.04738*.

Weihua Hu, Matthias Fey, Marinka Zitnik, Yuxiao Dong, Hongyu Ren, Bowen Liu, Michele Catasta, and Jure Leskovec. 2020a. Open graph benchmark: Datasets for machine learning on graphs. *Advances in neural information processing systems*, 33:22118–22133.

Ziniu Hu, Yuxiao Dong, Kuansan Wang, Kai-Wei Chang, and Yizhou Sun. 2020b. Gpt-gnn: Generative pre-training of graph neural networks. In *Proceedings of the 26th ACM SIGKDD International Conference on Knowledge Discovery & Data Mining*, pages 1857–1867.

Wen-Chin Huang, Chia-Hua Wu, Shang-Bao Luo, Kuan-Yu Chen, Hsin-Min Wang, and Tomoki Toda. 2021. Speech recognition by simply fine-tuning bert. In *ICASSP 2021-2021 IEEE International Conference on Acoustics, Speech and Signal Processing (ICASSP)*, pages 7343–7347. IEEE.

Klicpera Johannes, Groß Janek, and Günnemann Stephan. 2020. Directional message passing for molecular graphs. In *International Conference on Learning Representations*.

Shengchao Liu, Hanchen Wang, Weiyang Liu, Joan Lasenby, Hongyu Guo, and Jian Tang. 2021. Pre-training molecular graph representation with 3d geometry. In *International Conference on Learning Representations*.

Yinhan Liu, Myle Ott, Naman Goyal, Jingfei Du, Mandar Joshi, Danqi Chen, Omer Levy, Mike Lewis, Luke Zettlemoyer, and Veselin Stoyanov. 2019. Roberta: A robustly optimized bert pretraining approach.

Shengjie Luo, Tianlang Chen, Yixian Xu, Shuxin Zheng, Tie-Yan Liu, Liwei Wang, and Di He. 2022. One transformer can understand both 2d & 3d molecular data. In *The Eleventh International Conference on Learning Representations*.

Alec Radford, Jong Wook Kim, Chris Hallacy, Aditya Ramesh, Gabriel Goh, Sandhini Agarwal, Girish Sastry, Amanda Askell, Pamela Mishkin, Jack Clark, Gretchen Krueger, and Ilya Sutskever. 2021. Learning transferable visual models from natural language supervision.

Alec Radford, Karthik Narasimhan, Tim Salimans, and Ilya Sutskever. 2018. Improving language understanding by generative pre-training.

Roshan Rao, Nicholas Bhattacharya, Neil Thomas, Yan Duan, Peter Chen, John Canny, Pieter Abbeel, and Yun Song. 2019. Evaluating protein transfer learning with tape. *Advances in neural information processing systems*, 32.

Alexander Rives, Joshua Meier, Tom Sercu, Siddharth Goyal, Zeming Lin, Jason Liu, Demi Guo, Myle Ott, C Lawrence Zitnick, Jerry Ma, et al. 2021. Biological structure and function emerge from scaling unsupervised learning to 250 million protein sequences. *Proceedings of the National Academy of Sciences*, 118(15):e2016239118.

Yu Rong, Yatao Bian, Tingyang Xu, Weiyang Xie, Ying Wei, Wenbing Huang, and Junzhou Huang. 2020. Self-supervised graph transformer on large-scale molecular data. *Advances in Neural Information Processing Systems*, 33:12559–12571.

Devendra Sachan, Yuhao Zhang, Peng Qi, and William L Hamilton. 2021. Do syntax trees help pre-trained transformers extract information? In *Proceedings of the 16th Conference of the European Chapter of the Association for Computational Linguistics: Main Volume*, pages 2647–2661.

Hannes Stärk, Dominique Beaini, Gabriele Corso, Prudencio Tossou, Christian Dallago, Stephan Günnemann, and Pietro Liò. 2022. 3d infomax improves gnns for molecular property prediction. In *International Conference on Machine Learning*, pages 20479–20502. PMLR.

Ashish Vaswani, Noam Shazeer, Niki Parmar, Jakob Uszkoreit, Llion Jones, Aidan N Gomez, Łukasz Kaiser, and Illia Polosukhin. 2017. Attention is all you need. *Advances in neural information processing systems*, 30.

Ashish Vaswani, Noam Shazeer, Niki Parmar, Jakob Uszkoreit, Llion Jones, Aidan N. Gomez, Lukasz Kaiser, and Illia Polosukhin. 2023. Attention is all you need.

Sheng Wang, Yuzhi Guo, Yuhong Wang, Hongmao Sun, and Junzhou Huang. 2019a. Smiles-bert: large scale unsupervised pre-training for molecular property prediction. In *Proceedings of the 10th ACM international conference on bioinformatics, computational biology and health informatics*, pages 429–436.

Sheng Wang, Yuzhi Guo, Yuhong Wang, Hongmao Sun, and Junzhou Huang. 2019b. Smiles-bert: Large scale unsupervised pre-training for molecular property prediction. In *Proceedings of the 10th ACM International Conference on Bioinformatics, Computational Biology and Health Informatics*, BCB '19, page 429–436, New York, NY, USA. Association for Computing Machinery.

Yuyang Wang, Jianren Wang, Zhonglin Cao, and Amir Barati Farimani. 2022. Molecular contrastive learning of representations via graph neural networks. *Nature Machine Intelligence*, 4(3):279–287.

Zhenqin Wu, Bharath Ramsundar, Evan N Feinberg, Joseph Gomes, Caleb Geniesse, Aneesh S Pappu, Karl Leswing, and Vijay Pande. 2018. Moleculenet: a benchmark for molecular machine learning. *Chemical science*, 9(2):513–530.

Jun Xia, Chengshuai Zhao, Bozhen Hu, Zhangyang Gao, Cheng Tan, Yue Liu, Siyuan Li, and Stan Z Li. 2022. Mole-bert: Rethinking pre-training graph neural networks for molecules. In *The Eleventh International Conference on Learning Representations*.

Minghao Xu, Zuobai Zhang, Jiarui Lu, Zhaocheng Zhu, Yangtian Zhang, Ma Chang, Runcheng Liu, and Jian Tang. 2022. Peer: a comprehensive and multi-task benchmark for protein sequence understanding. *Advances in Neural Information Processing Systems*, 35:35156–35173.

Chengxuan Ying, Tianle Cai, Shengjie Luo, Shuxin Zheng, Guolin Ke, Di He, Yanming Shen, and Tie-Yan Liu. 2021. Do transformers really perform badly for graph representation? *Advances in Neural Information Processing Systems*, 34:28877–28888.

Yuning You, Tianlong Chen, Yang Shen, and Zhangyang Wang. 2021. Graph contrastive learning automated. In *International Conference on Machine Learning*, pages 12121–12132. PMLR.

Yanqiao Zhu, Dingshuo Chen, Yuanqi Du, Yingze Wang, Qiang Liu, and Shu Wu. 2022. Featurizations matter: a multiview contrastive learning approach to molecular pretraining. In *ICML 2022 2nd AI for Science Workshop*.

ALMol: Aligned Language-Molecule Translation LLMs through Offline Preference Contrastive Optimisation

Dimitris Gkoumas
Queen Mary University of London, London, UK
d.gkoumas@qmul.ac.uk

Abstract

The field of chemistry and Artificial Intelligence (AI) intersection is an area of active research that aims to accelerate scientific discovery. The integration of large language models (LLMs) with scientific modalities has shown significant promise in this endeavour. However, challenges persist in effectively addressing training efficacy and the out-of-distribution problem, particularly as existing approaches rely on larger models and datasets. In this context, we focus on machine language-molecule translation and deploy a novel training approach called contrastive preference optimisation, which avoids generating translations that are merely adequate but not perfect. To ensure generalisability and mitigate memorisation effects, we conduct experiments using only 10% of the data. Our results demonstrate that our models achieve up to a 32% improvement compared to counterpart models. Finally, we introduce a fine-grained, domain-agnostic evaluation method to assess hallucination in LLMs and promote responsible use.

1 Introduction

The world is facing unprecedented complexity in the form of global challenges such as climate change, healthcare, and pandemics. Innovative scientific solutions are urgently needed to address these challenges. Chemistry has been at the forefront of developing such solutions, pioneering new drugs (Ferguson and Gray, 2018), creating advanced materials (Kippelen and Brédas, 2009), or enhancing chemical processes (Zhong et al., 2023). However, these frontiers are vast and require the involvement of Artificial Intelligence (AI) technology to navigate them effectively.

Large language models (LLMs) have shown promising potential for accelerating scientific discovery across various domains, including chemistry, biology, and materials science (Zhang et al., 2023; AI4Science and Quantum, 2023). Existing work has applied successful paradigms from natural language processing (NLP) and multimodal representation learning to the chemistry domain. One common approach involves converting the inherent three-dimensional structures of molecules into SMILES, which provide a mapping to symbolic character-level representations. Subsequently, researchers have explored learning language-molecule representations either in separate yet coordinated spaces (Edwards et al., 2022, 2021; Liu et al., 2023a), in a joint space (Liu et al., 2023b), or through hybrid approaches (Luo et al., 2023; Christofidellis et al., 2023). In light of the recent significant advancements in the field, none of the above approaches effectively tackle the inherent challenges in training such models. Instead, they rely on sparse or noisy synthetic data, often necessitating exponentially more data than is typically used in NLP tasks (Edwards et al., 2024).

However, training on larger models and datasets does not necessarily guarantee higher performance. A successful paradigm that augments the capabilities of LLMs across multiple NLP tasks is Reinforcement Learning with Human Feedback (RLHF) (Ouyang et al., 2022). Although initially challenged by issues of slowness and instability, recent research has addressed many of these challenges by shifting towards closed-form losses that operate directly on offline preference data (Rafailov et al., 2024). RLHF has demonstrated superior performance compared to standard minimising cross-entropy optimisation approaches.

In this context, we address challenges related to effectively training robust language models when integrated with scientific modalities. We deploy a novel way of training LLMs for language-molecule translation that avoids generating translations that are only adequate but not perfect, called contrastive preference optimisation (CTO) (Xu et al., 2024). CTO is based on offline preferences instead of su-

Proceedings of the 1st Workshop on Language + Molecules (L+M 2024), pages 22–28
August 15, 2024

pervised fine-tuning, mimicking reference translations. To ensure that our models can effectively generalise instead of memorising patterns, we conduct experiments using only 10% of the L+M-24 dataset (Edwards et al., 2024). Our contributions have as follows:

- Our models achieve significant performance improvements across various evaluation metrics compared to models trained on extensive in-distribution and out-of-distribution data (§ 4.4).
- We showcase their robustness through experiments comparing pivot and minor cross-modals. Our empirical results demonstrate that our models consistently outperform the leading baseline, Meditron, which is trained on the entire dataset, even in agnostic cross-modal scenarios (§ 4.4).
- We propose a fine-grained evaluation method that is domain-independent, assessing factual consistency in generated captions using a question-answering evaluation metric and measuring overlaps of unigrams in generated molecules against references (§ 3.3). Our analysis shows that our models achieve improved factual consistency and character-level unigram overlaps for caption and molecule generation (§ 4.5).

2 Background

Reinforcement Learning with Human Feedback (RLHF) optimisation (Ouyang et al., 2022) operates with a triple dataset $\mathcal{D} = \{x, y_w, y_l\}$, where y_w and y_l represent preferred and dis-preferred outputs, corresponding to input x, such that $y_w \succ y_l$ for x. The probability of y_w over y_l in pairwise comparisons is typically computed using the Bradley-Terry model (Bradley and Terry, 1952):

$$p^*(y_w \succ y_l|x) = \sigma(r^*(x, y_w) - r^*(x, y_l)) \quad (1)$$

where σ is the logistic function, and r^* denotes the reward function that underlies the preferences.

As obtaining the reward directly from a human would be prohibitively expensive, a reward model r_ϕ is trained to act as a surrogate by minimising the negative log-likelihood of the preference data:

$$\mathcal{L}(r_\phi) = -\mathbb{E}_{(x,y_w,y_l)\sim\mathcal{D}}[\log \sigma(r_\phi(x, y_w) - r_\phi(x, y_l))] \quad (2)$$

Additionally, the Kullback-Leibler (KL) divergence between the outputs generated by π_{ref} and the parameterised π_θ models serves as an additional reward signal, ensuring that the generated responses closely align with the reference model. Consequently, an optimal model π_θ is one that maximises:

$$\mathbb{E}_{(x\in\mathcal{D},y\in\pi_\theta)}[r_\phi(x, y)] - \beta\mathcal{D}_{\text{KL}}(\pi_\theta(y|x)||\pi_{\text{ref}}(y|x)) \quad (3)$$

where β is the temperature parameter typically $\in [0.1, 0.5]$.

RLHF can present challenges due to its inherent slowness and instability, especially in distributed settings (Zheng et al., 2024). Recent work has shifted towards closed-form losses to align LLMs with human preferences. Here, we experiment with contrastive preference optimisation that adopts a closed-form loss for RLHF.

3 Methodology

3.1 Task Formulation

Let (x, y) be a pair of source and target sequences mapped to X and Y spaces, respectively. We cast the problem of language-molecule translation as a cross-modal translation task that operates on offline preference data $\mathcal{D} = \{x^{(i)}, y_w^{(i)}, y_l^{(i)}\}_{i=1}^N$, where x is an input, y_w are preferred (e.g. human gold standard) and y_l dis-preferred outputs (typically synthetic, obtained from an appropriate translation model), and N is the total number of pairs. The goal is to learn an optimal function $f : X \leftrightarrow Y$ through a model π_θ parameterised by θ. We coordinate the two spaces through instructional modelling to regulate the translation process in both directions. Specifically, for LMolT, we use instructions for language-to-molecule and molecule-to-language translation (see Appx. A).

3.2 Contrastive Preference Optimisation

Contrastive preference optimisation (CTO) (Xu et al., 2024) addresses challenges stemming from the inherent limitation in RLHF, as discussed in § 2, and from the necessity of high-quality data. CTO is a general approximation of Eq. 3 using a uniform reference model, which assumes equal likelihood for all possible generated outputs:

$$\mathcal{L}(\pi_\theta; U) = -\mathbb{E}_{(x,y_w,y_l)\sim D} \left[\log \sigma\Big(\beta \log \pi_\theta(y_w|x) - \beta \log \pi_\theta(y_l|x)\Big)\right] \quad (4)$$

where π_θ is parameterised model by θ and β hyper-parameter (please refer § 2). Eq. 4 implies that the loss is calculated based on how well the generated translations match this uniform distribution of possible translations, rather than being biased towards any particular translation. To maintain π_θ close to the preferred data distribution, a behaviour cloning (BC) (Hejna et al., 2023) regulariser is introduced:

$$\min_\theta \mathcal{L}(\pi_\theta, U) \quad \text{s.t.}$$
$$\mathbb{E}_{(x,y_w)\sim D}\Big[\mathbb{KL}(\pi_w(y_w|x)||\pi_\theta(y_w|x))\Big] < \epsilon, \quad (5)$$

Here, ϵ denotes a small positive constant, and $\mathbb{KL}$ signifies the Kullback-Leibler divergence. The regulariser is enhanced with an additional SFT term on the preferred data, bolstering the CPO loss as:

$$\mathcal{L}_{\text{CPO}} = \min_\theta \underbrace{\mathcal{L}(\pi_\theta, U)}_{\mathcal{L}_{\text{prefer}}} - \underbrace{\mathbb{E}_{(x,y_w)\sim D}[\log \pi_\theta(y_w|x)]}_{\mathcal{L}_{\text{NLL}}} \quad (6)$$

3.3 Proposed Evaluation Methodology

Prior studies have utilised embedding representations, for assessing the semantics in chemical-domain models (Jaeger et al., 2018; Edwards et al., 2021; Christofidellis et al., 2023). However, these approaches require domain adaptation for out-of-distribution data (Edwards et al., 2024) and might lead to opaque and arbitrary outcomes (Steck et al., 2024). We address these limitations by introducing a scalable fine-grained evaluation methodology for assessing the presence of hallucinations[1] in generated outputs.

Language Evaluation: For molecule-to-language translation, we deploy the QAFactEval (Fabbri et al., 2022) metric to evaluate the factual consistency of generated captions. QAFactEval first selects noun phrases and named entities (NER) from the generated outputs. A question generation (QG) model then formulates associated questions, which a question answering (QA) model addresses based on the reference text. QAFactEval measures the semantic overlap between the QA model's responses and the selected answers to produce the final metric score. An example is illustrated in Fig. 1. Here, we report the semantic *overlap*, the f_1 *accuracy* between the QA model and the selected answer, and *answerability*, which is the probability of the question being answered by the reference caption.

[1]Hallucination in LLMs refers to a phenomenon where the generated outputs are inaccurate, nonsensical, or contradictory to the provided factual information.

Reference Caption
It belongs to the orexin receptor modulator class of molecules.
Generated Caption
The molecule is an antiviral.
Selected Answer
an antiviral
Generated Question
What is the molecule?
QA Output
Orexin receptor modulator
Scores
Overlap: 0.5, f1: 0.0, Is answered: 0.5

Figure 1: A toy example illustrating a factual inconsistency between a generated and a reference caption. The QAFactEval metric selects a noun-phrase answer from the generated caption. A QG model then generates an associated question that a QA model answers based on the reference caption. The scores measure the semantic overlap between the QA model's answer and the selected answer from the generated caption

Molecule Evaluation: For language-to-molecule translation, we employ the Chr-F metric, an F-score statistic, to evaluate character n-gram matches between prediction-reference pairs (Popović, 2015). This metric assesses the matches in generated molecules against their references by averaging the scores of unigram, bigram, and trigram matches. A higher Chr-F score indicates better performance.

Bias Evaluation: We also calculate the character and token length bias in generated-reference pairs of molecules and captions, respectively, to investigate potential length bias in the evaluated LLMs.

4 Experiments

4.1 Data

We conduct experiments on the *L+M-24* benchmark dataset, which encompasses both molecule and linguistic modalities (Edwards et al., 2024). It is divided into four categories, each with significant applications in small-molecule domain; biomedical; light and electricity; human interaction and organoleptics; and agriculture and industry. The training and validation subsets consist of approximately 127k and 34k language-molecule pairs, respectively. Here, we utilise 10% of these subsets for training and validation. To operationalise CTO, we recreate a triples dataset consisting of preferred and dis-preferred outputs (see § 2), where the former are the golden references and the latter are generated from MolT5 (Edwards et al., 2022). For evaluation, we randomly selected 3k unseen pairs from a distinct dataset provided by the research group of L+M-24.[2]

4.2 Bechmark Models

We compare our results with established language-molecule models as captured in the literature:

- TxtChem-T5 (Christofidellis et al., 2023): A T5 model trained on both linguistic and molecule modalities with a multi-task objective across various datasets, including the CheBI-20 dataset (Edwards et al., 2022), akin to *L+M-24*.
- Chem-LLM (Zhang et al., 2024): An InternLM2-Base-7B model, trained on an extensive chemical domain knowledge dataset, with the direct preference optimisation objective (Rafailov et al., 2024), achieves results comparable to GPT-4.
- Meditron (Chen et al., 2023): A Meditron-7B model fine-tuned on the entire *L+M-24* for unidirectional language-molecule translation.
- SFT-Meditron: We fine-tune Meditron-7B on a 10% subset of *L+M-24* for bi-directional machine language-molecule translation.

4.3 Experimental Settings

Here, we train Meditron with CTO on a 10% subset of *L+M-24*. We experiment with both language and molecule weight initialisation obtained from Meditron trained on the entire data (Edwards et al., 2024). We refer to them as CTO-Meditron$_{\overrightarrow{Lan.}}$ and CTO-Meditron$_{\overrightarrow{Mol.}}$, respectively. We train the models with QLoRA (Dettmers et al., 2024). For evaluation, we adopt established metrics in (Edwards et al., 2022).

4.4 Experiment Results

Table 2 presents a summary of the molecule-to-language results. We observed a significant decrease in performance for benchmark models trained on extensive data with SFT when tested on out-of-distribution data. Among the baseline models, Meditron demonstrated the highest performance, likely due to its training on the entire *L+M-24* dataset utilised in our experiments. Training Meditron with SFT for bi-directional language-molecule translation has demonstrated neither effectiveness (see Table 1) nor efficiency (refer to Appx. B). This suggests that the performance in our experiments is not dependent on memorised patterns from Meditron trained on the entire dataset. In contrast, our models trained with the CTO objective on only 10% of *L+M-24* achieved a remarkable improvement in performance across diverse evaluation metrics, up to 32% compared to Meditron trained on the entire dataset. This improvement is consistent, as our model consistently enhances performance when initialised from agnostic cross-modals, i.e., CTO-Meditron$_{\overrightarrow{Lan}}$ in Table 1.

We observed similar performance patterns for language-to-molecule translation as reported in Table 2. However, even though our model achieved better performance compared to Meditron when initialised from agnostic cross-modals, it struggled to learn molecular patterns (see CTO-Meditron$_{\overrightarrow{Mol.}}$ in Table 2). This suggests that language plays a pivotal role in the molecule modality. In the future, we aim to explore more advanced initialised methods to address this challenge.

4.5 Evaluation Results

Fig. 2 illustrates the evaluation results on the factual consistency of generated captions against references for the molecule-to-language task. CTO-Meditron$_{\overrightarrow{Mol.}}$, trained on 10% of the available data, exhibited superior factual consistency, achieving a semantic overlap of 2.08, $f1$ accuracy of 0.34, and answerability of 0.68, compared to 1.34, 0.20, and 0.51, respectively, for Meditron trained on the entire dataset. CTO-Meditron$_{\overrightarrow{Lan.}}$ also outperformed Meditron but showed lower performance than CTO-Meditron$_{\overrightarrow{Mol.}}$. We attribute this to the model being initialised by agnostic cross-modals.

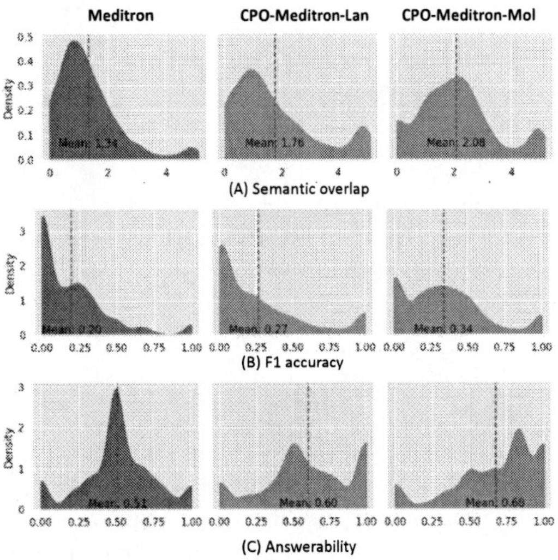

Figure 2: Factual consistency in generated captions against references, assessed through (A) semantic overlap, (B) F1 accuracy, and (C) answerability using QAFactEval (§ 3.3) across various LLMs.

[2]Sampling is conducted from a distinct subset.

Model	Blue-2 ↑	Blue-4 ↑	Rouge-1 ↑	Rouge-2 ↑	Rouge-L ↑	METEOR ↑
TxtChem-T5	0.08	0.09	0.19	0.06	0.17	0.16
Chem-LLM	0.03	0.00	0.11	0.02	0.09	0.14
Meditron	0.42	0.30	0.63	0.47	0.49	0.54
SFT-Meditron	0.37	0.26	0.54	0.39	0.38	0.60
CTO-Meditron$_{\overrightarrow{Lan}}$	0.62 (+0.20)	0.45 (+0.15)	0.67 (+0.03)	0.50 (+0.03)	0.48 (-0.01)	0.62 (+0.08)
CTO-Meditron$_{\overrightarrow{Mol}}$	0.74 (+0.32)	0.53 (+0.23)	0.76 (+0.10)	0.56 (+0.09)	0.53 (+0.04)	0.71(+0.17)

Table 1: Molecule-to-language translation results. Arrows next to metrics indicate the higher value the better performance. Numbers in parentheses show deviations from Meditron trained on the entire dataset.

Model	BLEU ↑	Exact ↑	Levenshtein ↓	MACCS FTS ↑	RDK FTS ↑	Morgan FTS ↑	FCD ↓	Validity ↑
TxtChem-T5	0.18	0.00	133.29	0.21	0.10	0.03	37.67	0.58
Chem-LLM	0.04	0.00	732.74	0.00	0.00	0.00	59.44	0.19
Meditron	0.43	0.00	66.16	0.35	0.29	0.19	13.64	0.57
SFT-Meditron	0.30	0.00	186.99	0.70	0.62	0.41	11.14	0.98
CTO-Meditron$_{\overrightarrow{Lan.}}$	0.71 (+0.28)	0.00	42.65 (-23.51)	0.78 (+0.43)	0.70 (+0.41)	0.48 (+0.29)	4.19 (-9.45)	1.00 (+0.43)
CTO-Meditron$_{\overrightarrow{Mol.}}$	0.52 (+0.09)	0.00	76.95 (+10.43)	0.52 (+0.17)	0.49 (+0.20)	0.37 (+0.18)	27.39 (+13.75)	0.58 (+0.01)

Table 2: Language-to-molecule translation results. Arrows next to metrics indicate whether higher or lower values denote better performance. Numbers in parentheses show deviations from Meditron trained on the entire dataset.

For the language-to-molecule task, we observed that both Meditron$_{\overrightarrow{Lan.}}$ and Meditron$_{\overrightarrow{Mol.}}$ achieved similar performance in terms of uni-, bi-, and tri-gram overlaps between generated and reference pairs, outperforming Meditron (see Fig. 3). However, when the model was initialized with known cross-modal weights, i.e., Meditron$_{\overrightarrow{Lan.}}$, it achieved a slightly increased performance

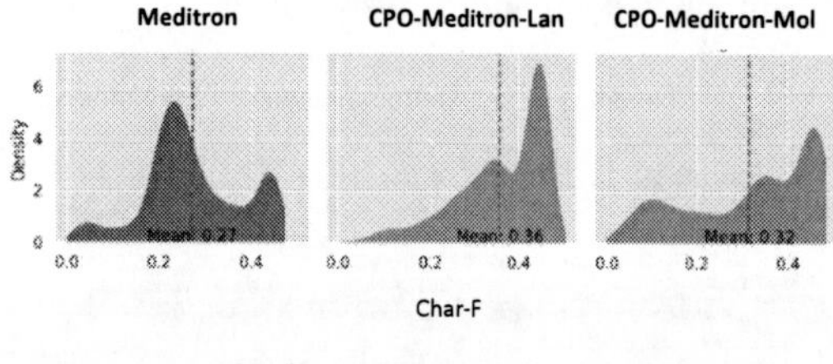

Figure 3: Overlaps of n-gram matches between generated and reference molecules as captured by the char-F (§ 3.3) score across various LLMs.

For the language-to-molecule task, we observed that Meditron and Meditron$_{\overrightarrow{Mol.}}$ generated significantly shorter and longer outputs, respectively (see Fig. 4). In contrast, Meditron$_{\overrightarrow{Lan.}}$ did not exhibit any length bias, producing outputs similar in length to the actual ones. Conversely, for the molecule-to-language task, our models did not show any significant length bias, while Meditron, trained on the entire dataset, generated significantly shorter answers against references.

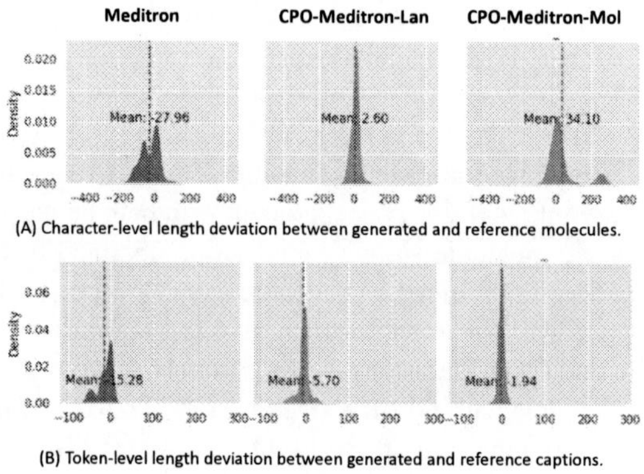

Figure 4: Length-bias across different LLMs.

5 Conclusion

This work address training efficacy and the out-of-distribution problem for automatic language-molecule translation. We train models using only 10% of available data and deploying contrastive preference optimisation which avoids generating translations that are merely adequate but not perfect. We achieve significant improvement in performance when compared with models trained on extensive in and out-of-the-distribution data. Finally, we propose a fine-grained, domain-agnostic evaluation method to assess hallucination in LLMs. Our models show superior factual consistency for caption generation and character-level unigram overlaps for molecule generation.

References

Microsoft Research AI4Science and Microsoft Azure Quantum. 2023. The impact of large language models on scientific discovery: a preliminary study using gpt-4. *arXiv preprint arXiv:2311.07361*.

Ralph Allan Bradley and Milton E Terry. 1952. Rank analysis of incomplete block designs: I. the method of paired comparisons. *Biometrika*, 39(3/4):324–345.

Zeming Chen, Alejandro Hernández Cano, Angelika Romanou, Antoine Bonnet, Kyle Matoba, Francesco Salvi, Matteo Pagliardini, Simin Fan, Andreas Köpf, Amirkeivan Mohtashami, et al. 2023. Meditron-70b: Scaling medical pretraining for large language models. *arXiv preprint arXiv:2311.16079*.

Dimitrios Christofidellis, Giorgio Giannone, Jannis Born, Ole Winther, Teodoro Laino, and Matteo Manica. 2023. Unifying molecular and textual representations via multi-task language modelling. In *International Conference on Machine Learning*, pages 6140–6157. PMLR.

Tim Dettmers, Artidoro Pagnoni, Ari Holtzman, and Luke Zettlemoyer. 2024. Qlora: Efficient finetuning of quantized llms. *Advances in Neural Information Processing Systems*, 36.

Carl Edwards, Tuan Lai, Kevin Ros, Garrett Honke, Kyunghyun Cho, and Heng Ji. 2022. Translation between molecules and natural language. In *Proceedings of the 2022 Conference on Empirical Methods in Natural Language Processing*, pages 375–413.

Carl Edwards, Qingyun Wang, Lawrence Zhao, and Heng Ji. 2024. L+m-24: Building a dataset for language+ molecules@ acl 2024. *arXiv preprint arXiv:2403.00791*.

Carl Edwards, ChengXiang Zhai, and Heng Ji. 2021. Text2mol: Cross-modal molecule retrieval with natural language queries. In *Proceedings of the 2021 Conference on Empirical Methods in Natural Language Processing*, pages 595–607.

Alexander Richard Fabbri, Chien-Sheng Wu, Wenhao Liu, and Caiming Xiong. 2022. Qafacteval: Improved qa-based factual consistency evaluation for summarization. In *Proceedings of the 2022 Conference of the North American Chapter of the Association for Computational Linguistics: Human Language Technologies*, pages 2587–2601.

Fleur M Ferguson and Nathanael S Gray. 2018. Kinase inhibitors: the road ahead. *Nature reviews Drug discovery*, 17(5):353–377.

Joey Hejna, Rafael Rafailov, Harshit Sikchi, Chelsea Finn, Scott Niekum, W Bradley Knox, and Dorsa Sadigh. 2023. Contrastive prefence learning: Learning from human feedback without rl. *arXiv preprint arXiv:2310.13639*.

Sabrina Jaeger, Simone Fulle, and Samo Turk. 2018. Mol2vec: unsupervised machine learning approach with chemical intuition. *Journal of chemical information and modeling*, 58(1):27–35.

Bernard Kippelen and Jean-Luc Brédas. 2009. Organic photovoltaics. *Energy & Environmental Science*, 2(3):251–261.

Shengchao Liu, Weili Nie, Chengpeng Wang, Jiarui Lu, Zhuoran Qiao, Ling Liu, Jian Tang, Chaowei Xiao, and Animashree Anandkumar. 2023a. Multimodal molecule structure–text model for text-based retrieval and editing. *Nature Machine Intelligence*, 5(12):1447–1457.

Zequn Liu, Wei Zhang, Yingce Xia, Lijun Wu, Shufang Xie, Tao Qin, Ming Zhang, and Tie-Yan Liu. 2023b. Molxpt: Wrapping molecules with text for generative pre-training. *arXiv preprint arXiv:2305.10688*.

Yizhen Luo, Kai Yang, Massimo Hong, Xingyi Liu, and Zaiqing Nie. 2023. Molfm: A multimodal molecular foundation model. *arXiv preprint arXiv:2307.09484*.

Long Ouyang, Jeffrey Wu, Xu Jiang, Diogo Almeida, Carroll Wainwright, Pamela Mishkin, Chong Zhang, Sandhini Agarwal, Katarina Slama, Alex Ray, et al. 2022. Training language models to follow instructions with human feedback. *Advances in neural information processing systems*, 35:27730–27744.

Maja Popović. 2015. chrf: character n-gram f-score for automatic mt evaluation. In *Proceedings of the tenth workshop on statistical machine translation*, pages 392–395.

Rafael Rafailov, Archit Sharma, Eric Mitchell, Christopher D Manning, Stefano Ermon, and Chelsea Finn. 2024. Direct preference optimization: Your language model is secretly a reward model. *Advances in Neural Information Processing Systems*, 36.

Harald Steck, Chaitanya Ekanadham, and Nathan Kallus. 2024. Is cosine-similarity of embeddings really about similarity? *arXiv preprint arXiv:2403.05440*.

Haoran Xu, Amr Sharaf, Yunmo Chen, Weiting Tan, Lingfeng Shen, Benjamin Van Durme, Kenton Murray, and Young Jin Kim. 2024. Contrastive preference optimization: Pushing the boundaries of llm performance in machine translation. *arXiv preprint arXiv:2401.08417*.

Di Zhang, Wei Liu, Qian Tan, Jingdan Chen, Hang Yan, Yuliang Yan, Jiatong Li, Weiran Huang, Xiangyu Yue, Dongzhan Zhou, et al. 2024. Chemllm: A chemical large language model. *arXiv preprint arXiv:2402.06852*.

X Zhang, L Wang, J Helwig, Y Luo, C Fu, Y Xie, M Liu, Y Lin, Z Xu, K Yan, et al. 2023. Artificial intelligence for science in quantum, atomistic, and continuum systems. arxiv 2023. *arXiv preprint arXiv:2307.08423*.

Chen Zheng, Ke Sun, Hang Wu, Chenguang Xi, and Xun Zhou. 2024. Balancing enhancement, harmlessness, and general capabilities: Enhancing conversational llms with direct rlhf. *arXiv preprint arXiv:2403.02513*.

Ming Zhong, Siru Ouyang, Yizhu Jiao, Priyanka Kargupta, Leo Luo, Yanzhen Shen, Bobby Zhou, Xianrui Zhong, Xuan Liu, Hongxiang Li, et al. 2023. Reaction miner: An integrated system for chemical reaction extraction from textual data. In *Proceedings of the 2023 Conference on Empirical Methods in Natural Language Processing: System Demonstrations*, pages 389–402.

A Language-molecule Translation Instructions

> Below is an instruction that describes a task, paired with an input that provides further context.
> Write a response that appropriately completes the request.
>
> ### Instruction: You are a researcher. You can come up captions based on your existing knowledge.
> Captions are given against the following input. You should be as detailed as possible.
>
> ### Input: Molecule: {source molecule}
> In that molecule, could you formulate a caption about?
>
> ### Response: {target caption}

Figure 5: Instruction for molecule to language translation, i.e., $M \to L$

> Below is an instruction that describes a task, paired with an input that provides further context.
> Write a response that appropriately completes the request.
>
> ### Instruction: You are a researcher. You can come up molecule smile strings based on your existing knowledge.
> Molecule smile strings are given against the following input. You should be as detailed as possible.
>
> ### Input: Caption: {source caption}
> In that caption, could you generate a molecule smile string?
>
> ### Response: {target molecule}

Figure 6: Instruction for language to molecule translation, i.e., $L \to M$

B Training Effectiveness and Efficiency

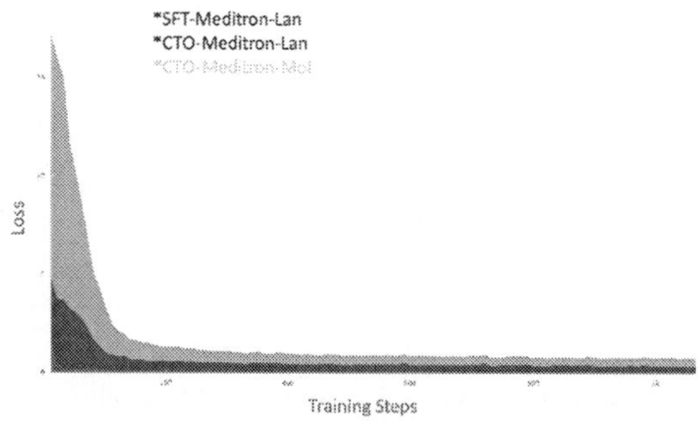

Figure 7: Training convergence

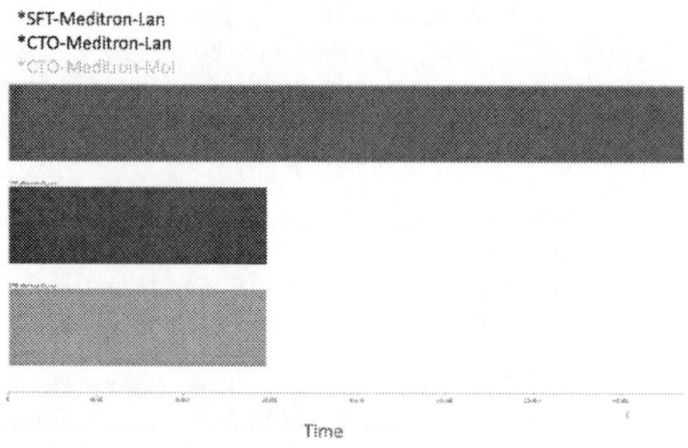

Figure 8: Training efficiency

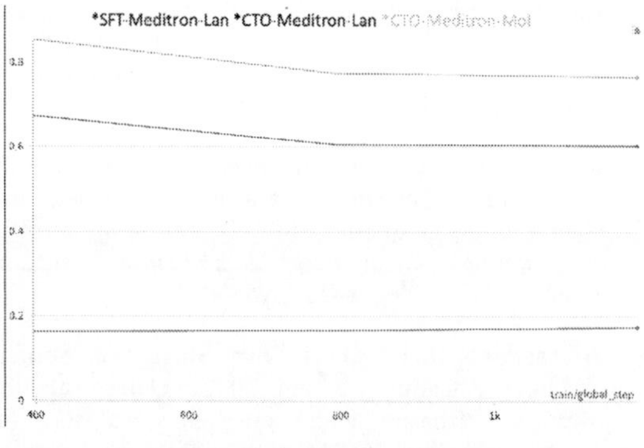

Figure 9: Validation loss

Evaluating Extrapolation Ability of Large Language Model in Chemical Domain

Taehun Cha and **Donghun Lee***
Department of Mathematics
Korea University
{cth127, holy}@korea.ac.kr

Abstract

Solving a problem outside the training space, i.e. extrapolation, has been a long problem in the machine learning community. The current success of large language models demonstrates the LLM's extrapolation ability to several unseen tasks. In line with these works, we evaluate the LLM's extrapolation ability in the chemical domain. We construct a data set measuring the material properties of epoxy polymers depending on various raw materials and curing processes. LLM should predict the material property when novel raw material is introduced utilizing its chemical knowledge. Through experiments, LLM tends to choose the right direction of adjustment but fails to determine the exact degree, resulting in poor MAE on some properties. But LLM can successfully adjust the degree with only a one-shot example. The results show that LLM can extrapolate to new unseen material utilizing its chemical knowledge learned through massive pre-training.

1 Introduction

Marcus (1998) depicted two aspects of the generalization: interpolation and extrapolation. The interpolation targets a problem *within* the training space, while the extrapolation targets the *outside*. Despite the rapid development of machine learning technology, even a modern deep-learning-based model struggles to extrapolate on some tasks that humans find easy (Lake and Baroni, 2018, Barrett et al., 2018 and Saxton et al., 2019).

Human reasoning involves the extrapolation ability (Webb et al., 2020), especially for knowledge discovery. Mitchell et al. (2018) exemplified Halley's prediction on the return of a comet: it was possible thanks to Newton's inverse square law of gravity and would be difficult with pre-Newtonian models. Newton found laws that went *beyond simply maximizing the fit* to the known set of planetary bodies (Mitchell et al., 2018), unlike usual machine learning models.

The current success of large language models (LLMs) shows hints of their extrapolation ability. Conneau and Lample (2019) reported that fine-tuning a multilingual language model on a monolingual classification data set can result in a strong multilingual classifier, which has never seen a multilingual classification data set. Wei et al. (2022) introduced an instruction tuning framework: by training LLM on multiple tasks to follow human instructions, the LLM shows improved zero-shot performance on several unseen tasks. These results suggest an emergent extrapolation ability of LLM utilizing its representation power learned through massive pre-training.

In this paper, we explore the extrapolation ability of LLM in the chemical domain. Our main research question is *Can LLM perform the extrapolation utilizing its internal chemical knowledge?* To examine this question, we suggest a novel task regressing material properties of epoxy polymers when a novel raw material is introduced. LLM should infer the effect of novel raw material on the epoxy polymer from natural language descriptions or SMILES.

2 Related Works

Several researchers adopted an LLM to the chemical domain by training it on a chemistry-related corpus. Fang et al. (2024) introduced a data set for instruction tuning including various molecule/protein-oriented tasks. Cao et al. (2023) and Zhao et al. (2023) integrated the graph structure of molecules into an LLM to improve its representation power. Ye et al. (2023) and Zhao et al. (2024) trained a dialogue model on chemical domain. Our goal is to verify the chemical ability of an existing LLM, not suggesting a new foundation model.

* corresponding author

Proceedings of the 1st Workshop on Language + Molecules (L+M 2024), pages 29–34

Guo et al. (2023) verified existing LLMs' ability on eight chemical tasks from name prediction to molecule captioning. They showed that GPT-4 (OpenAI, 2024) showed the best performance on most tasks showing comparable performance with SOTA, task-specific models. Our work is an extension of their work while differing on two points: (1) Their work focused on molecule-level tasks, while our work is compound-level. As more information should be considered, compound-level tasks require more complex reasoning than the molecule-level. (2) Unlike classic tasks, we focus on the extrapolation ability of an LLM, which is also more challenging.

3 Problem Statement

Let $(\mathcal{X}, \mathcal{Y})$ be a domain of independent and dependent variables of train data. We have our train data $\mathcal{D}_{train} = \{(x_i, y_i)\}_{i=1}^{N_{train}}, x_i \in \mathcal{X}, y_i \in \mathcal{Y}$. Let $\mathcal{X}'$ be a domain of additional independent variables. Set a domain of independent variables of test data as $\mathcal{X} \times \mathcal{X}'$. Then we have our test data $\mathcal{D}_{test} = \{(x_i, x'_i, y_i)\}_{i=1}^{N_{test}}, x_i \in \mathcal{X}, x'_i \in \mathcal{X}', y_i \in \mathcal{Y}$.

Let $f : \mathcal{X} \times \mathcal{X}' \rightarrow \mathcal{Y}$ be a model trained on $\mathcal{D}_{train}$ with $\mathbb{E}_{(x,y)\sim\mathcal{D}_{train}} [\mathcal{L}(f(x, \phi), y)]$, where $\mathcal{L}$ is a loss function. We measure an *extrapolation ability* of a model f as $\mathbb{E}_{(x,x',y)\sim\mathcal{D}_{test}} [\mathcal{L}(f(x, x'), y)]$, when $X \bigcap X' = \phi$.

A model should infer the relationship between x' and other variables to extrapolate successfully. Our research hypothesis is *Can we utilize LLM's internal chemical knowledge for extrapolation, by providing additional information, e.g. SMILES of an additional raw material?* We test this hypothesis through experiments in the next section.

4 Experiments

4.1 Experimental Setup

We collect 917 data points with lab experiments measuring three dynamic mechanical analysis (DMA) properties, glass transition temperature (T_g), tan delta peak (δ), and cross-link density (v_c). Each data point contains 6 independent variables regarding raw materials (ratio between resin A: resin B_1: resin B_2: resin B_3: curing agent: catalyst) and 4 regarding curing processes (first and second curing temperature and time).

To evaluate the extrapolation ability of LLM, we construct a regression task. Our goal is to predict the DMA properties of test data given train data from a different domain, e.g. different raw materials. LLM should extrapolate the train data utilizing its chemical knowledge.

We test two extrapolation setups: (1) Additional epoxy resin. A model should infer the effect of a new epoxy resin B_i mixed with the original resin A. (2) Replaced epoxy resin. A model should infer the effect of a new epoxy resin B_2 replacing the original resin A. In both settings, train data only utilize the original resin A.

For LLM, we utilize *gpt-4-turbo* (OpenAI, 2024) with 10-shot examples for in-context learning. We select examples based on the cosine similarity of the feature vector between the train set and each test data point.

For baselines, we utilize four regression models, linear regression (**LR**), ridge regression (**RR**), random forest (**RF**, Ho, 1995), and XGBoost (**XGB**, Chen and Guestrin, 2016). To perform extrapolation with baseline regressors, we use the ratio of all epoxy resins ($A + B_1 + B_2 + B_3$) as a proxy variable.

4.2 Additional Epoxy Resin

Here, we evaluate the extrapolation ability of LLM for an additional raw material. Train and test data consists of 4 curing process variables (first and second curing temperature and time). Also, train data consists of 3 raw material-related variables as following:

- Resin A (DGEBA-based oligomer): a standard liquid bisphenol A epoxy resin with SMILES CC(C)(C1=CC=C(C=C1)OCC2CO 2)C3=CC=C(C=C3)OCC4CO4
- Curing agent (Dicyandiamide): C(#N)N=C (N)N
- Catalyst: CC1=C(C=C(C=C1)NC(=O)N(C)C) NC(=O)N(C)C

However, test data contains one additional variable, the ratio of resin B_i. Here is a brief explanation of resin B_i:

- Resin B_1: CTBN(Carboyl-Terminated Butadiene Acrylonitrile) modified epoxy resin, where resin A is chemically combined with CTBN, with SMILES O=C(OCC(O)C)CC(C#N)C/C=C/CC(OCC(O)C)=O

	Resin B_1			Resin B_2			Resin B_3		
	T_g	δ	v_c	T_g	δ	v_c	T_g	δ	v_c
LR	4.61	0.0667	0.000347	4.31	0.0539	**0.000225**	8.42	0.0536	0.000329
RR	**4.58**	**0.0666**	0.000349	**4.20**	**0.0537**	0.000228	8.42	**0.0520**	0.000336
RF	5.70	0.0730	0.000310	4.99	0.0760	0.000311	9.79	0.0572	0.000301
XGB	5.61	0.0718	0.000315	4.60	0.0761	0.000237	9.00	0.0559	0.000304
Ours	7.32	0.0859	**0.000299**	5.62	0.0816	0.000288	**6.40**	0.0778	**0.000251**

Table 1: Mean absolute error (MAE) on extrapolative regression results when additional epoxy resin is added. Reported values are the average of MAE on 5 trials.

- Resin B_2: MBS type core shell rubber (CSR) modified epoxy resin, where resin A is physically combined with CSR with a ratio of 65:35 (resin A: CSR).
- Resin B_3: Dimer acid modified epoxy resin with SMILES OC(COC([R]C(OCC(O)COC1=CC=C(C(C)(C)C2=CC=C(OCC3CO3)C=C2)C=C1)=O)=O)COC(C=C4)=CC=C4C(C)(C)C5=CC=C(OCC6CO6)C=C5

LLM's goal is to predict the effect of additional resin on DMA properties only with train data and the chemical information provided above.

As a result, we obtain 385 train data with 7 independent variables and 30 test data (for each i) with 8 independent variables. The example prompt is on Appendix A. The results are on Table 1.

LLM shows superior extrapolation ability on v_c while failing on δ. Performance on T_g highly depends on the type of resin B_i. However, LLM's error shows relatively low volatility (5.62 to 7.32), unlike baseline regressors' which show high volatility (4.20 to 9.79). The result suggests that LLM can be a low-risk extrapolator, unlike utilizing regression models with proxy variables.

By examining the LLM prediction, we find out that LLM tends to adjust its prediction depending on resin type and target value. To quantitatively examine this phenomenon, we compute term frequency adjusting its final prediction. We count the number of tokens indicating its adjustment (*'increase', 'increased', 'higher', 'addition'* for ↑ and *'decrease', 'decreased', 'lower', 'reduction'* for ↓) in sentences mentioning 'resin B'. To verify the validity of the adjustment direction, we also report the average material property values of train and test sets. The results are on Table 2.

		Average			Frequency	
		Train		Test	↑	↓
B_1	T_g	161.3	↓	158.8	92	**358**
	δ	0.68	↑	0.72	**456**	322
	v_c	0.0013	↓	0.0011	67	**483**
B_2	T_g	161.3	↓	156.6	91	**248**
	δ	0.68	↑	0.74	**271**	151
	v_c	0.0013	↓	0.0011	61	**307**
B_3	T_g	161.3	↓	151.0	91	**542**
	δ	0.68	↑	0.74	**350**	527
	v_c	0.0013	↓	0.0009	117	**545**

Table 2: Term frequency analysis when additional epoxy resin is introduced. 'Average' column is the average value of target material properties (e.g. T_g) for each data set. Arrows between two columns represent the required adjustment direction (increase/decrease) from the train to the test set. 'Frequency' column is the term frequency on each word group representing increase/decrease. We mark the frequency in the right direction with bold.

Except for B_3 - δ case, LLM tends to use words mentioning *right direction* (↑ or ↓) more frequently. In other words, LLM captures the right adjustment direction. Though LLM chooses the right direction, LLM tends to overestimate the degree of adjustment and, as a result, shows higher MAEs. Moreover, the ratio between words in the right and wrong directions on δ is relatively low compared to T_g and v_c. These may suggest the reason why LLM's extrapolation ability on δ is relatively low.

An example answer is presented on Table 3.

4.3 Replaced Epoxy Resin

We present the extrapolation ability of an LLM when replacing epoxy resin from A to B_2. It is more challenging as the material properties of a

(...) CTBN is a rubbery polymer that is typically used to improve the toughness of epoxy resins. The incorporation of CTBN into an epoxy resin generally **results in a decrease in $\mathbf{T_g}$** because the CTBN phase is softer and more flexible compared to the rigid epoxy network formed by DGEBA-based resins. (...) The SMILES of Resin B indicates the presence of butadiene and acrylonitrile groups, which contribute to the elastomeric properties of the resin. This further supports the expectation of **a lower $\mathbf{T_g}$** due to increased flexibility and reduced crosslink density. (...)

Table 3: An example answer from LLM for adding resin B_1. LLM utilizes its chemical knowledge of CTBN and its SMILES to extrapolate existing data and predict a decrease in T_g.

	T_g	δ	v_c
LR	12.87	0.1606	0.001094
RR	12.78	0.1573	0.001097
RF	**12.62**	**0.1107**	0.000718
XGB	13.35	0.1199	0.000779
Ours	21.17	0.1116	**0.000467**
Ours (1 shot)	12.14	0.1080	0.000389

Table 4: MAE on extrapolative regression result when the epoxy resin A is replaced by B_2. Reported values are the average of MAE on 5 trials. The last line shows LLM's result with the 1 shot correction.

		Average			Frequency	
		Train		Test	↑	↓
B_2	T_g	161.3	↓	146.26	18	**151**
	δ	0.68	↑	0.71	**176**	106
	v_c	0.0013	↓	0.0007	13	**230**

Table 5: Term frequency analysis when epoxy resin A is replaced by B_2.

product on test data would be much more different from train data. The experimental setting is almost the same with Section 4.2, except that the ratio of resin A is 0 in the test data. We obtain 385 train data and 20 test data. The example prompt is on Appendix A. The results are on Table 4. We also perform the term frequency analysis on Table 5.

Similar to Section 4.2, LLM shows superior performance on extrapolating v_c. LLM also shows the same pattern on term frequency as in Table 2. The result suggests LLM chooses the right adjustment direction utilizing its chemical knowledge. However, MAE on T_g is high compared to baseline regressors, suggesting a similar conclusion: the direction is right, but the degree is wrong.

To check the correctability of the degree, we supply one test data point (with ground truth answer) and the previous LLM's answer for the data point back to LLM. The example prompt is on Appendix A and the result is on the last line of Table 4.

We can verify that LLM can successfully modify its degree of adjustment. As a result, LLM shows the best extrapolation ability with only one-shot correction.

5 Conclusion

In this paper, we evaluate the extrapolation ability of LLM in the chemical domain. We focus on regressing three material properties of epoxy compound when a novel raw material is introduced. We build a data set involving various raw materials and curing conditions from lab experiments. Compared to baseline regressors, LLM shows superior extrapolation ability in predicting cross-link density (v_c), while failing on tan δ peak. By examining the tokens used in LLM prediction, we find out that LLM tends to capture the right adjustment direction while failing to grasp the exact degree of adjustment. We also show that LLM successfully adjusts the degree with only 1-shot example. This result shows the potential applicability of LLM's extrapolation ability in chemical knowledge discovery.

Acknowledgements

This work was supported by the Ministry of Trade, Industry and Energy (MOTIE), Korea Institute for Advancement of Technology (KIAT) through the Virtual Engineering Platform Program (P0022334).

References

David Barrett, Felix Hill, Adam Santoro, Ari Morcos, and Timothy Lillicrap. 2018. Measuring abstract reasoning in neural networks. In *Proceedings of the 35th International Conference on Machine Learning*, volume 80 of *Proceedings of Machine Learning Research*, pages 511–520. PMLR.

He Cao, Zijing Liu, Xingyu Lu, Yuan Yao, and Yu Li. 2023. Instructmol: Multi-modal integration for building a versatile and reliable molecular assistant in drug discovery.

Tianqi Chen and Carlos Guestrin. 2016. Xgboost: A scalable tree boosting system. In *Proceedings of the 22nd ACM SIGKDD International Conference on Knowledge Discovery and Data Mining*, KDD '16. ACM.

Alexis Conneau and Guillaume Lample. 2019. Cross-lingual language model pretraining. In *Advances in Neural Information Processing Systems*, volume 32. Curran Associates, Inc.

Yin Fang, Xiaozhuan Liang, Ningyu Zhang, Kangwei Liu, Rui Huang, Zhuo Chen, Xiaohui Fan, and Huajun Chen. 2024. Mol-instructions: A large-scale biomolecular instruction dataset for large language models. In *ICLR*. OpenReview.net.

Taicheng Guo, Kehan Guo, Bozhao Nan, Zhenwen Liang, Zhichun Guo, Nitesh V Chawla, Olaf Wiest, and Xiangliang Zhang. 2023. What can large language models do in chemistry? a comprehensive benchmark on eight tasks. In *Thirty-seventh Conference on Neural Information Processing Systems Datasets and Benchmarks Track*.

Tin Kam Ho. 1995. Random decision forests. In *Proceedings of 3rd international conference on document analysis and recognition*, volume 1, pages 278–282. IEEE.

Brenden Lake and Marco Baroni. 2018. Generalization without systematicity: On the compositional skills of sequence-to-sequence recurrent networks. In *Proceedings of the 35th International Conference on Machine Learning*, volume 80 of *Proceedings of Machine Learning Research*, pages 2873–2882. PMLR.

Gary F. Marcus. 1998. Rethinking eliminative connectionism. *Cognitive Psychology*, 37(3):243–282.

Jeff Mitchell, Pontus Stenetorp, Pasquale Minervini, and Sebastian Riedel. 2018. Extrapolation in NLP. In *Proceedings of the Workshop on Generalization in the Age of Deep Learning*, pages 28–33, New Orleans, Louisiana. Association for Computational Linguistics.

OpenAI. 2024. Gpt-4 technical report.

David Saxton, Edward Grefenstette, Felix Hill, and Pushmeet Kohli. 2019. Analysing mathematical reasoning abilities of neural models. In *7th International Conference on Learning Representations, ICLR 2019, New Orleans, LA, USA, May 6-9, 2019*. OpenReview.net.

Taylor W. Webb, Zachary Dulberg, Steven M. Frankland, Alexander A. Petrov, Randall C. O'Reilly, and Jonathan D. Cohen. 2020. Learning representations that support extrapolation. In *Proceedings of the 37th International Conference on Machine Learning*, ICML'20. JMLR.org.

Jason Wei, Maarten Bosma, Vincent Zhao, Kelvin Guu, Adams Wei Yu, Brian Lester, Nan Du, Andrew M. Dai, and Quoc V Le. 2022. Finetuned language models are zero-shot learners. In *International Conference on Learning Representations*.

Geyan Ye, Xibao Cai, Houtim Lai, Xing Wang, Junhong Huang, Longyue Wang, Wei Liu, and Xiangxiang Zeng. 2023. Drugassist: A large language model for molecule optimization. *arXiv preprint arXiv:2401.10334*.

Haiteng Zhao, Shengchao Liu, Chang Ma, Hannan Xu, Jie Fu, Zhi-Hong Deng, Lingpeng Kong, and Qi Liu. 2023. GIMLET: A unified graph-text model for instruction-based molecule zero-shot learning. In *Thirty-seventh Conference on Neural Information Processing Systems*.

Zihan Zhao, Da Ma, Lu Chen, Liangtai Sun, Zihao Li, Hongshen Xu, Zichen Zhu, Su Zhu, Shuai Fan, Guodong Shen, Xin Chen, and Kai Yu. 2024. Chemdfm: Dialogue foundation model for chemistry.

A Example Prompts

Prompt for Section 4.2

Predict the *[PROPERTY]* of an epoxy product with the following information. You should infer the effect of a new resin B.:
Epoxy resin A (DGEBA-based oligomer) is a standard liquid bisphenol A epoxy resin with SMILES CC(C)(C1=CC=C(C=C1)OCC2CO2)C3=CC=C(C=C3)OCC4CO4.
Epoxy resin B is a CTBN(Carboyl-Terminated Butadiene Acrylonitrile) modified epoxy resin, where resin A is chemically combined with CTBN, with SMILES O=C(OCC(O)C)CC(C#N)C/C=C/CC(OCC(O)C)=O.
SMILES of curing agent (Dicyandiamide) is C(#N)N=C(N)N.
SMILES of catalyst is CC1=C(C=C(C=C1)NC(=O)N(C)C)NC(=O)N(C)C.
The following is another data point measuring the *[PROPERTY]*.
Ratio ((resin A: resin B): curing agent: catalyst)	First curing condition	Second curing condition	*[PROPERTY]*
(93.02: 0.0): 6.05: 0.93	1.0 hour in 100.0°C	0.5 hour in 130.0°C	*[PROPERTY1]*
(93.02: 0.0): 6.05: 0.93	1.0 hour in 100.0°C	1.5 hour in 130.0°C	*[PROPERTY2]*
(...)
Fill in the '?'.
| (83.72: 9.3): 6.05: 0.93 | 1.5 hour in 100.0°C | 1.0 hour in 130.0°C | ? |

Prompt for Section 4.3

Predict the *[PROPERTY]* of an epoxy product with the following information. You should infer the effect of a new resin B.:
Epoxy resin A (DGEBA-based oligomer) is a standard liquid bisphenol A epoxy resin with SMILES CC(C)(C1=CC=C(C=C1)OCC2CO2)C3=CC=C(C=C3)OCC4CO4.
Epoxy resin B is an MBS type core shell rubber (CSR) modified epoxy resin, where resin A is physically combined with CSR with a ratio of 65:35 (resin A:CSR).
SMILES of curing agent (Dicyandiamide) is C(#N)N=C(N)N.
SMILES of catalyst is CC1=C(C=C(C=C1)NC(=O)N(C)C)NC(=O)N(C)C.
The following is another data point measuring the *[PROPERTY]*.
Ratio ((resin A: resin B): curing agent: catalyst)	First curing condition	Second curing condition	*[PROPERTY]*
(93.02: 0.0): 5.12: 1.86	1.0 hour in 100.0°C	1.0 hour in 120.0°C	*[PROPERTY1]*
(93.02: 0.0): 5.12: 1.86	1.0 hour in 90.0°C	1.0 hour in 130.0°C	*[PROPERTY2]*
(...)
Fill in the '?'.
| (0.0: 93.65): 4.35: 2.01 | 1.0 hour in 90.0°C | 1.5 hour in 120.0°C | ? |

Additional Prompt for 1-shot Correction

Note that for the data point: | (0.0: 93.65): 4.35: 2.01 | 1.0 hour in 90.0°C | 1.5 hour in 120.0°C |, your answer was *[PREVIOUS ANSWER]*.
But the true value was *[PROPERTY3]*.

Table 6: Example prompts for experiments. *[PROPERTY]* can be a glass transition temperature (T_g), tan delta peak (δ), or cross-link density (v_c).

Design Proteins Using Large Language Models: Enhancements and Comparative Analyses

Kamyar Zeinalipour[1], **Neda Jamshidi**[1], **Monica Bianchini**[1], **Marco Maggini**[1], **Marco Gori**[1],

[1]University of Siena, DIISM, Via Roma 56, 53100 Siena, Italy

Correspondence: kamyar.zeinalipour2@unisi.it

Abstract

Pre-trained LLMs have demonstrated substantial capabilities across a range of conventional natural language processing (NLP) tasks, such as summarization and entity recognition. In this paper, we explore the application of LLMs in the generation of high-quality protein sequences. Specifically, we adopt a suite of pre-trained LLMs, including `Mistral-7B`[1], `Llama-2-7B`[2], `Llama-3-8B`[3], and `gemma-7B`[4], to produce valid protein sequences. All of these models are publicly available.[5] Unlike previous work in this field, our approach utilizes a relatively small dataset comprising 42,000 distinct human protein sequences. We retrain these models to process protein-related data, ensuring the generation of biologically feasible protein structures. Our findings demonstrate that even with limited data, the adapted models exhibit efficiency comparable to established protein-focused models such as ProGen varieties, ProtGPT2, and ProLLaMA, which were trained on millions of protein sequences. To validate and quantify the performance of our models, we conduct comparative analyses employing standard metrics such as pLDDT, RMSD, TM-score, and REU. Furthermore, we commit to making the trained versions of all four models publicly available, fostering greater transparency and collaboration in the field of computational biology.

1 Introduction

In recent years, the field of natural language processing (NLP) has achieved remarkable progress, particularly through the development and utilization of large pre-trained language models. These sophisticated models represent a significant leap forward, primarily due to their ability to understand and generate human-like text based on training from extensive datasets. Typically, these models are trained using unsupervised learning techniques, where they learn to predict the next word or token in a sequence by examining the tokens that precede it. This method has propelled them to the forefront of various NLP applications, including chatbots (Wei et al., 2024), text summarization (Zhang et al., 2024; Tang et al., 2023), and advanced information extraction tasks (Dagdelen et al., 2024). Among the intriguing avenues explored with these models is their application in the field of bioinformatics, specifically in protein generation (Madani et al., 2020). Indeed, the protein alphabet is composed of twenty common amino acids, each represented by a single character. Regarding their primary structure, proteins, which are vital biological molecules, are made up of chains of amino acids, thus forming sequences of letters and drawing a parallel to the structure of natural languages. As in natural languages, protein sequences have directionality and are typically composed of reused modular elements that exhibit slight variations. Moreover, common protein motifs and domains, which are the basic building blocks of proteins, are similar to words, phrases, and sentences in human language. This similarity suggests that language models, which excel in handling sequential data, could effectively generate amino acid chains, or proteins.

The primary objective of our research lies in advancing the understanding and application of medium-sized language models, particularly those in the 7 billion to 8 billion parameter range, including `Mistral-7B`, `Llama-2-7B`, `Llama-3-8B`, and `gemma-7B`, for the generation of high-quality protein sequences. Our hypothesis, backed by preliminary studies, suggests that these models, even when trained with considerably small datasets, can produce accurate and viable protein sequences effectively.

[1]huggingface.co/Kamyar-zeinalipour/P-Mistral-7B

[2]huggingface.co/Kamyar-zeinalipour/P-Llama2-7B

[3]https://huggingface.co/Kamyar-zeinalipour/P-Llama3-8B

[4]huggingface.co/Kamyar-zeinalipour/P-gemma-7B

[5]github.com/KamyarZeinalipour/protein-design-LLMs

Proceedings of the 1st Workshop on Language + Molecules (L+M 2024), pages 35–48
August 15, 2024 ©2024 Association for Computational Linguistics

Furthermore, we extend our investigation to encompass a comparative analysis utilizing established protein-focused language models such as ProGen (Nijkamp et al. (2023); Madani et al. (2020)), ProtGPT2 (Ferruz et al. (2022)), and ProLLaMA (Lv et al. (2024)). By applying the same experimental conditions across different models, we aim to provide quantitative and qualitative comparisons of their performance and effectiveness.
Ultimately, this study seeks to validate the capability of medium-sized models in protein design, emphasizing the potential of employing more compact, cost-efficient language models as powerful tools in bioinformatics research. This approach may significantly expedite scientific research and practical applications, spanning from drug design to precision medicine to other interdisciplinary fields.

This paper makes the following contributions:

- **Exploration of Medium-sized LLMs –** We investigate the efficacy of medium-sized language models, with 7-8 billion parameters, in generating functionally viable protein sequences;
- **Adaptation to Small Data Sets –** We show that these models can achieve high performance even when trained with small datasets;
- **Comparative Analysis –** We provide a thorough comparative analysis of the performance of our models against established models in the field under identical experimental conditions;
- **Accessibility of Trained Models –** We commit to making all four trained language models developed for this study available to the scientific community to encourage further research and development.

The layout of this document is as follows: Section 2 reviews previous research. Our methods are detailed in Section 3. Experimental results are discussed in Section 4, while conclusions and future perspectives are collected in Section 5.

2 Related Works

The integration of natural language processing (NLP) techniques, traditionally applied to human languages, into bioinformatics, has transformative potential, particularly in the analysis of biological sequences such as DNA, RNA, and proteins. These biological data, sharing similarities with linguistic texts in their structured and functional building blocks, are highly amenable to computational methodologies. The impactful success seen in NLP through transformer-based models has led to breakthroughs in specialized models geared toward understanding the complexities of these biological sequences. By utilizing extensive databases such as UniProt (Consortium, 2019), ENSEMBL (Cunningham et al., 2022), and GenBank (Benson et al., 2012), these models harness rich data to enhance both predictive and analytical capabilities in bioinformatics.
The realm of protein sequences has seen notable advancements through the adoption of both supervised and unsupervised learning models. Language models have been increasingly leveraged and employed in the domain of protein design (Ferruz and Höcker, 2022). Supervised learning approaches refine models by training them with labeled data, which is invaluable for accurately predicting protein stability or identifying structural similarities among sequences (Bepler and Berger, 2021; Alley et al., 2019). On the other hand, the introduction of transformer technology has been pivotal in popularizing unsupervised learning methods (Vaswani et al., 2017). These methods involve the strategic corruption of input sequences which are then used to train models to predict and reconstruct the NATURAL sequence. Leading models such as ESM (Rives et al., 2021), ProtTrans (Elnaggar et al., 2021), and ProteinBERT (Brandes et al., 2022) demonstrate this approach, offering powerful embeddings that prove critical in supporting a wide array of downstream biochemical tasks (Yang et al., 2024; Rao et al., 2019). These tasks include, but are not limited to, analyzing protein-protein interactions, predicting molecular functions, and identifying potential sites for drug binding. In addition to these developments, the adoption of autoregressive models — widely recognized for their ability to generate coherent, long-form text in classical NLP settings — has been successfully applied to the domain of protein sequencing. Prototypes like ProGen (Nijkamp et al., 2023; Madani et al., 2020), ProtGPT2 (Ferruz et al., 2022) and ProLLaMA (Lv et al., 2024) capitalize on this capability, employing autoregressive algorithms to effectively predict the future elements of protein sequences from given contexts. This predictive ability is critical for sophisticated applications such as protein design, where the generation of novel and function-

ally effective proteins is required.
In this study, we employ some pre-trained language models, which we further fine-tune for protein generation tasks, by retraining both the tokenizers and the entire models. We then compare the results with those from other large language models (LLMs) currently available for protein generation tasks.

3 Methodology

In this section, we delineate the methodologies employed to adapt pre-trained LLMs for the generation of protein sequences. Our approach involved refining the tokenizer based on the Byte-Pair Encoding (BPE) methodology, followed by fine-tuning the entire pre-trained model using a designated dataset of protein sequences. Subsequently, this fine-tuned model was utilized to generate new protein sequences. It's important to note that base models such as LLMs, while powerful, are not inherently capable of designing novel proteins. Their success in this domain is achieved through a specialized fine-tuning process, which involves not only adapting the model to a specific task using a smaller, task-specific dataset but also modifying the tokenizer. This is because the tokens that LLMs were initially trained on are natural language tokens, whereas our domain requires a different set of tokens. Therefore, we also need to train the tokenizer to handle this new domain effectively. Verification of these sequences was carried out by generating their respective PDB structures using DeepMind's AlphaFold (Jumper et al., 2021). We assessed the quality of these structures using various metrics such as pLDDT, RMSD, TM-Score and REU. The performance of the models — namely `Mistral-7B` (Jiang et al., 2023), `Llama-2-7B` (Touvron et al., 2023), `Llama-3-8B` , and `gemma-7B` (Team et al., 2024) — was then compared with previous studies that employed language models for protein sequence generation. We have also evaluated the potential fitness of our generated sequences in comparison to natural and random sequences in the context of pLDDT, Rosetta-Relax scores, RMSD and TM-Scores, thereby providing a comparative analysis. Figure 1 illustrates this methodology. Subsequently, we will provide a detailed description of all these steps, focusing on the training of the LLMs and their validation.

3.1 From LLMs to Proteins

Large language models, such as transformers, are sophisticated algorithms trained on extensive textual datasets. These models utilize their predictive capability primarily to determine the subsequent token based on the preceding ones. Given their training on a vast amount of text data, LLMs are highly adaptable and can be finely tuned for specialized tasks, including summarizing specific document types like legal texts. An interesting application of these models is in the domain of protein generation. Proteins, being amino acid sequences, differ significantly from standard text data. This difference necessitates the retraining of tokenizers to achieve more accurate tokenization for proteins, enhancing the model ability to recognize and predict relevant patterns in amino acid sequences. Following the retraining, these adapted tokenizers are used to refine the parameters of pre-trained LLMs. This fine-tuning process tailors the LLMs to predict protein sequences effectively by generating valid protein structures. In subsequent sections, we will elaborate on the methodologies applied for tokenizer retraining, describe the various LLMs utilized, and discuss their specific fine-tuning.

Tokenizer retraining In situations where the corpus significantly diverges from that utilized during the initial training of a language model, it becomes imperative to retrain the model from scratch. This process necessitates adjusting the tokenizer to accommodate the nuances of the new dataset. A tokenizer serves the critical function of converting textual data into numerical representations suitable for computational processing by language models. For the retraining of our tokenizer, we employed the Byte-Pair Encoding (BPE) method. BPE is a hybrid between a character-level and word-level tokenizer. It starts with a base vocabulary of individual characters and iteratively merges the most frequently adjacent pairs of characters or character sequences. Through this methodology, BPE effectively manages the vocabulary size, allowing for efficient handling of unknown words by breaking them down into recognizable subwords. This is particularly beneficial in managing morphologically rich languages or corpora with specialized jargon. In our adaptation process, we retained the original vocabulary size of the tokenizer used in prior models to maintain consistency and optimize integration with the pre-trained configurations. This approach ensures that the retrained models sustain

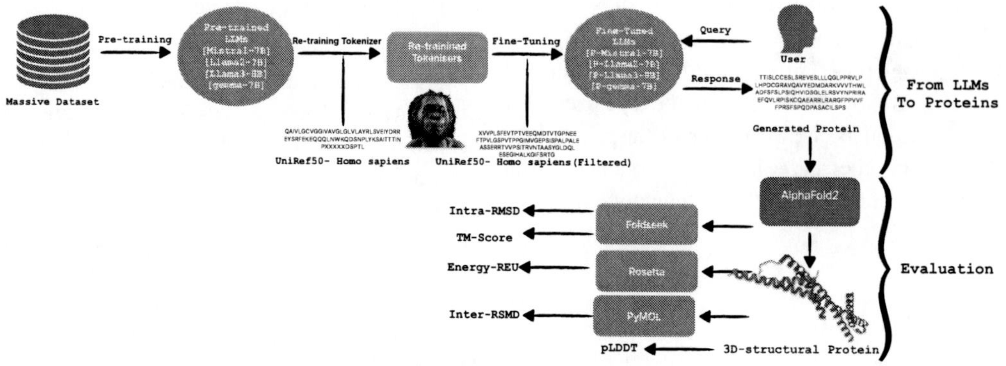

Figure 1: A comprehensive overview of our methodology employed for training, evaluating, and validating the protein sequence generation model. We initially retrained tokenizers for four distinct large language models — `Mistral-7B`, `Llama-2-7B`, `Llama-3-8B`, and `gemma-7B` — using the UniRef50-Homo sapiens dataset employing the Byte-Pair Encoding (BPE) technique. Subsequently, we fine-tuned these models on a filtered subset of the UniRef50-Homo sapiens dataset, aiming to minimize the loss associated with predicting subsequent protein sequences. For evaluation, model output was validated using AlphaFold 2 to construct 3D protein structures, followed by assessments of the generated protein structural accuracy using metrics such as per-residue confidence score (pLDDT) from AlphaFold 2, RMSD (Root Mean Square Deviation), and TM-Score to compare topological similarities with known protein structures applied using FoldSeek. Additional evaluation included the use of Rosetta-Relax for analyzing the energetic profiles of the generated proteins. Finally, protein structural comparisons within each dataset were conducted using PyMOL to calculate the intra-dataset RMSD.

compatibility with existing frameworks while benefiting from a tokenizer that is fine-tuned to the specific features of the new dataset.

Fine-Tune Pre-trained LLMs In this research, our objective was to assess the capabilities of various pre-trained language models in the specialized task of protein generation. To this end, we fine-tuned four distinct models: `Mistral-7B`, `Llama-2-7B`, `Llama-3-8B`, and `gemma-7B`. Each model is based on the transformer architecture, which is renowned for its effectiveness in handling sequence-to-sequence tasks and operates under a causal framework conducive to generative tasks.

The four models were specifically chosen to represent a bandwidth of computational capacities predominantly ranging between 7 billion and 8 billion parameters, enabling a focused analysis on how parameter scale influences model performance in biological sequence generation. `Mistral-7B`, developed by MistralAI, contains precisely 7 billion parameters. In contrast, both `Llama-2-7B` and the newer `Llama-3-8B` are products from Meta, featuring 7 billion and 8 billion parameters, respectively. The latter represents an advanced iteration within the LLama series, potentially offering enhancements in learning efficiency and output refinement. Finally, `gemma-7B` from Google, also with 7 billion parameters, extends our model diversity, providing an additional perspective from another leading tech giant's approach to language model development.

By employing these models, we aim to conduct a thorough comparative analysis, examining not just the quantitative outcomes in terms of accuracy and efficiency in protein generation, but also qualitative aspects such as the fidelity and usability of generated sequences. Given the similar parameter size, any observed differences in performance can be more directly attributed to architectural nuances and training methodologies between the models. This study not only advances our understanding of the capabilities of high-capacity language models in biosciences but also guides future developments in computational biology and the deployment of AI-driven tools for scientific discovery.

Firstly, we observe that each of these language models employs variants of the cross-entropy loss function. Throughout the fine-tuning process, the objective is to minimize this loss, which effectively maximizes the probability of predicting subsequent tokens accurately, based on the context provided by previous tokens. This optimization directly enhances the model ability to generate coherent and contextually appropriate text.

Given a sequence of tokens, the cross-entropy loss predicts the probability of each subsequent token based on the previous context, i.e., given $x_1, x_2, ..., x_n$ in training data, the model is able to predict each subsequent token x_{t+1} based on previous tokens $x_1, ..., x_t$. The formula for the loss across an entire sequence of length N is:

$$\mathcal{L} = -\sum_{t=1}^{N} \log(p_{\text{model}}(x_{t+1} \mid x_1, x_2, ..., x_t))$$

where $p_{\text{model}}(x_{t+1} \mid x_1, ..., x_t)$ is the probability assigned by the model to the correct next token x_{t+1}, conditioned on the sequence $x_1, ..., x_t$.
This loss not only encourages the correct prediction of the next token but also indirectly learns the contextual dependencies among the tokens in the sequence, which is crucial for the generation of coherent and contextually appropriate outputs in language models.

3.2 Evaluation

In this section, we describe each evaluation method implemented in our study following the generation of proteins. Initially, protein sequences generated using tuned LLMs were structurally modeled using AlphaFold2[6], which provided three-dimensional structures along with per-residue confidence scores (pLDDT). Subsequently, the topological similarity of these structures to known protein configurations was assessed using the TM-Score computed by FoldSeek [7]Additionally, Rosetta -Relax [8]was employed to analyze the energetic profiles of the modeled proteins, enhancing our understanding of their stability and viability. For intra-dataset structural comparisons, RMSD calculations were conducted using PyMOL[9] . Detailed descriptions and analyses of these metrics are provided in the following sections.

Alphafold2 (pLDDT) In the initial phase of the evaluation, we utilized AlphaFold2 to predict the structures of the generated proteins and compute their predicted Local Distance Difference Test (pLDDT) scores. AlphaFold2, developed by DeepMind, represents a significant advancement in protein structure prediction by leveraging sophisticated deep learning methodologies. It predicts protein structures from amino acid sequences, using extensive training datasets of known protein structures and incorporating a self-attention mechanism. Moreover, pLDDT scores can be obtained, which provide valuable insight into structural accuracy, with values below 50 indicative of disordered regions, scores between 50 and 90 suggesting regions with some order, and scores above 90 denoting well-ordered regions.

Foldseek (TM-Score, Intra RMSD) To evaluate the accuracy of predicted protein structures, we utilized Foldseek, a robust tool designed for the comparison and analysis of three-dimensional protein structures. Foldseek is a tool for searching a set of query protein structures through a set of target protein structures. It uses a fast and sensitive k-mer and ungapped alignment prefilter from MMseqs2 on the 3Di sequences of the query and target structures to quickly identify candidate structures that are similar to the query. By submitting our predicted protein models to Foldseek, we computed two critical metrics: the TM-score and Root Mean Square Deviation (RMSD). The TM-score, ranging from 0 to 1, quantifies the global topological similarity between two protein structures, with higher scores indicating greater structural resemblance. Specifically, a TM-score above 0.5 generally indicates that the structures share the same fold, while a score below 0.3 suggests random structural similarity. Conversely, RMSD is a widely used metric in structural biology that assesses the similarity between two protein structures by comparing the positional differences of corresponding atoms, typically those in the backbone, after optimal superimposition. This metric provides insight into structural similarity from the perspective of atomic distances. In this study, we refer to this measure as 'Intra RMSD,' emphasizing the comparison between each predicted model and its respective known structure.A lower score is generally more desirable
Figure 2 (a) illustrates an instance where the generated protein structure has limited similarity to the protein structure matched by Foldseek, as indicated by the green line in the figure. The protein structure in Figure 2 (a) achieves a relatively low TM-Score of 0.28, indicating a weak resemblance to the matched protein structure. Furthermore, the substantial RMSD of 26.2 Å highlights a significant deviation and misalignment between the generated and matched structures. In contrast, Figure 2 (b)

[6]deepmind.google/technologies/alphafold/
[7]search.foldseek.com/
[8]www.rosettacommons.org/software
[9]pymol.org/

showcases a successful example of protein structure generation, where the generated structure has a high degree of similarity to the matched protein structure. The generated protein structure attains a high TM-Score of 0.90, signifying a strong structural similarity to the matched protein. Additionally, the low RMSD of 1.55 Å suggests that the generated structure has a high degree of precision and alignment with the matched structure.

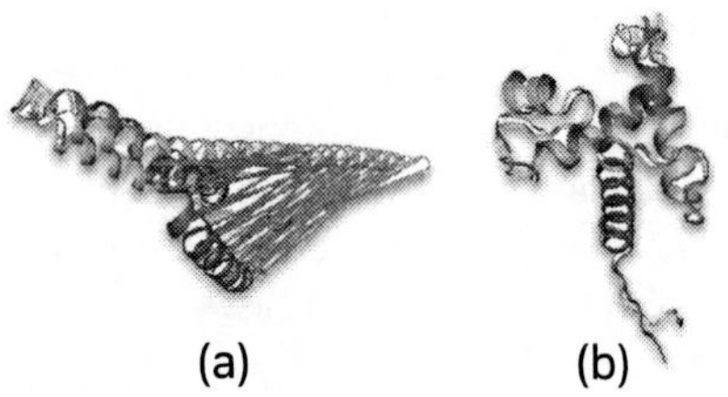

Figure 2: Illustration of High TM-Score and low Intra RMSD Compared to Low TM-Score and high Intra RMSD

Rosetta-Relax (REU) To comprehensively assess the quality of our predicted protein structures, we initiated the process by relaxing the native template. This initial relaxation ensures that the structure is energetically optimized from the outset, facilitating more accurate subsequent evaluations. Following the relaxation of the native template, we applied Rosetta-RelaxBB across all datasets. Rosetta-RelaxBB employs a Monte Carlo optimization approach that explores a range of backbone and rotamer conformations to minimize the Rosetta Energy function, which is based on biophysical principles and constraints. During each design iteration, amino acid side chains are substituted while maintaining fixed carbon backbone torsions. Energy minimization and relaxation are performed after threading the amino acid sequence through the known structure, allowing the backbone to transition into a potentially more stable energy state. Conformers with lower Rosetta Energy values indicate more relaxed and stable structures. The latest Rosetta Energy Forcefield (REF2015) shows a strong correlation with experimental parameters such as heat capacity, density, and enthalpy, providing a robust scoring function indicative of the thermodynamic stability of protein conformations.For a refined structure of this size, a score of -100 REU to -300 REU is typical. The lower the score, the more stable the structure is likely to be for a given protein.

PyMOL (Inter RMSD) For the fourth phase of our evaluation, we utilized PyMOL, a sophisticated molecular visualization software equipped with extensive tools for protein structure analysis and comparison. PyMOL's features facilitate detailed examination of molecular structures and enable various quantitative assessments, such as calculating the Root Mean Square Deviation (RMSD). Specifically, we determined the Inter RMSD, which quantifies the RMSD for each trajectory within our datasets.As previously mentioned a lower score is generally more desirable.

4 Experimental results

In this section, we delineate the experiments conducted in this study, presenting an evaluation of the results garnered from the protein sequences we generated. Additionally, we discuss the regeneration of proteins utilizing language-based models specifically designed for protein generation tasks, including ProGen in four distinct sizes, ProtGPT2, and ProLLaMA.

Initially, we explore the dataset utilized in our experiments, which is notably smaller than those used in other models, followed by a detailed exposition of our training setup. Finally, we present a comprehensive analysis of the evaluation results employing various metrics such as pLDDT, RMSD, TM-Score and REU.

4.1 Dataset

In this study, the **UniRef50** dataset, originating from the UniProt databases, has been utilized. The UniProt Reference Cluster (UniRef) databases systematically organize clustered sets of protein sequences from UniProtKB [10] and selected UniParc records, aiming to reduce redundancy and provide comprehensive coverage of sequence space. This is achieved through varying levels of sequence identity across three datasets, facilitating faster similarity searches among proteins.

Specific attention was given to the Homo sapiens subset within UniRef50, which initially comprised over 60,000 protein sequences. Given the constraints of computational resources and the criteria of our intended language models, a sequence length

[10] https://www.uniprot.org

filter was applied. Only sequences below 512 tokens, as determined by our pre-trained tokenizer, were retained, narrowing the pool to 60,000 sequences.

For training and evaluation purposes, 42,000 sequences were allocated to the training set while the remaining 1,480 were designated for testing.[11]

This careful selection and allocation of sequences effectively optimized our computational resources and facilitated robust training and validation of our predictive models on protein sequences.

4.2 Training Setup

The training methodology employed in this study involved training Language Models (LMs) specifically tailored for protein generation utilizing four Nvidia A6000 GPUs. The training configuration utilized a sequence length of 512, with a maximum training step limit of 2000 and a batch size of 1, coupled with a gradient accumulation step size of 16 for enhanced training efficiency. The learning rate was set at 5e-5, and a cosine learning rate scheduler was employed to adaptively adjust the learning rate. Furthermore, a weight decay of 0.01 and a num warm-up step value of 150 were applied to stabilize the training process. The utilization of the bfloat16 data format contributed to faster computation due to reduced precision, enhancing overall training performance. We employed DeepSpeed (Rasley et al., 2020), a deep learning optimization library developed by Microsoft, to facilitate efficient training and optimization of the models. and also we applied FlashAttention 2 (Dao, 2023).

Four distinct LLMs models, namely `Mistral-7B`, `Llama-2-7B`, `Llama-3-8B`, and `gemma-7B` were trained using this meticulously tuned training configuration. The selection of appropriate hyperparameters and the utilization of multiple GPUs facilitated efficient and timely training of these models. The strategic incorporation of the cosine learning rate scheduler and weight decay mechanism bolstered the models' convergence and performance during training, ultimately leading to the successful generation of protein sequences.

4.3 Results Evaluation

In this section, we randomly selected 250 proteins, each with a length between 70 to 140 amino acids, from each of the under-investigation models for structure prediction and subsequent evaluation. In order to initiate the protein generation process, we input a special token, known as the beginning-of-sequence (BOS) token. Once this token is fed into the model, it begins to generate protein sequences, leveraging the patterns and knowledge it has acquired during its training phase. These proteins were submitted to AlphaFold2, which generated 3D structural models with corresponding pLDDT scores for each protein. Examples of these 3D structures and corresponding pLDDT can be seen in Figure 3. We proceeded to randomly select 20 3D structural proteins from each of the under-investigated models for a more in-depth analysis. The chosen proteins were then subjected to further evaluations, including the calculation of Intra RMSD, Inter RMSD, TM-Score, and REU with selected proteins. This multi-faceted approach to evaluation has allowed us to thoroughly assess the performance of our models and the quality of our 3D protein structure predictions.

To evaluate the pLDDT score for each protein, AlphaFold2 generates five 3D structural models with corresponding pLDDT scores. We then calculated the mean of the five pLDDT scores to obtain a representative pLDDT score for each protein. We present the evaluation results using all the metrics discussed in Section 4. Table 1 summarizes the mean values of each evaluation metric for each model. Notably, P-Mistral consistently outperforms all other models across various metrics. Detailed information on these metrics, as well as corresponding plots and tables, are provided in the Appendix A.

The most significant difference between the trained models and randomly generated proteins We procedurally generated a set of proteins in a random manner, with each of these proteins being composed of a sequence of 20 amino acids, is observed in the pLDDT metric, as depicted in Figure 4. Our models,`P-Llama2` and `P-Llama3`, exhibit a distribution similar to the NATURAL data. Additionally, we observed a significant disparity between randomly generated proteins and other models when evaluating the TM-score metric, as illustrated in Figure 5. Other metrics, such as Inter and Intra RMSD, are shown in Figures 8 and 6.

Furthermore, for the REU metric, we identified an optimal range between -100 and -300. The randomly generated proteins fall significantly outside this interval, whereas the models we introduced

[11] huggingface.co/datasets/Kamyar-zeinalipour/UniRef50-HumanProteins/settings

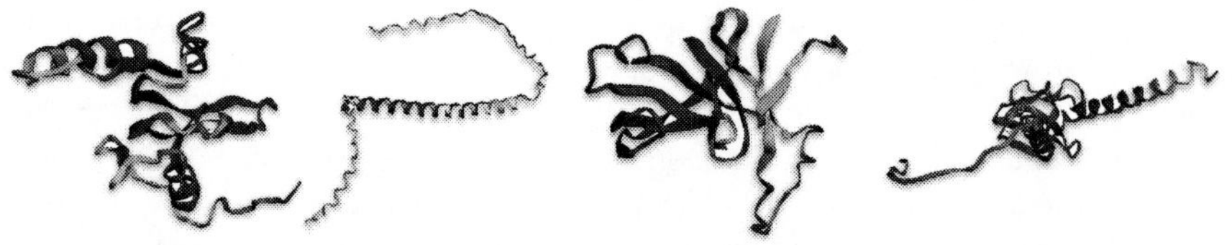

Figure 3: Examples of the 3D structure of proteins generated by each introduced model

Model	#param	train size	pLDDT ↑	Intra↓ RMSD	REU ↓	TM ↑ -Score	Inter ↓ RMSD
NATURAL	–	–	67.77	–	-153.06	–	4.40
RANDOM	–	–	39.71	9.88	-197.22	0.41	6.81
P-Llama2	7B	42K	65.39	7.02	-153.31	0.63	4.76
P-Llama3	8B	42K	62.99	7.38	-132.50	0.65	**4.30**
P-Mistral	7B	42K	**72.03**	**5.42**	-197.40	**0.68**	4.70
P-gemma	7B	42K	62.24	5.80	-141.60	0.65	5.83
PROLLAMA	7B	–	55.80	9.46	-126.65	0.47	5.66
PROTGPT2	774M	49.8M	64.50	6.52	-146.23	0.52	5.52
PROGENSMALL	151M	280M	58.35	11.46	-212.22	0.48	6.76
PROGENMEDIUM	764M	280M	58.98	11.64	-240.89	0.59	11.20
PROGENLARGE	2.7B	280M	61.78	7.65	-158.18	0.58	5.47
PROGENXLARGE	6.4B	280M	68.04	10.37	**-251.37**	0.54	6.05

Table 1: Mean of the analyzed Metrics for each model.

predominantly fall within the same range as the NATURAL data, as seen in Figure 8. The most intriguing finding of our study is that we were able to achieve and even surpass the performance of models trained on massive protein datasets, using a significantly smaller dataset. This was demonstrated across various evaluation metrics.

5 Conclusion

In this study, we introduced four novel models designed to generate high-quality protein sequences by leveraging pre-trained language models. This research is motivated by the growing demand for efficient and accurate tools that can assist in understanding and engineering protein structures, which are pivotal in numerous biological and medical applications. Our approach involved a meticulous design and training phase, followed by rigorous testing and validation processes to assess the performance of each model.

To provide a thorough evaluation, we conducted comprehensive experiments comparing our models with a range of existing models that also utilize language models for protein sequence generation. Comparative analyses were performed, which were grounded on diverse criteria, including sequence quality, diversity, and fidelity to biological functions. These analyses also incorporated several structural assessment metrics such as pLDDT (predicted Local Distance Difference), TM-Score (to assess structural similarity), RMSD (Root Mean Square Deviation), and REU (Rosetta Energy Unit). Our findings revealed that some of our proposed models, particularly `P-Mistral`, exhibited superior performance compared to existing models, even surpassing those trained on considerably larger datasets. This remarkable performance underscores the potential of our models to offer significant advancements in the field of protein sequence generation.

We are committed to the principles of open science and reproducibility. Consequently, we will make all four models publicly available to the research community. This accessibility will empower other

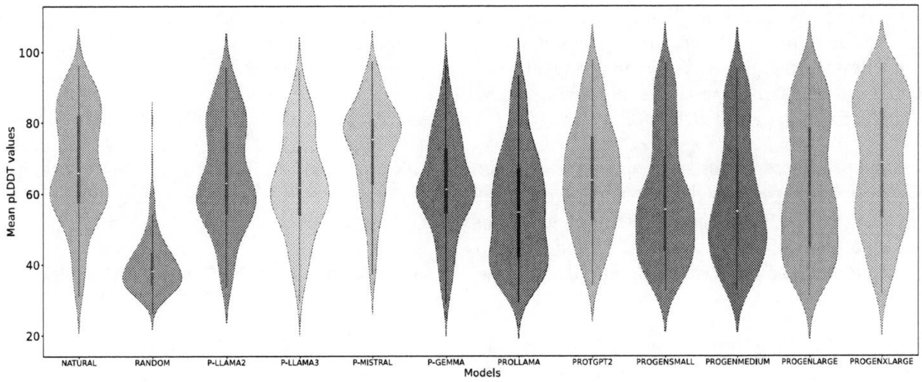

Figure 4: Violin plot of pLDDT

researchers to utilize and build upon our work, fostering further advancements in the field of protein sequence generation.
Moreover, We aim to extend the capabilities of these models by incorporating instruction tuning to generate proteins with specific constraints. This will involve refining the models to adhere to certain criteria, such as ensuring the sequences have particular structural or functional properties. Such advancements could be pivotal in various applications, including drug design, synthetic biology, and understanding protein interactions at a deeper level. While our current implementation of LLMs for protein generation excels in unconditional generation, there is a need to explore and develop methods for generating conditional proteins. This would allow us to guide the generation process toward specific protein characteristics or functions, thereby enhancing the practical utility of our model.

Acknowledgments

The funding for this paper was provided by the TAILOR project and the HumanE-AI-Net projects, both supported by the EU Horizon 2020 research and innovation program under GA No 952215 and No 952026, respectively.

References

Ethan C Alley, Grigory Khimulya, Surojit Biswas, Mohammed AlQuraishi, and George M Church. 2019. Unified rational protein engineering with sequence-based deep representation learning. *Nature methods*, 16(12):1315–1322.

Dennis A Benson, Mark Cavanaugh, Karen Clark, Ilene Karsch-Mizrachi, David J Lipman, James Ostell, and Eric W Sayers. 2012. Genbank. *Nucleic acids research*, 41(D1):D36–D42.

Tristan Bepler and Bonnie Berger. 2021. Learning the protein language: Evolution, structure, and function. *Cell systems*, 12(6):654–669.

Nadav Brandes, Dan Ofer, Yam Peleg, Nadav Rappoport, and Michal Linial. 2022. Proteinbert: a universal deep-learning model of protein sequence and function. *Bioinformatics*, 38(8):2102–2110.

UniProt Consortium. 2019. Uniprot: a worldwide hub of protein knowledge. *Nucleic acids research*, 47(D1):D506–D515.

Fiona Cunningham, James E Allen, Jamie Allen, Jorge Alvarez-Jarreta, M Ridwan Amode, Irina M Armean, Olanrewaju Austine-Orimoloye, Andrey G Azov, If Barnes, Ruth Bennett, et al. 2022. Ensembl 2022. *Nucleic acids research*, 50(D1):D988–D995.

J. Dagdelen, A. Dunn, S. Lee, et al. 2024. Structured information extraction from scientific text with large language models. *Nature Communication*, 15(1418).

Tri Dao. 2023. Flashattention-2: Faster attention with better parallelism and work partitioning. *arXiv preprint arXiv:2307.08691*.

Ahmed Elnaggar, Michael Heinzinger, Christian Dallago, Ghalia Rehawi, Yu Wang, Llion Jones, Tom Gibbs, Tamas Feher, Christoph Angerer, Martin Steinegger, et al. 2021. Prottrans: Toward understanding the language of life through self-supervised learning. *IEEE transactions on pattern analysis and machine intelligence*, 44(10):7112–7127.

Noelia Ferruz and Birte Höcker. 2022. Controllable protein design with language models. *Nature Machine Intelligence*, 4(6):521–532.

Noelia Ferruz, Steffen Schmidt, and Birte Höcker. 2022. Protgpt2 is a deep unsupervised language model for protein design. *Nature communications*, 13(1):4348.

Albert Q Jiang, Alexandre Sablayrolles, Arthur Mensch, Chris Bamford, Devendra Singh Chaplot, Diego de las Casas, Florian Bressand, Gianna Lengyel, Guillaume Lample, Lucile Saulnier, et al. 2023. Mistral 7b. *arXiv preprint arXiv:2310.06825*.

John Jumper, Richard Evans, Alexander Pritzel, Tim Green, Michael Figurnov, Olaf Ronneberger, Kathryn Tunyasuvunakool, Russ Bates, Augustin Žídek, Anna Potapenko, et al. 2021. Highly accurate protein structure prediction with alphafold. *Nature*, 596(7873):583–589.

Liuzhenghao Lv, Zongying Lin, Hao Li, Yuyang Liu, Jiaxi Cui, Calvin Yu-Chian Chen, Li Yuan, and Yonghong Tian. 2024. Prollama: A protein large language model for multi-task protein language processing. *arXiv preprint arXiv:2402.16445*.

Ali Madani, Bryan McCann, Nikhil Naik, Nitish Shirish Keskar, Namrata Anand, Raphael R Eguchi, Po-Ssu Huang, and Richard Socher. 2020. Progen: Language modeling for protein generation. *arXiv preprint arXiv:2004.03497*.

Erik Nijkamp, Jeffrey A Ruffolo, Eli N Weinstein, Nikhil Naik, and Ali Madani. 2023. Progen2: exploring the boundaries of protein language models. *Cell systems*, 14(11):968–978.

Roshan Rao, Nicholas Bhattacharya, Neil Thomas, Yan Duan, Peter Chen, John Canny, Pieter Abbeel, and Yun Song. 2019. Evaluating protein transfer learning with tape. *Advances in neural information processing systems*, 32.

Jeff Rasley, Samyam Rajbhandari, Olatunji Ruwase, and Yuxiong He. 2020. Deepspeed: System optimizations enable training deep learning models with over 100 billion parameters. In *Proceedings of the 26th ACM SIGKDD International Conference on Knowledge Discovery & Data Mining*, pages 3505–3506.

Alexander Rives, Joshua Meier, Tom Sercu, Siddharth Goyal, Zeming Lin, Jason Liu, Demi Guo, Myle Ott, C Lawrence Zitnick, Jerry Ma, et al. 2021. Biological structure and function emerge from scaling unsupervised learning to 250 million protein sequences. *Proceedings of the National Academy of Sciences*, 118(15):e2016239118.

L. Tang, Z. Sun, B. Idnay, et al. 2023. Evaluating large language models on medical evidence summarization. *Digital Medicine*, 6(158).

Gemma Team, Thomas Mesnard, Cassidy Hardin, Robert Dadashi, Surya Bhupatiraju, Shreya Pathak, Laurent Sifre, Morgane Rivière, Mihir Sanjay Kale, Juliette Love, et al. 2024. Gemma: Open models based on gemini research and technology. *arXiv preprint arXiv:2403.08295*.

Hugo Touvron, Louis Martin, Kevin Stone, Peter Albert, Amjad Almahairi, Yasmine Babaei, Nikolay Bashlykov, Soumya Batra, Prajjwal Bhargava, Shruti Bhosale, et al. 2023. Llama 2: Open foundation and fine-tuned chat models. *arXiv preprint arXiv:2307.09288*.

Ashish Vaswani, Noam Shazeer, Niki Parmar, Jakob Uszkoreit, Llion Jones, Aidan N Gomez, Łukasz Kaiser, and Illia Polosukhin. 2017. Attention is all you need. *Advances in neural information processing systems*, 30.

Jing Wei, Sungdong Kim, Hyunhoon Jung, and Young-Ho Kim. 2024. Leveraging large language models to power chatbots for collecting user self-reported data. *Proceedings of the ACM on Human-Computer Interaction*, 8(CSCW1):1–35.

Kevin K Yang, Nicolo Fusi, and Alex X Lu. 2024. Convolutions are competitive with transformers for protein sequence pretraining. *Cell Systems*, 15(3):286–294.

Tianyi Zhang, Faisal Ladhak, Esin Durmus, Percy Liang, Kathleen McKeown, and Tatsunori B. Hashimoto. 2024. Benchmarking large language models for news summarization. *Transactions of the Association for Computational Linguistics*, 12:39–57.

A Appendix

In this appendix, we have included violin plots and descriptive statistics for all the evaluation metrics utilized throughout this study. The violin plots offer a visual representation of the distribution and density of the data, enabling an in-depth comparison between different models or methods. Additionally, the descriptive statistics provide a comprehensive summary of the central tendency, dispersion, and shape of the distribution of each metric, including measures such as mean, median, standard deviation, and interquartile range. These tools together facilitate a thorough understanding of the performance and variability of the metrics used, thereby supporting a robust assessment of the study results.

pLDDT The violin plot of the mean pLLDDTs of each model is shown in Figure 4, while its descriptive statistics are collected in Table 2.

TM-Score The violin plot of the TM-Score of each model is shown in Figure 5, while its descriptive statistics are collected in Table 3.

Intra RMSD The violin plot of the Intra RMSD of each model is shown in Figure˚6, while its descriptive statistics are collected in Table 4.

Inter RMSD The violin plot of the Inter RMSD of each model is shown in Figure 7, while its descriptive statistics are collected in Table 5.

Model	Q1	Q3	mean	median	min	max
NATURAL	57.85	81.69	67.77	65.93	31.1	96.10
RANDOM	34.62	42.95	39.71	38.12	26.52	80.74
P-Llama2	54.55	78.15	65.39	62.95	33.58	95.26
P-Llama3	54.12	73	62.99	61.71	29.46	94.68
P-Mistral	62.82	80.83	72.03	75.22	35.06	96.98
P-gemma	54.76	72.26	62.24	61.17	29.1	96.00
PROLLAMA	42.3	66.68	55.80	54.7	29.52	93.34
PROTGPT2	52.73	75.45	64.50	63.72	34.02	97.46
PROGENSMALL	43.68	70.09	58.35	55.51	32.46	96.68
PROGENMEDIUM	45.27	71.71	58.98	54.96	32.56	95.20
PROGENLARGE	45.06	78.14	61.78	58.78	31.06	95.84
PROGENXLARGE	53.43	83.45	68.04	68.56	31.56	96.52

Table 2: Summary statistics for pLDDT

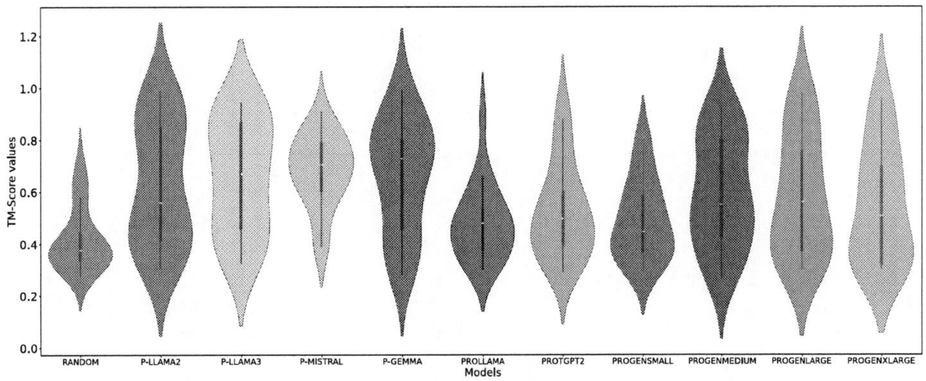

Figure 5: Violin plot of TM-Score

REU The violin plot of the REU of each model is shown in Figure 8, while its descriptive statistics are collected in Table 6.

Model	Q1	Q3	mean	median	min	max
RANDOM	0.33	0.44	0.41	0.37	0.27	0.71
P-Llama2	0.41	0.84	0.63	0.55	0.30	0.99
P-Llama3	0.46	0.86	0.65	0.66	0.32	0.94
P-Mistral	0.60	0.78	0.68	0.70	0.38	0.91
P-gemma	0.45	0.79	0.65	0.72	0.28	0.99
PROLLAMA	0.37	0.52	0.47	0.47	0.30	0.90
PROTGPT2	0.39	0.59	0.52	0.49	0.29	0.92
PROGENSMALL	0.37	0.58	0.48	0.44	0.29	0.80
PROGENMEDIUM	0.42	0.79	0.59	0.55	0.26	0.92
PROGENLARGE	0.37	0.75	0.58	0.56	0.30	0.98
PROGENXLARGE	0.32	0.69	0.54	0.50	0.30	0.96

Table 3: Summary statistics for TM-Score

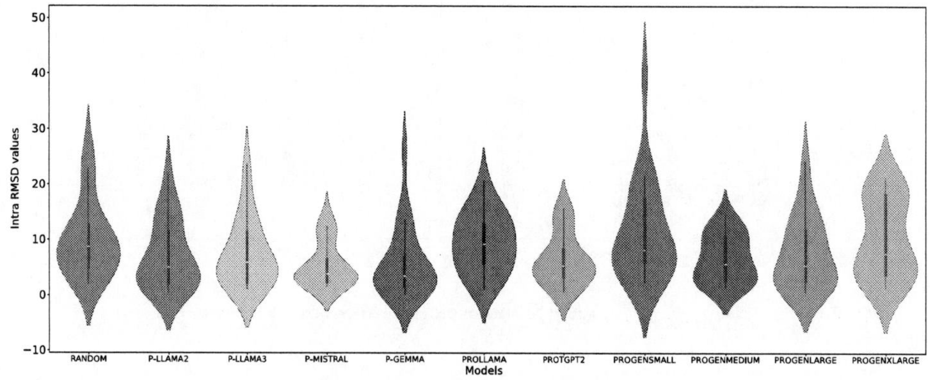

Figure 6: Violin plot of Intra RMSD

Model	Q1	Q3	mean	median	min	max
RANDOM	4.95	12.59	9.88	8.66	1.97	26.71
P-Llama2	2.01	11.43	7.02	4.98	0.39	21.88
P-Llama3	2.2	11.36	7.38	5.87	0.94	23.58
P-Mistral	2.28	6.42	5.42	3.79	1.55	14.20
P-gemma	1.73	6.74	5.80	3.45	0.11	26.20
PROLLAMA	5.74	12.78	9.46	9.21	1.07	20.59
PROTGPT2	3.35	8.29	6.52	5.31	0.69	15.65
PROGENSMALL	6.06	17.49	11.46	8.16	2.3	39.45
PROGENMEDIUM	2.68	10.62	11.64	5.69	1.42	14.46
PROGENLARGE	2.72	11.67	7.65	5.4	0.63	24.19
PROGENXLARGE	3.79	18.16	10.37	7.53	1.2	21.20

Table 4: Summary statistics for Intra RMSD

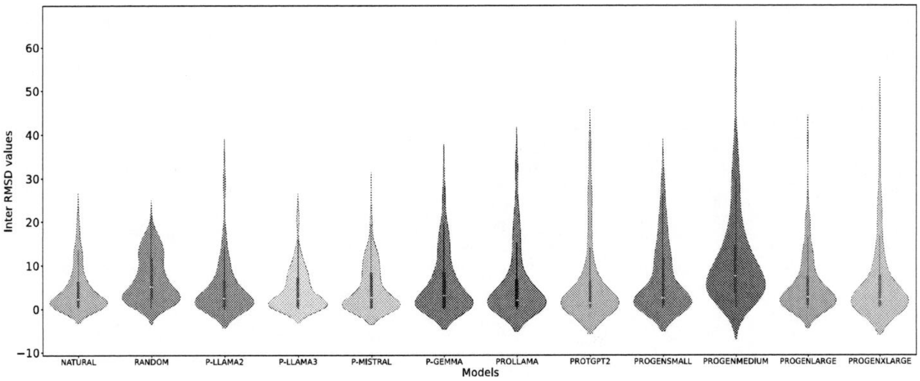

Figure 7: Violin plot of Inter RMSD

Model	Q1	Q3	Mean	Median	Min	max
NATURAL	0.87	6.04	4.40	2.24	0.23	22.98
RANDOM	2.41	11.34	6.81	5.15	0.16	21.18
P-Llama2	0.92	6.41	4.76	2.46	0.02	34.70
P-Llama3	0.76	6.94	4.30	2.41	0.11	23.11
P-Mistral	0.55	8.08	4.70	2.61	0.18	27.59
P-gemma	0.63	8.15	5.83	3.09	0.05	32.91
PROLLAMA	0.64	6.45	5.66	1.99	0.08	36.26
PROTGPT2	0.67	6.00	5.52	1.32	0.20	39.84
PROGENSMALL	1.02	11.29	6.76	2.45	0.20	33.43
PROGENMEDIUM	3.85	14.27	11.20	7.49	0.23	58.57
PROGENLARGE	1.10	7.11	5.47	2.66	0.07	39.71
PROGENXLARGE	0.88	7.37	6.05	2.06	0.16	46.93

Table 5: Summary statistics for Inter RMSD

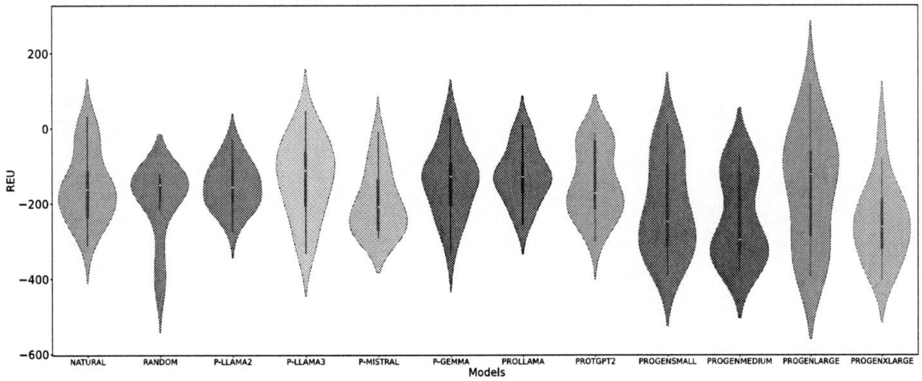

Figure 8: Violin plot of REU

Model	Q1	Q3	mean	median	min	max
NATURAL	-233,48	-115,43	-153,06	-163,30	-310,23	31.00
RANDOM	-193,85	-136,43	-197,22	-151,57	-434,25	-123.39
P-Llama2	-196,79	-105,67	-153,31	-156,82	-274,14	-30.49
P-Llama3	-205,03	-65,05	-132,50	-111,15	-331,44	45.39
P-Mistral	-269,91	-138,11	-197,40	-209,21	-289,82	-9.69
P-gemma	-204,11	-95,08	-141,60	-127,84	-333,33	27.28
PROLLAMA	-169,56	-96,10	-126,65	-129,17	-255,91	6.38
PROTGPT2	-215,40	-34,31	-146,23	-173,36	-301,04	-12.90
PROGENSMALL	-313,85	-101,59	-212,22	-249,00	-389,56	10.17
PROGENMEDIUM	-334,72	-119,91	-240,89	-297,72	-380,75	-70.46
PROGENLARGE	-286,13	-63,01	-158,18	-123,29	-391,96	115.96
PROGENXLARGE	-318,06	-191,64	-251,37	-263,17	-403,92	10.98

Table 6: Summary statistics for REU

Enhanced BioT5+ for Molecule-Text Translation: A Three-Stage Approach with Data Distillation, Diverse Training, and Voting Ensemble

Qizhi Pei[1], **Lijun Wu**[2*], **Kaiyuan Gao**[3], **Jinhua Zhu**[4], **Rui Yan**[1,5*]
[1]Gaoling School of Artificial Intelligence, Renmin University of China
[2]Microsoft Research [3]Huazhong University of Science and Technology
[4]University of Science and Technology of China
[5]Engineering Research Center of Next-Generation Intelligent Search and Recommendation, Ministry of Education
{qizhipei,ruiyan}@ruc.edu.cn apeterswu@gmail.com
im_kai@hust.edu.cn teslazhu@mail.ustc.edu.cn

Abstract

This paper presents our enhanced BioT5+ method for the Language + Molecules shared task at the ACL 2024 Workshop. The task involves "translating" between molecules and natural language, including molecule captioning and text-based molecule generation using the *L+M-24* dataset. Our method consists of three stages. In the first stage, we distill data from various models. In the second stage, combined with *extra* version of the provided dataset, we train diverse models for subsequent voting ensemble. We also adopt Transductive Ensemble Learning (TEL) to enhance these base models. Lastly, all models are integrated using a voting ensemble method. Experimental results demonstrate that BioT5+ achieves superior performance on *L+M-24* dataset. On the final leaderboard[1], our method (team name: **qizhipei**) ranks **first** in the text-based molecule generation task and **second** in the molecule captioning task, highlighting its efficacy and robustness in translating between molecules and natural language. The pre-trained BioT5+ models are available at https://github.com/QizhiPei/BioT5.

1 Introduction

With the development of Large Language Models (LLMs) (Touvron et al., 2023a,b; OpenAI, 2023; Taori et al., 2023; Chowdhery et al., 2023), the integration of molecules with natural language has garnered increasing attention in recent research efforts (Edwards et al., 2021, 2022; Zeng et al., 2022; Luo et al., 2023; Tang et al., 2023; Liu et al., 2023b; Zhao et al., 2023; Liu et al., 2023a,d,c; Pei et al., 2023, 2024a). Notably, two critical generative tasks have emerged: molecule captioning (*i.e., mol2text*) and text-based molecule generation (*i.e., text2mol*) (Edwards et al., 2022). These tasks are pivotal for biologists and chemists, as they facilitate the interpretation and creation of molecular structures through natural language descriptions.

Table 1: Statistics of *L+M-24* dataset. We use $\mathcal{B}$ to represent molecule-text paired datasets and $\mathcal{D}$ to represent datasets only containing molecules or text.

Split	Symbol	*mol2text*	*text2mol*
#Training	$\mathcal{B}$	126,864	126,864
#Training-*extra*	$\mathcal{B}_+$	533,953	533,953
#Validation	$\mathcal{B}_{valid}$	33,696	33,696
#Test	D_{test}	21,942	21,805

To leverage the advantages of natural language for molecular design and understanding (Zhang et al., 2024; Liao et al., 2024; Pei et al., 2024b; AI4Science and Quantum, 2023), Language + Molecules Workshop at ACL 2024 has been organized. A shared molecule-text translation task and the corresponding paired dataset are presented to accelerate research in this field.

1.1 Dataset Description

In the provided *L+M-24* dataset, each sample is a molecule-text pair, with the molecule represented by SMILES (Weininger, 1988; Weininger et al., 1989) and the text generated from collected molecular properties based on templates written by GPT-4 (OpenAI, 2023). An *extra* version of *L+M-24* is also available, with each molecule having five additional captions. We use the training split of this version (*i.e.*, training-*extra*) and remove dupli-

* Corresponding authors: Lijun Wu (apeterswu@gmail.com) and Rui Yan (ruiyan@ruc.edu.cn)

[1] https://language-plus-molecules.github.io/#leaderboard

Proceedings of the 1st Workshop on Language + Molecules (L+M 2024), pages 49–55
August 15, 2024

cates. The fundamental statistics of the *L+M-24* are shown in Table 1, with more details about its construction described in Edwards et al. (2024).

1.2 Task Description

Mol2text The goal of the *mol2text* task is to generate a caption for a given molecule. Participants are required to submit generated captions for the test split of *mol2text*. Evaluation metrics include widely used text generation metrics such as BLEU (Papineni et al., 2002), ROUGE (Lin, 2004), and METEOR (Banerjee and Lavie, 2005), in addition to the Text2Mol metric (Edwards et al., 2021, 2022). These metrics assess the similarity between the generated molecular captions and the ground truth. Classification metrics including Precision, Recall, and F-1 value are also used to evaluate property-specific *mol2text* results.

Text2mol The goal of the *text2mol* task is to generate a molecule that fits a given description. Participants are required to submit the generated molecule SMILES for the test split of *text2mol*. Evaluation metrics include BLEU (Papineni et al., 2002), exact match percentages, Levenshtein distance, fingerprints (FTS) similarity score (MACCS (Durant et al., 2002), RDK (Landrum et al., 2023), Morgan (Rogers and Hahn, 2010)), FCD score (Preuer et al., 2018), Text2Mol (Edwards et al., 2021, 2022) score, and validity. These metrics evaluate the similarity between the generated molecule and the ground truth.

1.3 Overview of our Method

Our proposed method, enhanced version of BioT5+, is designed to tackle the *mol2text* and *text2mol* tasks using a comprehensive three-stage approach. The first stage involves data distillation, where we generate synthetic datasets from trained models to enrich the training data. In the second stage, we perform diverse training by finetuning various models on different combinations of distilled and extra datasets. We also employ Transductive Ensemble Learning (TEL) to further enhance these models by leveraging unlabeled data. In the final stage, we integrate these models using a voting ensemble method, which selects the best predictions based on perplexity scores. This multi-faceted strategy ensures that our models are robust, diverse, and capable of achieving superior performance across both tasks.

2 Methodology

In this section, we give a detailed introduction to our three-stage methodology.

Notations. We use SELFIES (Krenn et al., 2020) as the sequence representation of the molecule. Compared to SMILES, SELFIES is a more robust molecular representation, which is beneficial for molecule generation tasks such as *text2mol*, as it ensures the generation of 100% valid molecules. The SMILES in the *L+M-24* dataset are converted to corresponding SELFIES using *selfies* toolkit[2]. Let M and T denote molecular SELFIES and text descriptions, respectively, and $\mathcal{M}$ and $\mathcal{T}$ denote the corresponding collection of all sequences. Let $\mathcal{B} = \{(m_i, t_i)\}_{i=1}^{|\mathcal{B}|}$ represent the molecule-text pairs from the training split of *L+M-24*, and $\mathcal{B}_+ = \{(m_i, t_i)\}_{i=1}^{|\mathcal{B}_+|}$ represent the molecule-text pairs from training-*extra* split, where $m_i \in \mathcal{M}$, $t_i \in \mathcal{T}$, and $|\mathcal{B}|$ and $|\mathcal{B}_+|$ represent the size of $\mathcal{B}$ and $\mathcal{B}_+$, respectively. Let $\mathcal{D}^m = \{m_j\}_{j=1}^{|\mathcal{D}^m|}$ denote the collection of molecules from the PubChem (Kim et al., 2019) database, where $m_j \in \mathcal{M}$ and $|\mathcal{D}^m| = 800\text{K}$ represents the number of sampled molecules. The text in $\mathcal{T}$ follows a specific format, so we directly use $\mathcal{D}^t = \{t_j\}_{j=1}^{|\mathcal{B}_+|}$, where the text $t_j \in \mathcal{B}_+$.

Our goal is to develop a *mol2text* translation model $f : \mathcal{M} \mapsto \mathcal{T}$, which generates a caption from T for a given molecule from M, and a reverse *text2mol* translation model $g : \mathcal{T} \mapsto \mathcal{M}$. In this paper, all models follow the T5 (Raffel et al., 2020)-large architecture. Our method consists of the following three stages:

Stage-1: Data Distillation. First, we train a *mol2text* translation model f_0 and a *text2mol* translation model g_0 on $\mathcal{B}$. Then, we use f_0 and g_0 to build the synthetic dataset:

$$\overline{\mathcal{B}}_{self} = \{(m, f_0(m)) \mid m \in \mathcal{D}_m\} \cup \{\ (g_0(t),\ t\ ) \mid\ t\ \in \mathcal{D}_t\ \}.$$

To further improve the diversity of the distilled data, we also use the officially provided Meditron-7B (Chen et al., 2023) *mol2text* model[3] f_{med} to build another synthetic dataset:

$$\overline{\mathcal{B}}_{med} = \{(m, f_{med}(m)) \mid m \in \mathcal{D}_m\}.$$

[2]https://github.com/aspuru-guzik-group/selfies

[3]https://huggingface.co/language-plus-molecules/Meditron7b-smiles2caption-LPM24

Model	BLEU-2	BLEU-4	ROUGE-1	ROUGE-2	ROUGE-L	METEOR	Text2Mol
Ground Truth							11.30
MolT5-Small	70.9	51.2	74.5	55.8	54.4	70.1	10.79
MolT5-Base	73.8	53.5	75.0	55.9	53.9	71.8	8.53
MolT5-Large	76.9	55.6	77.7	58.0	55.7	74.3	10.06
Meditron-7B	79.2	57.6	79.7	60.2	57.5	75.7	**11.91**
BioT5+	**79.8**	**57.9**	**81.2**	**61.7**	**58.4**	**77.7**	11.36

Table 2: Results for *mol2text* task on the validation set of *L+M-24*.

Model	Overall			Biomedical			Light+Electro			Human Interaction			Agr.+Industry			Held-out Combos		
	P	R	F-1	P	R	F-1	P	R	F-1	P	R	F-1	P	R	F-1	P	R	F-1
MolT5-Small	29.83	3.48	3.12	15.13	4.18	4.29	12.42	4.85	3.27	46.77	0.57	0.56	45.00	4.32	4.36	0.00	0.00	0.00
MolT5-Base	35.36	5.18	4.69	14.58	4.84	4.97	16.08	5.82	3.36	**63.94**	5.01	5.18	**46.85**	5.05	5.27	0.00	0.00	0.00
MolT5-Large	33.32	7.72	6.95	15.27	7.94	7.82	16.96	10.90	7.39	62.77	5.99	6.27	38.29	6.06	6.31	0.00	0.00	0.00
Meditron-7B	25.27	11.56	16.8	23.86	14.91	35.00	26.51	16.48	17.49	29.54	7.52	7.07	21.18	7.35	7.40	12.35	0.29	0.56
BioT5+	**35.50**	**20.69**	**20.93**	**56.91**	**38.22**	**39.27**	**36.20**	**27.43**	**28.22**	29.46	**9.09**	**8.42**	19.41	**8.03**	**7.82**	**17.61**	**0.73**	**1.40**

Table 3: Results for property-specific *mol2text* task on the validation set of *L+M-24*.

Model	P	R	F-1	P	R	F-1	P	R	F-1	P	R	F-1	P	R	F-1	P	R	F-1
	X-icides			**Toxins**			**Light**			**Electricity**			**X-inhibitors**			**anti-X**		
MolT5-Small	0.00	0.00	0.00	0.00	0.00	0.00	24.85	9.69	6.54	0.00	0.00	0.00	3.42	0.43	0.09	1.96	0.00	0.00
MolT5-Base	0.00	0.00	0.00	67.45	8.51	8.84	28.00	11.51	6.52	4.17	0.12	0.20	2.20	0.58	0.11	9.70	0.23	0.15
MolT5-Large	0.00	0.00	0.00	**69.42**	10.29	10.85	15.77	12.28	8.16	18.14	9.52	6.62	8.90	2.28	1.13	4.32	1.16	0.61
Meditron-7B	0.00	0.00	0.00	48.79	11.75	11.05	29.10	20.64	20.64	23.93	12.33	14.34	35.69	19.91	22.65	14.79	9.34	8.98
BioT5+	0.00	0.00	0.00	47.93	**13.42**	**12.55**	**38.29**	**30.32**	**30.68**	**34.12**	**24.53**	**25.76**	**48.00**	**31.05**	**32.58**	**33.96**	**13.04**	**15.34**
	X-modulator			**X-agonist**			**X-antagonist**			**X-treatment**			**X-disease**			**X cancer**		
MolT5-Small	0.00	0.00	0.00	0.00	0.00	0.00	0.00	0.00	0.00	55.49	1.99	1.70	87.44	50.08	49.94	71.86	21.03	24.27
MolT5-Base	0.00	0.00	0.00	0.00	0.00	0.00	0.00	0.00	0.00	58.90	2.25	1.80	94.61	55.16	59.18	45.06	25.49	24.54
MolT5-Large	21.30	0.58	0.88	5.91	1.96	1.23	14.30	0.58	0.42	14.27	2.67	2.22	97.18	81.07	81.86	65.76	52.06	51.56
Meditron-7B	42.43	21.24	24.98	39.19	23.23	26.35	34.22	18.98	21.15	28.75	11.35	15.13	**97.34**	81.11	82.02	**79.80**	68.65	72.62
BioT5+	**55.32**	**42.83**	**44.76**	**53.02**	**36.96**	**37.09**	**50.06**	**32.79**	**34.18**	**46.83**	**18.99**	**24.47**	96.61	**81.75**	**82.05**	77.77	**73.48**	**75.25**

Table 4: Results for selected subproperty group-specific *mol2text* task on the validation set of *L+M-24*.

Model	BLEU-2	BLEU-4	ROUGE-1	ROUGE-2	ROUGE-L	METEOR
MolT5-Small	66.82	48.29	72.80	54.44	53.33	68.14
MolT5-Base	69.83	50.56	73.34	54.55	52.86	69.86
MolT5-Large	73.63	53.20	75.79	56.47	54.42	72.16
Meditron-7B	75.16	54.72	77.97	58.75	56.33	73.69
BioT5+	**75.58**	**54.77**	**79.41**	**59.89**	**57.46**	**75.43**

Table 5: Results for *mol2text* task on the test set of *L+M-24*.

Table 6: Model combinations. $\mathcal{B}_+ \rightarrow \mathcal{B}$ means the model is first trained on $\mathcal{B}_+$ followed by $\mathcal{B}$.

Model	Dataset	Initialization
f_0, g_0	$\mathcal{B}$	BioT5+
f_1, g_1	$\mathcal{B} \cup \mathcal{B}_+$	BioT5+
f_2, g_2	$\mathcal{B} \cup \overline{\mathcal{B}}_{self}$	BioT5+
f_3, g_3	$\mathcal{B} \cup \overline{\mathcal{B}}_{med}$	BioT5+
f_4, g_4	$\mathcal{B}_+ \rightarrow \mathcal{B}$	BioT5+
f_1^*, g_1^*	$\overline{\mathcal{B}}^*$	f_1, g_1
f_2^*, g_2^*	$\overline{\mathcal{B}}^*$	f_2, g_2
f_3^*, g_3^*	$\overline{\mathcal{B}}^*$	f_3, g_3
f_4^*, g_4^*	$\overline{\mathcal{B}}^*$	f_4, g_4

In summary, despite $\mathcal{B}$, we have three additional synthetic datasets: $\mathcal{B}_+$, $\overline{\mathcal{B}}_{self}$, and $\overline{\mathcal{B}}_{med}$.

Stage-2: Diverse Training. Based on the datasets mentioned above, we train various types of *mol2text* and *text2mol* models on different combinations of these datasets, as shown in Table 6. We first train $\{f_i\}_{i=1}^4$ based on the distilled datasets in Stage-1. Then we adopt the Transductive Ensemble Learning (TEL) method to get $\{f_i^*\}_{i=1}^4$, which involves predicting labels for unlabeled data and subsequently fine-tuning models on these predictions to enhance performance (Wang et al., 2020). Taking the *mol2text* models as an example (the *text2mol* models follow a similar process), for each f_i in $\{f_i\}_{i=1}^4$, we select τ top-performing checkpoints $\{f_{ij}\}_{j=1}^{\tau}$ based on their validation BLEU scores from its training trajectory. We use $\{f_{ij}\}_{j=1}^{\tau}$ to caption the molecules from $\mathcal{B}_{valid}$ and $\mathcal{D}_{test}$, resulting in two synthetic datasets:

$$\overline{\mathcal{B}}_{valid,i} = \{(m, f_{ij}(m)) \mid m \in \mathcal{B}_{valid}, 1 \leq j \leq \tau\},$$
$$\overline{\mathcal{B}}_{test,i} = \{(m, f_{ij}(m)) \mid m \in \mathcal{D}_{test}, 1 \leq j \leq \tau\}.$$

Then we fine-tune model f_i^* on $\overline{\mathcal{B}}^* = \cup_{i=1}^4 \{\overline{\mathcal{B}}_{valid,i} \cup \overline{\mathcal{B}}_{test,i}\}$, where f_i^* is initialized from f_i. f_i^* generally performs better

Model	BLEU↑	Exact↑	Levenshtein↓	MACCS FTS↑	RDK FTS↑	Morgan FTS↑	FCD↓	Text2Mol↑	Validity↑
Ground Truth	100.0	100.0	0.00	100.0	100.0	100.0	0.00	11.26	100.0
MolT5-Small	56.56	0.00	56.34	64.22	58.10	37.44	NaN	0.49	80.52
MolT5-Base	68.38	0.00	44.79	76.03	65.23	47.46	NaN	7.06	**100.0**
MolT5-Large	56.42	0.00	55.40	75.70	65.01	39.51	17.52	7.69	99.44
Meditron-7B	69.40	**0.01**	46.49	77.16	69.34	50.07	**2.46**	7.80	99.63
BioT5+*	**73.97**	**0.01**	**40.87**	77.69	70.51	**51.58**	3.22	**13.83**	**100.0**
BioT5+	73.10	**0.01**	41.47	**78.06**	**70.93**	51.49	3.29	13.73	**100.0**

Table 7: Results for *text2mol* task on the validation set of *L+M-24*. * denotes model from TEL in Stage-2.

Model	BLEU↑	Exact↑	Levenshtein↓	MACCS FTS↑	RDK FTS↑	Morgan FTS↑	FCD↓	Text2Mol↑	Uniqueness↑	Validity↑
Ground Truth	100.0	100.0	0.00	100.0	100.0	100.0	0.0	23.05	100.0	100.0
MolT5-Small	22.80	0.00	54.14	8.99	5.19	3.48	NaN	5.79	10.14	39.79
MolT5-Base	29.51	0.00	48.91	38.78	19.73	14.21	NaN	21.60	5.13	**100.0**
MolT5-Large	24.37	0.00	63.44	41.56	24.23	15.71	NaN	**23.77**	12.72	97.82
Meditron-7B	28.04	0.00	53.44	40.90	27.42	16.82	3.91	22.46	**74.81**	98.58
BioT5+*	**33.35**	**0.10**	**43.65**	41.52	28.05	17.53	**3.52**	22.91	51.05	**100.0**
BioT5+	31.89	**0.10**	46.14	**42.57**	**29.50**	**18.01**	3.88	**23.77**	48.22	**100.0**

Table 8: Results for *text2mol* task on the subset of held-out combinations from the validation set of *L+M-24*. * denotes model from TEL in Stage-2.

Model	BLEU↑	Exact↑	Levenshtein↓	MACCS FTS↑	RDK FTS↑	Morgan FTS↑	FCD↓	Validity↑
MolT5-Small	55.44	0.0	57.21	63.06	56.83	36.69	nan	81.03
MolT5-Base	67.04	0.0	45.71	74.61	63.7	46.29	nan	99.89
MolT5-Large	55.31	0.0	56.47	74.14	63.4	38.54	17.63	99.12
Meditron	68.84	**0.01**	46.47	75.59	67.66	48.72	**2.44**	99.54
BioT5+	**73.17**	**0.01**	**41.05**	**76.05**	**68.70**	**50.05**	3.13	**100.0**

Table 9: Results for *text2mol* task on the test set of *L+M-24*.

than f_i as f_i^* due to its ability to leverage the collective knowledge and complementary strengths of ensemble learning, leading to improved generalization and robustness. The comparison between f_i and f_i^* is shown in Table 10. In total, as shown in Table 6, we obtain eight types of models $\{f_i\}_{i=1}^4$ and $\{f_i^*\}_{i=1}^4$ in Stage-2.

Stage-3: Voting Ensemble. In the final stage, we combine the strengths of the models trained in Stage-2 through a voting ensemble approach. This method leverages multiple models to improve the reliability and accuracy of the predictions. We illustrate this process using the *mol2text* test dataset as an example, but the same methodology applies to *text2mol* and validation datasets.

Let $\mathcal{F} = \{\hat{f}_j\}_{j=1}^{|\mathcal{F}|}$, where $\hat{f}_j$ is derived from the Stage-2 models in Table 6. Each $\hat{f}_j$ generates captions for the molecules in $\mathcal{D}_{test}$, resulting in a corresponding set of datasets:

$$\mathcal{S} = \left\{ \overline{\mathcal{D}}_{test,j} = \left\{ (m, \hat{f}_j(m)) \mid m \in \mathcal{D}_{test} \right\} \mid \hat{f}_j \in \mathcal{F} \right\}.$$

For each dataset in $\mathcal{S}$, we compute the perplexity (PPL) score of each caption using all models in $\mathcal{F}$. The perplexity of a model $\hat{f}_j$ on a molecule-text pair (m, t) is defined as:

$$\text{PPL}_{\hat{f}_j}(m, t) = \exp\left(-\frac{1}{N} \sum_{i=1}^{N} \log P_{\hat{f}_j}(t_i \mid t_{<i}, m) \right),$$

where N is the length of the caption t, and $P_{\hat{f}_j}(t_i \mid t_{<i}, m)$ is the probability of the i-th token in the caption given the preceding tokens and the molecule m. Next, we average the PPL scores across all models in $\mathcal{F}$ for each molecule-text pair in each dataset in $\mathcal{S}$. The average perplexity for a given molecule-text pair (m, t) in the dataset $\overline{\mathcal{D}}_{test,j}$ is calculated as:

$$\overline{\text{PPL}}(m, t) = \frac{1}{|\mathcal{F}|} \sum_{k=1}^{|\mathcal{F}|} \text{PPL}_{\hat{f}_k}(m, t).$$

Finally, for each molecule m in the test dataset $\mathcal{D}_{test}$, we select the caption $\hat{t}(m)$ with the lowest average PPL from each dataset in $\mathcal{S}$ as the final prediction: $\hat{t}(m) = \arg\min_{(m,t) \in \mathcal{S}} \overline{\text{PPL}}(m, t)$. This selection process ensures that we leverage the most reliable caption according to the ensemble's evaluation. By using this voting ensemble approach, we improve the robustness and accuracy of the predictions, leveraging the strengths of multiple models trained in Stage-2.

Model	BLEU-2	BLEU-4	ROUGE-1	ROUGE-2	ROUGE-L	METEOR
BioT5+†	79.53	57.44	80.69	61.10	57.98	76.86
BioT5+*	79.63	57.70	80.95	61.18	58.11	77.06
BioT5+	79.79	57.87	81.23	61.70	58.38	77.71

Table 10: Ablation results for *mol2text* task on the validation set of *L+M-24*. † denotes the model before TEL in Stage-2. * denotes the model after TEL in Stage-2.

Model Configuration. Following Pei et al. (2024a), we pre-train a large version of BioT5+ with 789M parameters, which is an enhanced version of BioT5 (Pei et al., 2023) with improved molecular understanding capabilities. As in Table 6, model $\{f_i\}_{i=0}^4$ are fine-tuned from this pre-trained BioT5+ model, and model $\{f_i^*\}_{i=1}^4$ are fine-tuned from $\{f_i\}_{i=1}^4$. We employ a greedy decoding strategy for all results, which selects the token with the highest probability at each time step without incorporating randomness or exploring multiple hypotheses.

3 Experiments

In this section, we present our main results for the *mol2text* and *text2mol* tasks. Baseline results on the validation set are derived from Edwards et al. (2024), and test set results are sourced from the official leaderboard. An ablation study is also conducted in Section 4 to demonstrate the efficacy of our methodology.

Mol2text. Results on the validation set are shown in Table 2, and results for the test set are shown in Table 5. Our method achieves the best performances on all metrics except for Text2Mol (Edwards et al., 2021, 2022) metric, with a BLEU-2 of 79.80 on the validation set and 75.58 on the test set. For the Text2Mol score on the validation set, both Meditron (Chen et al., 2023) and our method exceed the ground truth score (11.30), with our method slightly underperforming Meditron. The property-specific and selected subproperty group-specific results on the validation set are presented in Table 3 and Table 4, where our method also outperforms the baselines in nearly all metrics. These results show that the generated captions of our method are highly accurate.

Text2mol. Unlike *mol2text*, our voting ensemble in Stage 3 for the *text2mol* task does not improve all metrics simultaneously. Therefore, we also report the BioT5+* results which is the model from TEL in Stage-2. Results on the validation and test sets are presented in Table 7 and 9. Results on the subset of held-out combinations from the validation set are shown in Table 8. Our method achieves superior performances in most metrics, demonstrating its efficacy and generalization ability.

4 Ablation Study

To validate the effectiveness of our TEL training and voting ensemble, we conduct an ablation study for the *mol2text* task on the validation set of *L+M-24*. The results, shown in Table 10, indicate that the model after TEL (BioT5+*) yields better results than model before TEL (BioT5+†). The BioT5+ model, derived from voting ensemble in Stage-3, achieves the best results overall.

5 Conclusion

In this paper, we introduce our enhanced BioT5+ model for the shared task of the Language + Molecules Workshop at ACL 2024. We adopt a three-stage approach: data distillation, diverse training, and voting ensemble. Our method effectively leverages diverse datasets and advanced ensemble techniques to enhance model performance in both molecule captioning and text-based molecule generation tasks. Experimental results show that our approach achieves superior performance across various evaluation metrics, highlighting the potential of our enhanced BioT5+ model for integrating molecules and text.

6 Acknowledgements

This work was supported by the National Natural Science Foundation of China (NSFC Grant No. 62122089), Beijing Outstanding Young Scientist Program NO. BJJWZYJH012019100020098, and Intelligent Social Governance Platform, Major Innovation & Planning Interdisciplinary Platform for the "Double-First Class" Initiative, Renmin University of China, the Fundamental Research Funds for the Central Universities, and the Research Funds of Renmin University of China. Qizhi Pei is supported by the Outstanding Innovative Talents Cultivation Funded Programs 2023 of Renmin University of China.

References

Microsoft Research AI4Science and Microsoft Azure Quantum. 2023. The impact of large language models on scientific discovery: a preliminary study using gpt-4. *arXiv preprint arXiv:2311.07361*.

Satanjeev Banerjee and Alon Lavie. 2005. METEOR: an automatic metric for MT evaluation with improved correlation with human judgments. In *Proceedings of the Workshop on Intrinsic and Extrinsic Evaluation Measures for Machine Translation and/or Summarization@ACL 2005, Ann Arbor, Michigan, USA, June 29, 2005*, pages 65–72. Association for Computational Linguistics.

Zeming Chen, Alejandro Hernández Cano, Angelika Romanou, Antoine Bonnet, Kyle Matoba, Francesco Salvi, Matteo Pagliardini, Simin Fan, Andreas Köpf, Amirkeivan Mohtashami, et al. 2023. Meditron-70b: Scaling medical pretraining for large language models. *arXiv preprint arXiv:2311.16079*.

Aakanksha Chowdhery, Sharan Narang, Jacob Devlin, Maarten Bosma, Gaurav Mishra, Adam Roberts, Paul Barham, Hyung Won Chung, Charles Sutton, Sebastian Gehrmann, et al. 2023. Palm: Scaling language modeling with pathways. *Journal of Machine Learning Research*, 24(240):1–113.

Joseph L Durant, Burton A Leland, Douglas R Henry, and James G Nourse. 2002. Reoptimization of mdl keys for use in drug discovery. *Journal of chemical information and computer sciences*, 42(6):1273–1280.

Carl Edwards, Tuan Manh Lai, Kevin Ros, Garrett Honke, Kyunghyun Cho, and Heng Ji. 2022. Translation between molecules and natural language. In *Proceedings of the 2022 Conference on Empirical Methods in Natural Language Processing, EMNLP 2022, Abu Dhabi, United Arab Emirates, December 7-11, 2022*, pages 375–413. Association for Computational Linguistics.

Carl Edwards, Qingyun Wang, Lawrence Zhao, and Heng Ji. 2024. L+m-24: Building a dataset for language+ molecules@ acl 2024. *arXiv preprint arXiv:2403.00791*.

Carl Edwards, ChengXiang Zhai, and Heng Ji. 2021. Text2mol: Cross-modal molecule retrieval with natural language queries. In *Proceedings of the 2021 Conference on Empirical Methods in Natural Language Processing, EMNLP 2021, Virtual Event / Punta Cana, Dominican Republic, 7-11 November, 2021*, pages 595–607. Association for Computational Linguistics.

Sunghwan Kim, Jie Chen, Tiejun Cheng, Asta Gindulyte, Jia He, Siqian He, Qingliang Li, Benjamin A Shoemaker, Paul A Thiessen, Bo Yu, et al. 2019. Pubchem 2019 update: improved access to chemical data. *Nucleic acids research*, 47(D1):D1102–D1109.

Mario Krenn, Florian Häse, AkshatKumar Nigam, Pascal Friederich, and Alan Aspuru-Guzik. 2020. Self-referencing embedded strings (selfies): A 100% robust molecular string representation. *Machine Learning: Science and Technology*, 1(4):045024.

Greg Landrum et al. 2023. Rdkit: Open-source cheminformatics. GitHub release.

Chang Liao, Yemin Yu, Yu Mei, and Ying Wei. 2024. From words to molecules: A survey of large language models in chemistry. *arXiv preprint arXiv:2402.01439*.

Chin-Yew Lin. 2004. Rouge: A package for automatic evaluation of summaries. In *Text summarization branches out*, pages 74–81.

Pengfei Liu, Yiming Ren, and Zhixiang Ren. 2023a. Git-mol: A multi-modal large language model for molecular science with graph, image, and text. *CoRR*, abs/2308.06911.

Shengchao Liu, Weili Nie, Chengpeng Wang, Jiarui Lu, Zhuoran Qiao, Ling Liu, Jian Tang, Chaowei Xiao, and Animashree Anandkumar. 2023b. Multi-modal molecule structure–text model for text-based retrieval and editing. *Nature Machine Intelligence*, 5(12):1447–1457.

Zequn Liu, Wei Zhang, Yingce Xia, Lijun Wu, Shufang Xie, Tao Qin, Ming Zhang, and Tie-Yan Liu. 2023c. Molxpt: Wrapping molecules with text for generative pre-training. In *The 61st Annual Meeting Of The Association For Computational Linguistics*.

Zhiyuan Liu, Sihang Li, Yanchen Luo, Hao Fei, Yixin Cao, Kenji Kawaguchi, Xiang Wang, and Tat-Seng Chua. 2023d. Molca: Molecular graph-language modeling with cross-modal projector and uni-modal adapter. In *Proceedings of the 2023 Conference on Empirical Methods in Natural Language Processing, EMNLP 2023, Singapore, December 6-10, 2023*, pages 15623–15638. Association for Computational Linguistics.

Yizhen Luo, Kai Yang, Massimo Hong, Xing Yi Liu, and Zaiqing Nie. 2023. Molfm: A multimodal molecular foundation model. *CoRR*, abs/2307.09484.

OpenAI. 2023. GPT-4 technical report. *CoRR*, abs/2303.08774.

Kishore Papineni, Salim Roukos, Todd Ward, and Wei-Jing Zhu. 2002. Bleu: a method for automatic evaluation of machine translation. In *Proceedings of the 40th Annual Meeting of the Association for Computational Linguistics, July 6-12, 2002, Philadelphia, PA, USA*, pages 311–318. ACL.

Qizhi Pei, Lijun Wu, Kaiyuan Gao, Xiaozhuan Liang, Yin Fang, Jinhua Zhu, Shufang Xie, Tao Qin, and Rui Yan. 2024a. Biot5+: Towards generalized biological understanding with iupac integration and multi-task tuning. *arXiv preprint arXiv:2402.17810*.

Qizhi Pei, Lijun Wu, Kaiyuan Gao, Jinhua Zhu, Yue Wang, Zun Wang, Tao Qin, and Rui Yan. 2024b. Leveraging biomolecule and natural language through multi-modal learning: A survey. *arXiv preprint arXiv:2403.01528*.

Qizhi Pei, Wei Zhang, Jinhua Zhu, Kehan Wu, Kaiyuan Gao, Lijun Wu, Yingce Xia, and Rui Yan. 2023. BioT5: Enriching cross-modal integration in biology with chemical knowledge and natural language associations. In *Proceedings of the 2023 Conference on Empirical Methods in Natural Language Processing*, pages 1102–1123, Singapore. Association for Computational Linguistics.

Kristina Preuer, Philipp Renz, Thomas Unterthiner, Sepp Hochreiter, and Günter Klambauer. 2018. Fréchet chemnet distance: A metric for generative models for molecules in drug discovery. *J. Chem. Inf. Model.*, 58(9):1736–1741.

Colin Raffel, Noam Shazeer, Adam Roberts, Katherine Lee, Sharan Narang, Michael Matena, Yanqi Zhou, Wei Li, and Peter J Liu. 2020. Exploring the limits of transfer learning with a unified text-to-text transformer. *The Journal of Machine Learning Research*, 21(1):5485–5551.

David Rogers and Mathew Hahn. 2010. Extended-connectivity fingerprints. *Journal of chemical information and modeling*, 50(5):742–754.

Xiangru Tang, Andrew Tran, Jeffrey Tan, and Mark B Gerstein. 2023. Mollm: A unified language model to integrate biomedical text with 2d and 3d molecular representations. *bioRxiv*, pages 2023–11.

Rohan Taori, Ishaan Gulrajani, Tianyi Zhang, Yann Dubois, Xuechen Li, Carlos Guestrin, Percy Liang, and Tatsunori B. Hashimoto. 2023. Stanford alpaca: An instruction-following llama model. `https://github.com/tatsu-lab/stanford_alpaca`.

Hugo Touvron, Thibaut Lavril, Gautier Izacard, Xavier Martinet, Marie-Anne Lachaux, Timothée Lacroix, Baptiste Rozière, Naman Goyal, Eric Hambro, Faisal Azhar, Aurélien Rodriguez, Armand Joulin, Edouard Grave, and Guillaume Lample. 2023a. Llama: Open and efficient foundation language models. *CoRR*, abs/2302.13971.

Hugo Touvron, Louis Martin, Kevin Stone, Peter Albert, Amjad Almahairi, Yasmine Babaei, Nikolay Bashlykov, Soumya Batra, Prajjwal Bhargava, Shruti Bhosale, et al. 2023b. Llama 2: Open foundation and fine-tuned chat models. *arXiv preprint arXiv:2307.09288*.

Yiren Wang, Lijun Wu, Yingce Xia, Tao Qin, ChengXiang Zhai, and Tie-Yan Liu. 2020. Transductive ensemble learning for neural machine translation. In *Proceedings of the AAAI Conference on Artificial Intelligence*, volume 34, pages 6291–6298.

David Weininger. 1988. Smiles, a chemical language and information system. 1. introduction to methodology and encoding rules. *Journal of chemical information and computer sciences*, 28(1):31–36.

David Weininger, Arthur Weininger, and Joseph L Weininger. 1989. Smiles. 2. algorithm for generation of unique smiles notation. *Journal of chemical information and computer sciences*, 29(2):97–101.

Zheni Zeng, Yuan Yao, Zhiyuan Liu, and Maosong Sun. 2022. A deep-learning system bridging molecule structure and biomedical text with comprehension comparable to human professionals. *Nature communications*, 13(1):862.

Qiang Zhang, Keyang Ding, Tianwen Lyv, Xinda Wang, Qingyu Yin, Yiwen Zhang, Jing Yu, Yuhao Wang, Xiaotong Li, Zhuoyi Xiang, et al. 2024. Scientific large language models: A survey on biological & chemical domains. *arXiv preprint arXiv:2401.14656*.

Haiteng Zhao, Shengchao Liu, Chang Ma, Hannan Xu, Jie Fu, Zhihong Deng, Lingpeng Kong, and Qi Liu. 2023. GIMLET: A unified graph-text model for instruction-based molecule zero-shot learning. In *Advances in Neural Information Processing Systems 36: Annual Conference on Neural Information Processing Systems 2023, NeurIPS 2023, New Orleans, LA, USA, December 10 - 16, 2023*.

ChatMol Copilot: An Agent for Molecular Modeling and Computation Powered by LLMs

Jinyuan Sun[1], **Auston Li**[1,2], **Yifan Deng**[1], **Jiabo Li**[1,2]

[1]ChatMol Team [2]Wecomput Technology Co., Ltd.

Correspondence: jinyuansun@chatmol.org; jiaboli@chatmol.org

Abstract

Large Language Models (LLMs) like ChatGPT excel at diverse tasks when given explicit instructions, yet they often struggle with specialized domains such as molecular science, lacking in-depth reasoning and sophisticated planning capabilities. To address these limitations, we introduce ChatMol Copilot, a chatbot-like agent specifically engineered for protein design and small molecule computations. ChatMol Copilot employs a multi-level abstraction framework to expand the LLM's capability. At the basic level, it integrates external computational tools through function calls, thus offloading complex tasks and enabling a focus on strategic decision-making. The second level is data abstraction. Large data sets (such as a large number of molecules created by a generative model) are stored in Redis cache, and the redis keys are referenced by LLMs for data sources involved in computation. The third level of abstraction allows the LLM to orchestrate these tools, either directly or via dynamically generated Python executables. Our evaluations demonstrate that ChatMol Copilot can adeptly manage molecular modeling tasks, effectively utilizing a variety of tools as directed. By simplifying access to sophisticated molecular modeling resources, ChatMol Copilot stands to significantly accelerate drug discovery and biotechnological innovation, empowering biochemists with advanced, user-friendly AI capabilities. The open-sourced code is available at https://github.com/ChatMol/ChatMol

1 Introduction

Large Language Models (LLMs) equipped with specialized tools are catalyzing significant advancements across various scientific fields. In chemistry research, platforms like Coscientist (Boiko et al., 2023) and Chemcrow (M. Bran et al., 2024) have revolutionized lab automation and computational tasks. Furthermore, the novel CodeAct approach, which utilizes "Code as Action," leverages the coding prowess of LLMs to automate complex processes (Wang et al., 2024). Similarly, tools such as AlphaFold 3 (Abramson et al., 2024) have achieved remarkable success in predicting protein interactions and structures, underscoring the potential of computational methods in molecular biology.

Despite these strides, significant challenges persist in the molecular engineering field, particularly regarding the execution of complex modeling tasks and the interpretation of their outcomes (Greener et al., 2022). These challenges stem from a need for greater automation and a more intuitive interaction with computational tools. In response, we introduce ChatMol Copilot, a dedicated platform that enhances molecular modeling computations. ChatMol Copilot is designed with a multi-level abstraction framework to maximize automation and user-friendliness. At its foundation, it integrates external computational tools via function calls, simplifying the interface to show only inputs, outputs, and functional descriptions, thereby isolating the LLM from complex computational details. The advanced layer of this framework allows the LLM to either orchestrate these tools directly or through dynamically generated Python executables. This paper demonstrates how ChatMol Copilot effectively manages molecular modeling tasks and delivers precise, actionable responses to user inquiries, significantly streamlining the computational workflow in molecular science.

2 ChatMol Copilot Architecture

The ChatMol Copilot is designed around the capabilities of Large Language Models (LLMs). The system architecture aims to optimize workflow efficiency and precision in molecular modeling tasks.

Workflow Overview (Figure 1): The process begins with user instructions, which are interpreted by the LLM. This interpretation step determines

Proceedings of the 1st Workshop on Language + Molecules (L+M 2024), pages 56–66
August 15, 2024 ©2024 Association for Computational Linguistics

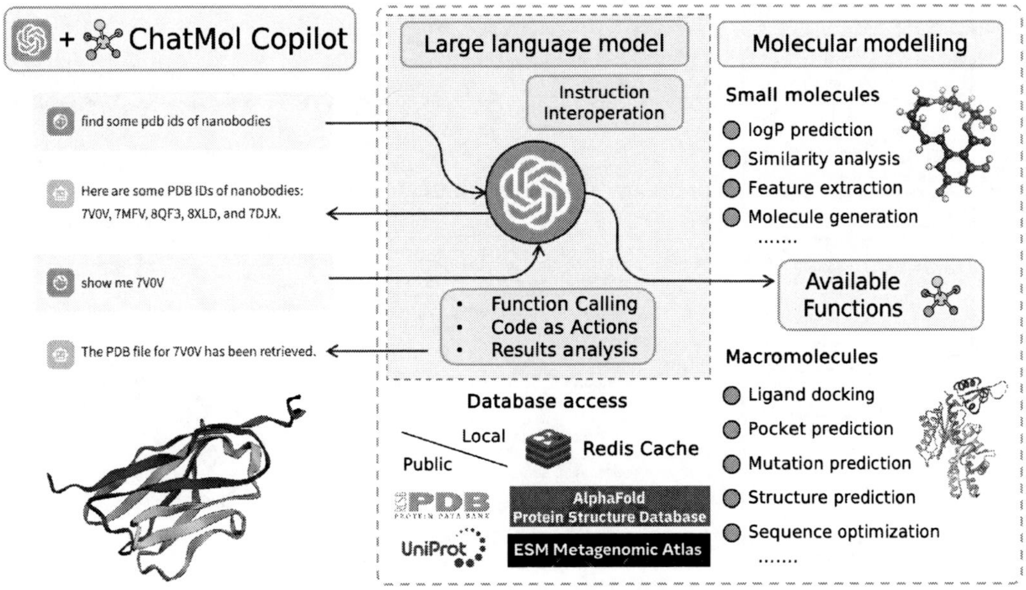

Figure 1: The general workflow of ChatMol Copilot.

whether the user's request can be directly answered or if it necessitates the use of specialized tools. ChatMol Copilot supports a broad range of molecular modeling applications, encompassing both small molecules (such as pharmaceuticals) and macromolecules (such as proteins and their interactions). In addition to pre-defined tools, the system can create new tools by writing and executing Python code. This significantly expands its capabilities beyond the predefined action space. Data abstraction is employed to alleviate the burden of data processing from LLMs. Besides internal data usage, the system has access to significant biological databases, enabling it to retrieve and utilize publicly available data as needed. As conversations progress, the integration of user demands with the computational capabilities of ChatMol Copilot facilitates the completion of increasingly complex tasks.

2.1 Equipped Tools

Numerous specialized neural networks have been developed for various molecular property prediction tasks (Wu et al., 2018). ChatMol Copilot integrates a range of tools to meet diverse computational needs, enabling comprehensive and efficient analysis.

Neural Network-Based Tools: For tools that utilize neural network inference, such as ESMFold (Lin et al., 2023) and ProteinMPNN (Dauparas et al., 2022), we have implemented publicly accessible APIs. This ensures minimal hardware requirements for users.

Local Execution Tools: For faster, Python-based tools, execution is handled locally on the user's computer. Examples include RDKit (Landrum et al., 2013) and TM-align (Zhang and Skolnick, 2005). Table 1 lists the primary tools integrated into the system for both small molecule and macromolecule analysis.

2.2 Integration with Microservices

Microservices are a staple in modern cloud computing architectures due to their scalability and modularity. Each microservice operates independently with a well-defined API and service description. In the ChatMol framework, we have developed a generic method for integrating these microservices into the ChatMol toolbox see Table 1.

For each microservice in our registry, Python code is generated based on the input parameter descriptions. This code is then wrapped into a standard function call, compiled on-the-fly, and added to our function calling list. As new microservices are registered, the function list is automatically updated, greatly enhancing the toolbox's capabilities while simplifying ongoing maintenance.

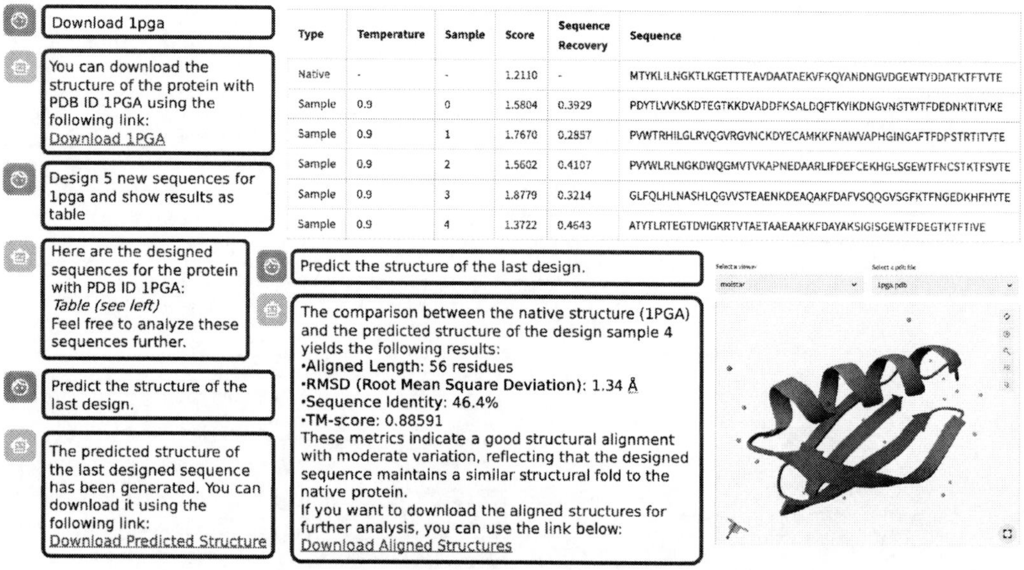

Figure 2: General protein design task. Text within purple boxes are instructions from users, and text within green boxes are answers given by ChatMol Copilot. Texts colored blue with underlines are hyperlinks for download files. The table and cartoon represented protein are real screen shots from the GUI of ChatMol Copilot.

2.3 Code as Actions and Redis Cache

Expanding the system's capabilities can be achieved through the automatic generation and execution of code, known as CodeAct. In ChatMol Copilot, we implemented a generic Python code executor and a universal data object access mechanism using Redis cache. Code generation can be based on task descriptions and knowledge from documents. Redis cache and generic data object read/write operations in code enabling the LLM to manage tasks and data flow much simpler by referencing data with their keys.

3 Use Cases of ChatMol Copilot for Molecular Modeling

This section showcases four examples demonstrating the wide-ranging capabilities of ChatMol Copilot in molecular modeling tasks. These use cases illustrate how ChatMol Copilot adheres to user instructions, utilizing appropriate tools from its equipped toolkit and microservices to meet the demands of biochemists, from protein modeling to small molecule *de novo* synthesis.

3.1 General Protein Design Task

Proteins, essential macromolecules in cells, perform various biological functions, including DNA duplication, metabolic reaction catalysis, and cell cycle regulation. They are also pivotal in healthcare as therapeutic agents like insulin and antibodies, and in various industries as catalysts for cleaner energy and chemicals (Huang et al., 2016).

A fundamental challenge in protein design is to find a sequence that folds into a desired structure (Dauparas et al., 2022). This task is complicated by epistasis, where residue-residue interactions can lead to misfolding and loss of function. To address this, we utilized ProteinMPNN (Dauparas et al., 2022) for sequence design and ESMFold (Lin et al., 2023) to predict the fold of the designed sequences. The effectiveness of the designs was validated by comparing their structures to the initial templates, with ChatMol Copilot presenting the results in a well-organized table format. Key metrics such as Root Mean Squared Error (RMSD) and TM-score are highlighted to assess the structural integrity of the designed sequences Figure 2.

3.2 Peptide/MHC-II Binding Affinity Prediction

The prediction of binding affinity between peptides and MHC-II complexes is critical for assessing the immunogenic potential of newly designed proteins (Jensen et al., 2018). In this use case, ChatMol Copilot was tasked with mutating a peptide sequence five times randomly, then calculating and tabulating the binding affinities of these variants

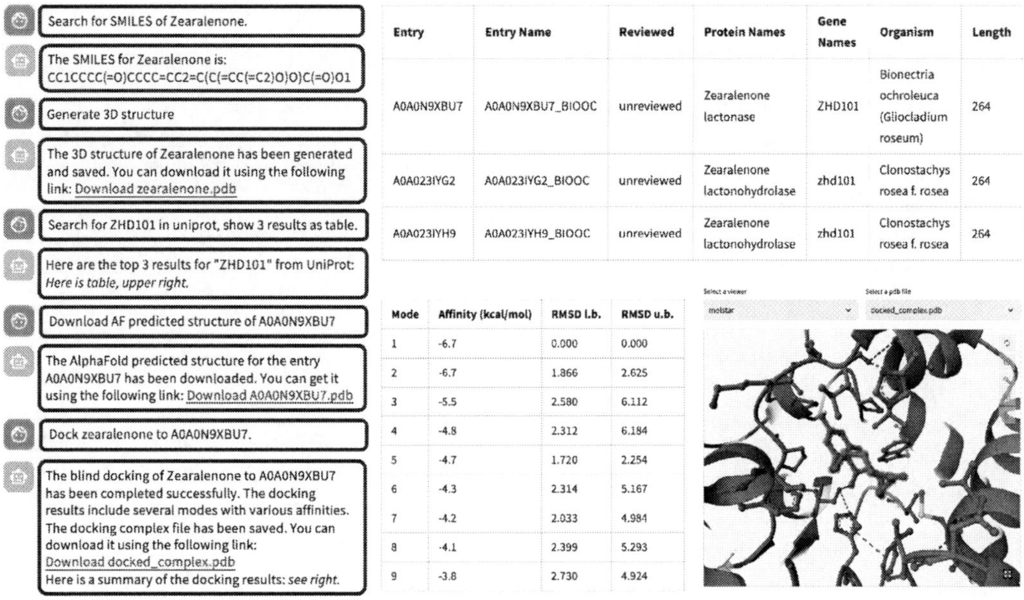

Entry	Entry Name	Reviewed	Protein Names	Gene Names	Organism	Length
A0A0N9XBU7	A0A0N9XBU7_BIOOC	unreviewed	Zearalenone lactonase	ZHD101	Bionectria ochroleuca (Gliocladium roseum)	264
A0A023IYG2	A0A023IYG2_BIOOC	unreviewed	Zearalenone lactonohydrolase	zhd101	Clonostachys rosea f. rosea	264
A0A023IYH9	A0A023IYH9_BIOOC	unreviewed	Zearalenone lactonohydrolase	zhd101	Clonostachys rosea f. rosea	264

Mode	Affinity (kcal/mol)	RMSD l.b.	RMSD u.b.
1	-6.7	0.000	0.000
2	-6.7	1.866	2.625
3	-5.5	2.580	6.112
4	-4.8	2.312	6.184
5	-4.7	1.720	2.254
6	-4.3	2.314	5.167
7	-4.2	2.033	4.984
8	-4.1	2.399	5.293
9	-3.8	2.730	4.924

Figure 3: Protein ligand docking task.

with the HLA-DPA10103-DPB10201 allele. This multi-step process, handled efficiently by a single user prompt, showcases ChatMol Copilot's ability to manage complex, multi-stage computational tasks effectively Figure 4.

3.3 Molecular docking task

In both designing of drugs or enzymes, molecular docking is commonly involved to determine the intermolecular interactions (Meng et al., 2011). A common molecular docking process requires input of: (1) receptor structure, (2) ligand conformer, (3) docking parameters including centre of box and the size of the box. We show that ChatMol Copilot will facilitate this multi-step task by using a set of related tools. With the name of a ligand provided, the copilot used the tool to search for SMILES and another tool to generate a conformer. After downloading the structure file of the receptor from the RCSB PDB database, the docking parameters were automatically determined under the help of the pocket prediction tool. Finally, the docked complex will be presented to the user Figure 3.

3.4 Molecule generation and filtering with generated Python code

Generating novel molecules with desired properties and structures is very important in drug discovery. A recently large molecule generation model SAFE (Noutahi et al., 2024) is open-sourced. There are 6 different modes for molecule generation, each is provided as an API service, and all the 6 APIs are integrated into ChatMol. In the following example, 200 molecules are requested to be generated with a common core. The molecules are stored in Redis cache with key 'SuperStructure_smiles'. Figure 5.

Molecular properties were calculated using a functional call, and the results were stored in Redis cache. To apply filtering with Lipinski's rule of 5 (Lipinski et al., 2012) to the generated molecules a Python function is created by GPT-4o: Figure 6.

In this code, the generated molecules with their properties were read from Redis, and the then Lipinski's rule of 5 is applied to remove molecules that violate the rules. The remaining molecules are saved into Redis. At the end of the code, the total number of the resulting molecules and the first 5 samples are returned.

4 Discussion and Conclusions

In this work, we present a practical solution how to leverage large language models to assist molecular design and computation, particularly for proteins. We also propose the architecture with multi-level abstraction so as to achieve a higher level of automation, which combines multiple steps in one shot. The automatic code generation and execution expands the systems capabilities beyond the predefined action space. The data abstraction with Redis cache makes the "Code as Actions" (Wang et al., 2024) more practical for molecular modeling and computation. Similar to the basic concept of "Code as Actions," we use LLMs to generate PyMOL commands in ChatMol based on user instructions, performing relatively complex molecular visualization tasks. Closed-source commercial models like GPT-4 and the Claude series can write PyMOL commands with high accuracy based on user instructions. Smaller open-source models, when fine-tuned with specific instructions, can also perform this task. As the capabilities of relatively smaller LLMs like phi-3 (Abdin et al., 2024) continue to improve, we can expect future open-source, affordable models to replace current commercial models for ChatMol Copilot needs, further democratizing this field. Even though our current experiments are primitive, we believe that the multi-level abstraction approach is a promising direction to achieve even higher intelligent for molecular design and computation.

References

Marah Abdin, Sam Ade Jacobs, Ammar Ahmad Awan, Jyoti Aneja, Ahmed Awadallah, Hany Awadalla, Nguyen Bach, Amit Bahree, Arash Bakhtiari, Harkirat Behl, et al. 2024. Phi-3 technical report: A highly capable language model locally on your phone. *arXiv preprint arXiv:2404.14219*.

Josh Abramson, Jonas Adler, Jack Dunger, Richard Evans, Tim Green, Alexander Pritzel, Olaf Ronneberger, Lindsay Willmore, Andrew J Ballard, Joshua Bambrick, et al. 2024. Accurate structure prediction of biomolecular interactions with alphafold 3. *Nature*, pages 1–3.

Daniil A Boiko, Robert MacKnight, Ben Kline, and Gabe Gomes. 2023. Autonomous chemical research with large language models. *Nature*, 624(7992):570–578.

Justas Dauparas, Ivan Anishchenko, Nathaniel Bennett, Hua Bai, Robert J Ragotte, Lukas F Milles, Basile IM Wicky, Alexis Courbet, Rob J de Haas, Neville Bethel, et al. 2022. Robust deep learning–based protein sequence design using proteinmpnn. *Science*, 378(6615):49–56.

Warren L DeLano et al. 2002. Pymol: An open-source molecular graphics tool. *CCP4 Newsl. Protein Crystallogr*, 40(1):82–92.

Justin Gilmer, Samuel S Schoenholz, Patrick F Riley, Oriol Vinyals, and George E Dahl. 2017. Neural message passing for quantum chemistry. In *International conference on machine learning*, pages 1263–1272. PMLR.

Joe G Greener, Shaun M Kandathil, Lewis Moffat, and David T Jones. 2022. A guide to machine learning for biologists. *Nature reviews Molecular cell biology*, 23(1):40–55.

Po-Ssu Huang, Scott E Boyken, and David Baker. 2016. The coming of age of de novo protein design. *Nature*, 537(7620):320–327.

Kamilla Kjaergaard Jensen, Massimo Andreatta, Paolo Marcatili, Søren Buus, Jason A Greenbaum, Zhen Yan, Alessandro Sette, Bjoern Peters, and Morten Nielsen. 2018. Improved methods for predicting peptide binding affinity to mhc class ii molecules. *Immunology*, 154(3):394–406.

Greg Landrum et al. 2013. Rdkit: A software suite for cheminformatics, computational chemistry, and predictive modeling. *Greg Landrum*, 8(31.10):5281.

Jiabo Li, Tedman Ehlers, Jon Sutter, Shikha Varma-O'Brien, and Johannes Kirchmair. 2007. Caesar: a new conformer generation algorithm based on recursive buildup and local rotational symmetry consideration. *Journal of chemical information and modeling*, 47(5):1923–1932.

Jiabo Li and Roy McWeeny. 2002. Vb2000: Pushing valence bond theory to new limits. *International journal of quantum chemistry*, 89(4):208–216.

Zeming Lin, Halil Akin, Roshan Rao, Brian Hie, Zhongkai Zhu, Wenting Lu, Nikita Smetanin, Robert Verkuil, Ori Kabeli, Yaniv Shmueli, et al. 2023. Evolutionary-scale prediction of atomic-level protein structure with a language model. *Science*, 379(6637):1123–1130.

Christopher A Lipinski, Franco Lombardo, Beryl W Dominy, and Paul J Feeney. 2012. Experimental and computational approaches to estimate solubility and permeability in drug discovery and development settings. *Advanced drug delivery reviews*, 64:4–17.

Andres M. Bran, Sam Cox, Oliver Schilter, Carlo Baldassari, Andrew D White, and Philippe Schwaller. 2024. Augmenting large language models with chemistry tools. *Nature Machine Intelligence*, pages 1–11.

Xuan-Yu Meng, Hong-Xing Zhang, Mihaly Mezei, and Meng Cui. 2011. Molecular docking: a powerful approach for structure-based drug discovery. *Current computer-aided drug design*, 7(2):146–157.

Emmanuel Noutahi, Cristian Gabellini, Michael Craig, Jonathan SC Lim, and Prudencio Tossou. 2024. Gotta be safe: a new framework for molecular design. *Digital Discovery*, 3(4):796–804.

Nicholas Rego and David Koes. 2015. 3dmol. js: molecular visualization with webgl. *Bioinformatics*, 31(8):1322–1324.

David Sehnal, Sebastian Bittrich, Mandar Deshpande, Radka Svobodová, Karel Berka, Václav Bazgier, Sameer Velankar, Stephen K Burley, Jaroslav Koča, and Alexander S Rose. 2021. Mol* viewer: modern web app for 3d visualization and analysis of large biomolecular structures. *Nucleic acids research*, 49(W1):W431–W437.

Jinyuan Sun, Tong Zhu, Yinglu Cui, and Bian Wu. 2023. Structure-based self-supervised learning enables ultrafast prediction of stability changes upon mutation at the protein universe scale. *bioRxiv*, pages 2023–08.

Renxiao Wang, Xueliang Fang, Yipin Lu, Chao-Yie Yang, and Shaomeng Wang. 2005. The pdbbind database: methodologies and updates. *Journal of medicinal chemistry*, 48(12):4111–4119.

Xingyao Wang, Yangyi Chen, Lifan Yuan, Yizhe Zhang, Yunzhu Li, Hao Peng, and Heng Ji. 2024. Executable code actions elicit better llm agents. *arXiv preprint arXiv:2402.01030*.

Zhenqin Wu, Bharath Ramsundar, Evan N Feinberg, Joseph Gomes, Caleb Geniesse, Aneesh S Pappu, Karl Leswing, and Vijay Pande. 2018. Moleculenet: a benchmark for molecular machine learning. *Chemical science*, 9(2):513–530.

Yang Zhang and Jeffrey Skolnick. 2005. Tm-align: a protein structure alignment algorithm based on the tm-score. *Nucleic acids research*, 33(7):2302–2309.

A Cases of using ChatMol Copilot

A.1 Protein stability engineering task

Enzyme stability engineering plays a crucial role in various biotechnological applications by enhancing the resilience of enzymes to environmental conditions and enabling them to maintain their catalytic activity over extended periods. This process involves modifying specific amino acid residues within the enzyme structure to improve its thermal stability, pH tolerance, resistance to proteolytic degradation, and overall performance under varying conditions.

In the process copilot performed, it searches the RCSB PDB database for the LinB enzyme and download it. Subsequently, stabilizing mutations are recommended based on the energy values calculated for each mutation in the provided protein structure according users instructions. These mutations represent amino acid substitutions that are predicted to increase the stability of the enzyme. By introducing these mutations, the enzyme's structural integrity can be enhanced, leading to improved enzymatic activity and potential applications in biocatalysis, drug development, and other biotechnological processes.

A.2 Generate a set of molecules, compute the molecular properties and display the results in a table

In this case, the *de novo* generation method is used to create a set of molecules. A set of molecular properties are computed for each molecule, and the results are collected for all molecules and a table is created. All these steps are accomplished with just one prompt.

B All tools

B.1 Ligand binding pocket prediction

A message passing nerual network (Gilmer et al., 2017) based pocket prediction tool was developed named PocketMPNN. Although many pocket prediction methods were available, a residue-level prediction tool was still in the absence. However, it is of significant importance to facilitate the molecular docking process. Therefore, we developed a neural network trained on the PDB-Bind database (Wang et al., 2005) for pocket residue prediction and a publicly available API was provided. We only took this as a demonstration due to it not being computation extensive and still having satisfactory accuracy.

B.2 Protein structure prediction

The public API provided by the ESM Metagenomic Atlas was used for structure prediction. The ESMFold is of good prediction accuracy and fast response compared with MSA-based prediction such AlphaFold2. Within the length of 400 aa, this API usually responds within 20 seconds. Additionally, ESMFold's reliance on evolutionary information enables it to handle diverse protein sequences and structural motifs with high fidelity.

B.3 Mutation effect prediction

The public API of Pythia (Sun et al., 2023) was used for mutation effect prediction. The Pythia is a ultra fast mutation effect predictor with good accuracy.

B.4 Protein structure visualisation

During the conversation, py3Dmol (Rego and Koes, 2015) is used to show a cartoon representation of a protein. For more interactive and general visualisation and interaction, the streamlit plugin of Mol* (Sehnal et al., 2021) was used.

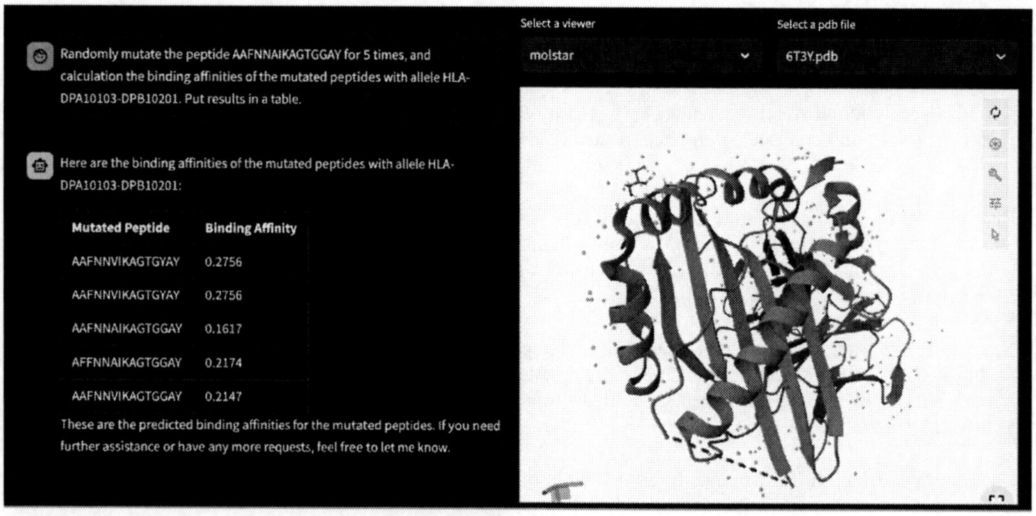

Figure 4: Using MHC binding affinity prediction tool

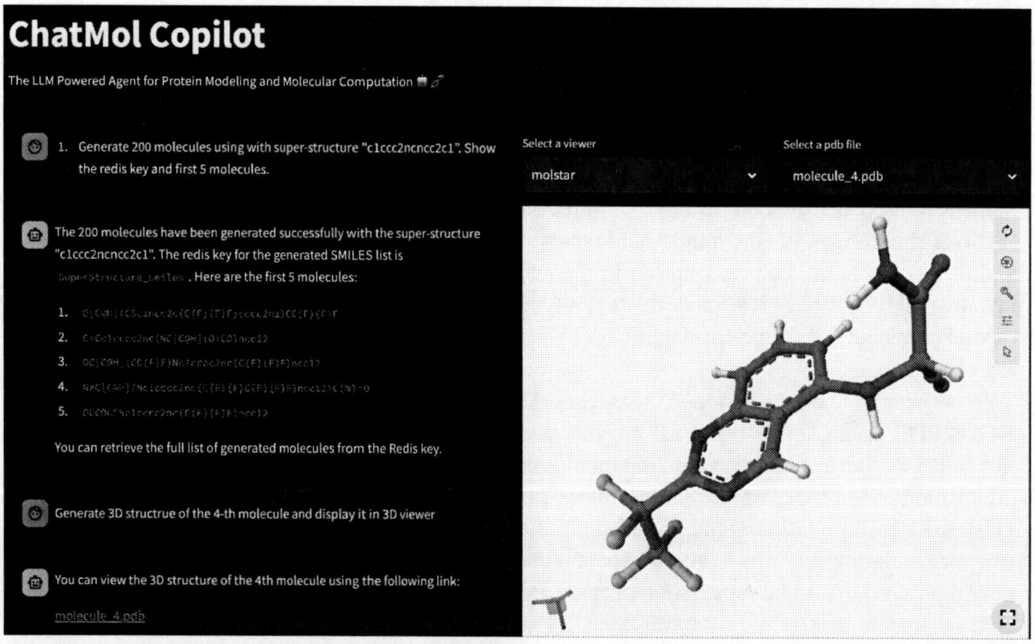

Figure 5: Using SAFE for molecular generation

B.5 Docking

The AutoDock Vina is a fast and widely applied docking tool. We implemented a RESTful API to make it adaptable in the form of a function calling for LLM to use this tool.

B.6 Blind Docking

During the docking process, it is necessary for the geometric centre of a pocket to be assigned. However, this inspection of a structure can be challenging without an experimentally determined protein-ligand complex. Here, we combined the pocket prediction with the Autodock Vina, using the geometric centre of predicted pocket residues as a hint for docking.

B.7 Protein sequence design

We use ProteinMPNN for protein sequence design. It is a neural network based on the message passing neural network, trained on protein structure to generate the native protein sequences and has been experimentally verified to be a robust tool. We also implemented a public accessible API for this copilot.

C Other details of ChatMol Copilot

C.1 Visualisation Components (Mol*, PyMOL and py3Dmol)

Visualisation is one of the most important components for the interactions between a user and ChatMol system. In ChatMol Copilot, three different visualisation components can be used. In addition to traditional interactions via the mouse, one important new way of using computers is to communicate with human natural language. This is made possible via LLMs, such as ChatGPT. The advantages of the three visualisation components are listed below:

PyMOL (DeLano et al., 2002) has high visual quality, and widely adopted by science communities.

MolStar (Mol*) serves as a basis for the next-generation data delivery and analysis tools for (not only) macromolecular structure data.

py3Dmol is a python package can be integrated easily in other python code.

We provide three options there so that users have choices according to their personal preferences.

C.2 Registry for computational services

To improve the interoperability of various computational services, all backend services are wrapped with FastAPI. For the convenience of usage and management of these services, a simple registry system for all FastAPI services is implemented. The registry itself is also a FastAPI service, which provides registration for new services, a map for finding and query the services, and for load balancing and routing. Each registry record contains a brief description of the service, the service name, the endpoint URL and the description of input/output parameters.

C.3 Function Calling and Agentic Approach

Agentic approach is the new trend of workflow automation and more deeply the road map to artificial general intelligence (AGI) as pointed out by Andrew Ng in his very recent talk at here.

As our initial approach in this new paradigm, we have implemented tool use and self reflection in our system design. In additional third party tools, all our internal computational tools which are already wrapped into FastAPI calls are further integrated into ChatMol as function calling services that can be orchestrated using LLMs, such as ChatGPT.

C.4 Registered Services

Registry This is the first service of the registry system. The main function of this service is to register other services. To register a server, the following information must be provided: service name, a brief description of the service, the URL for the service endpoint, a list of input parameter names, and the description of the parameters. **AlphaConf** A super-fast 3D conformation generation method developed by ChemXAI. The input is a file of molecules in SDF format, and the output is a file of generated 3D conformations. It takes less than 30 minutes to generate conformations for all ChEMBL database molecules on a 16-core linux machine. The conformation quality as measured by the coverage of bioactive conformers is comparable or even better than the best commercially available products, such as Omega or ConfGenX. AlphaConf follows a divide-n-conquer and build-up strategy similar to CAESAR algorithm (Li et al., 2007). A highly efficient 3D conformation storage technology is used to compress storage by factor up to 3 orders of magnitude. 100,000 conformations/second (16 core machine). 142M confs of ChEMBL storage:

**Python function to filter molecules based on Lipinski's rule of five:

```python
def filter_by_lipinski():
    from chatmol_fn import redis_reader, redis_writer
    import pandas as pd

    # Read the molecule properties data from Redis
    mol_property_table = redis_reader("mol_property_table")

    # Filter according to Lipinski's rule of five
    filtered_data = [mol for mol in mol_property_table if
                     mol['HBD (Hydrogen Bond Donors)'] <= 5 an
                     mol['HBA (Hydrogen Bond Acceptors)'] <= 1
                     mol['Molecular Weight'] < 500 and
                     mol['LOGP'] <= 5]

    # Write the filtered data to Redis
    redis_writer("filtered_lipinski_molecules", filtered_data)

    # Return the total number of molecules and the first 5 molecu
    return {"total_filtered_molecules": len(filtered_data),
            "first_5_molecules": filtered_data[:5]}

# Note: Do not execute this function yet, pending approval.
```

Please review the Python function code above. If it looks good to you, I will proceed with executing it.

Figure 6: Python code generated for Lipinski's rule of five

Table 1: Integrated Tools in ChatMol Copilot

Macromolecules	Description	Small Molecules	Description
PocketMPNN	Ligand binding pocket prediction	SAFE	Molecule generation
ESM Atlas	Protein structure prediction	generate 3D conformation	3D conformation by RDKit
Pythia	Mutation effect prediction	get smiles feature	Calculate features of molecules
py3Dmol, Mol*	Visualizer	predict logp from smiles	Prediction logP for molecules
Autodock	Docking simulation	smiles similarity	Compare molecular similarity
ProteinMPNN	Protein sequence design	AlphaConf	Fast conformation generation
BAPrediction	Peptide-MHC-II binding affinity	AlphaShape	Shape based virtual screening
search rcsb, query uniprot, fetch asked pdb, get smiles from name	Query databases	VB2000	Ab initio valence bond calculation

2.7GB.

AlphaShape Shape and pharmacophore based virtual screening with GPU acceleration. 1000,000 molecule shape comparison/second on a 2-RTX4090 GPU machine.

VB2000 3.0 This is a completely new implementation of early work VB2000 (Li and McWeeny, 2002). A modern *ab initial* valence bond calculation program. The first version was released in year 2000, and the current version is 3.0. More information of VB2000 from the official website at here.

BAPrediction Binding affinity prediction of peptide-MHC-II molecules. The prediction model is trained with the latest data sets, which include both binding affinity data (BA) and eluted ligand binding data. A combination of XGBoost and a novel feature engineering method has been used to improve the prediction accuracy. It provides better results than the published results in literature.

Molecule Generation SAFE is a very recently released open-source molecular generation model is used. The model has 87M parameters and is trained with 1.1 billion compounds in SAFE representations. The SAFE model provides 4 modes for molecule generation: 1) DenovoGen (*de novo* molecular generation). Random generation of molecules with no constraints. The output is a set of SMILES strings of the generated molecules. The input parameter is the number of molecules to be generated. 2) SuperStructure. In super structure generation, new molecules are generated based on a starting core. A smiles of the starting core need to be provided. 3) MotifExtend. In motif extension, we are interested in generating a molecule containing a given motif as a starting point. The extension point of the motif need to be labelled. 4) LinkerGen. Linker generation for linking two fragments. The smiles of two terminal fragments need to be provided in the inputs.

C.5 ChatMol in PyMOL

As an example of "code as action" and the utilization of open-source LLMs, we demonstrate a case where LLMs are directly used to generate PyMOL command lines and perform corresponding molecular visualization tasks in PyMOL. This case involves the use of two LLMs: GPT-4o and a fine-tuned Llama-3-8B-instruct. Both models correctly execute the commands "download 1pga" and "remove waters." However, GPT-4o produced an incorrect response Figure 7 when handling the command "color it by secondary structures".

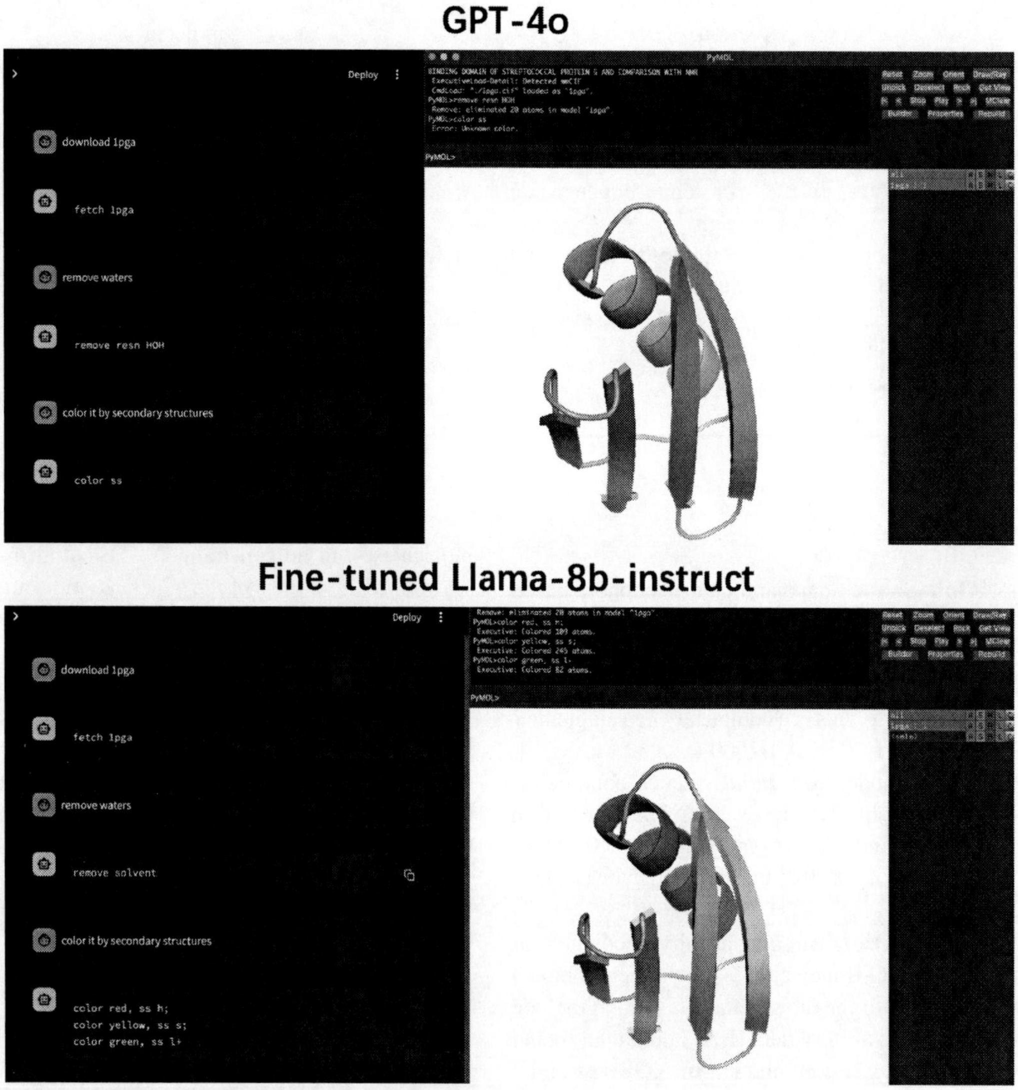

Figure 7: Performing same task using GPT-4o and fine-tuned llama-3-8b instruct

SciMind: A Multimodal Mixture-of-Experts Model for Advancing Pharmaceutical Sciences

Zhaoping Xiong[1], Xintao Fang[1], Haotian Chu[2], Xiaozhe Wan[2], Liwei Liu[2], Yameng Li[1], Wenkai Xiang[3] and Mingyue Zheng[4]

[1]ProtonUnfold Tech. Co. Ltd.
[2]Huawei Technologies Ltd.
[3]Lingang Laboratory
[4]Shanghai Institute of Materia Medica

[1]{xiongzhaoping, fangxintao, liyameng}@protonunfold.com
[2]{chuhaotian2, wanxiaozhe, liuliwei5}@huawei.com
[3]{xiangwenkai}@lglab.ac.cn
[4]{myzheng}@simm.ac.cn

Abstract

Large language models (LLMs) have made substantial strides, but their use in reliably tackling issues within specialized domains, particularly in interdisciplinary areas like pharmaceutical sciences, is hindered by data heterogeneity, knowledge complexity, unique objectives, and a spectrum of constraint conditions. In this area, diverse modalities such as nucleic acids, proteins, molecular structures, and natural language are often involved. We designed a specialized token set and introduced a new Mixture-of-Experts (MoEs) pre-training and fine-tuning strategy to unify these modalities in one model. With this strategy, we've created a multi-modal mixture-of-experts foundational model for pharmaceutical sciences, named SciMind. This model has undergone extensive pre-training on publicly accessible datasets including nucleic acid sequences, protein sequences, molecular structure strings, and biomedical texts, and delivers good performance on biomedical text comprehension, promoter prediction, protein function prediction, molecular description, and molecular generation.

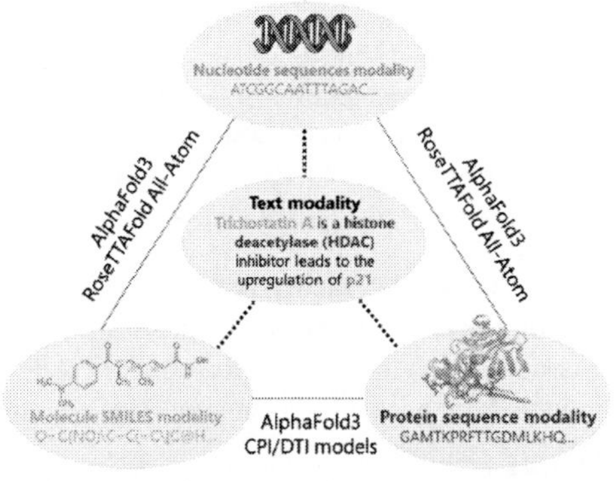

Figure 1: An overview of the four modalities in pharmaceutical sciences. The three traditional modalities, including nucleic acids (DNA/RNA), proteins, and small molecules, are typically modeled independently. Recent advancements have been made in the realm of cross-modal modeling, as indicated by the solid lines. However, there is a gap domain. In recent times, the natural language modality has surfaced as a highly promising method to describe nucleotide sequences, small molecules, and proteins, and it is swiftly garnering attention.

1 Introduction

Large language models (LLMs) have made substantial strides, providing a versatile, task-agnostic base for a variety of applications[1], [2], [3]. However, their use in reliably tackling issues within specialized domains, particularly in interdisciplinary areas like pharmaceutical sciences, is hindered by several obstacles. These include data heterogeneity, knowledge complexity, unique objectives, and a spectrum of constraint conditions, which block the creation of groundbreaking applications[4], [5], [6]. This research aims to lay the groundwork for a large-scale model within the pharmaceutical sciences. In this area, four diverse modalities including nucleic acids, proteins, molecular structures, and natural language are involved. Of them, nucleic acids, proteins and molecular structures are the common modalities modeled by the pharmaceutical science community. Predicting the properties of a molecule or a protein[7], [8], [9], designing and optimizing for new ones[10], [11], [12], and understanding how

Proceedings of the 1st Workshop on Language + Molecules (L+M 2024), pages 67–74
August 15, 2024 ©2024 Association for Computational Linguistics

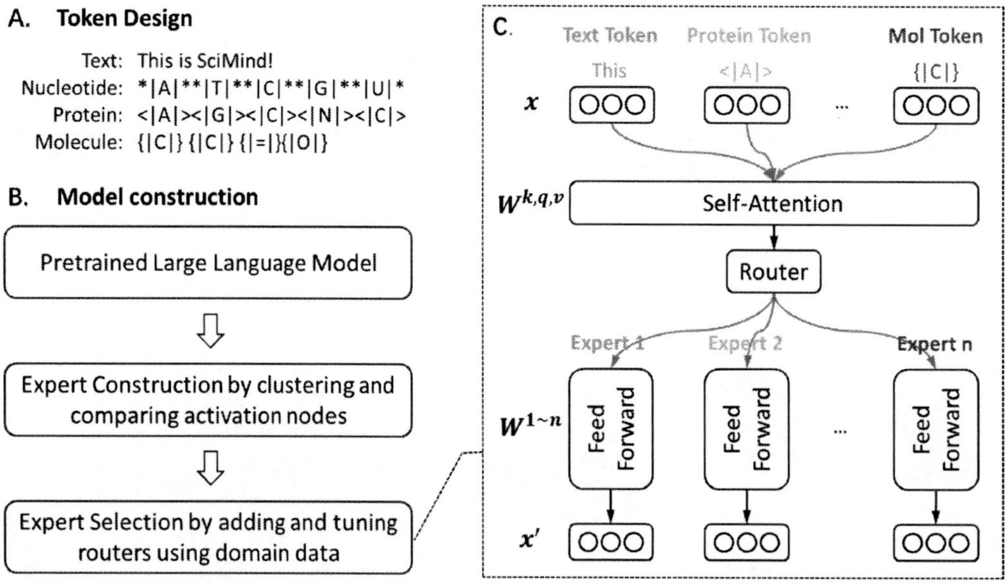

Figure 2: SciMind multi-modal model overview. A, there are four modalities in SciMind, and different modality was designated with different tokens to represent their sequences; B, based on llama-2-7B, 16 experts are split using restricted K-Means clustering according to the feedforward layer weights. A routing layer is added before the feedforward layer of the original model, and domain data is used to pretrain or fine-tune the routing layer to achieve the selection of different experts for different tokens.

they interact with each other [13], [14], [15] are common tasks and have made great progress. For example, AlphaFold3 and RosettaFold All-Atom models can even predict all interactions among these modalities.

However, a gap exists between these interactions and biological functions. While binding is common between proteins and molecules, the effects it may cause are rare and often expressed in natural language after experimentation, making standardization for modeling challenging. The effects a molecule can cause by binding to a protein are diverse, including competitive inhibition, non-competitive inhibition, agonizing, antagonizing, allosteric regulation, covalent modification, transport, and chelation, among others[16]. These effects are interconnected yet distinct from one another. Modeling each effect separately requires standardization and a separate classification or regression model, often leading to a loss of semantic meaning in the labels. In contrast, natural language descriptions provide an abstract and meaningful form of labeling for data, capable of conveying rich information.

Recent advancements in LLMs have propelled the development of cross-modal models between language and other modalities[4], [17], [17], [18], [19], [20]. These models, which include language-molecule, language-protein, and language-nucleic acids modalities, extend our capabilities to predict molecule functions, generate or optimize molecules with flexible constraints, annotate protein functions, and create or optimize proteins. However, their modality fusion is limited to two modalities.

In the field of pharmaceutical sciences, multiple modalities can be integrated, as depicted in Figure 1. If a model capable of managing all these modalities exists, then all biomedical text knowledge could be stored in a richly informative format. To address this, we've developed a specialized token set designed to individually tokenize different modalities. We also introduce a novel pre-training and fine-tuning strategy that harnesses the benefits of large-parameter models while minimizing their costs. This strategy, based on previous work MoEfication[21], involves two key components: (1) splitting the parameters of Feed-Forward Networks (FFNs) into multiple functional partitions called experts, and (2) building expert routers to determine which experts will be used for each input. By adopting a selective unequal number of expert activation strategy on different tokens, this approach enables data from different modalities to choose the most appropriate processing path. This approach not only results in a sparser model architecture, thereby reducing inference costs, but also circumvents modal alignment and potential performance decreases due to model size reduction. The main contributions of our work are as follows:

1) We've created a multi-modal mixture-of-expert foundational large model for pharmaceutical sciences, named SciMind. This model has undergone extensive pre-training on publicly accessible datasets including nucleic acids, protein sequences, molecular structures strings, and biomedical texts, and could be fine-tuned for downstream tasks involving all modalities in pharmaceutical sciences.
2) SciMind achieves state-of-the-art performance on benchmarks of molecular captioning and molecular generation by description.

2 Related works

In this section, we will provide a concise overview of the related work on cross-modal models in the field of pharmaceutical sciences.

2.1 Cross Language-Molecule Modalities

The pioneering work of MolT5 has paved the way for research in molecular captioning and generation by description, introducing the ChEBI benchmark dataset for this purpose[18]. Subsequent models such as MoSu[22], MolXPT[23], BioT5[24], and Mol-instruction[25] have expanded the scope of tasks to include numeric molecular property prediction. However, the scarcity of language-molecule pair datasets remains a challenge. To address this, the PubchemSTM[19] and L+M-24[26] datasets have been introduced, leading to improvements in molecular retrieval and editing constrained by language.

2.2 Cross Language-Protein Modalities

ProteinDT[27] and Mol-Instruction[25] are examples of multi-modal frameworks that leverage semantically related text for protein annotation and design. BioTranslator[28], a cross-modal model, is specifically designed for annotating biological entities such as gene expression vectors, protein networks, and protein sequences based on user-provided text. Building on the blip2 framework, Mistral and ESM2 have been used to create FAPM[29], which has achieved state-of-the-art results in protein functional Go Terms prediction and demonstrates strong generalization to proteins with few homologs.

3 SciMind

In this section, we will detail the design and training of our multi-modal mixture-of-experts model, SciMind. The overview of the pre-training is illustrated in Figure 2. Unlike existing models, our focus is on integrating all modalities into a single model. To this end, we have designed specialized token sets for each modality. However, each modality has a different level of complexity and requires a different number of parameters to avoid overfitting. To leverage the many open-source pretrained language models, we have chosen to construct a Mixture-of-Experts model by splitting the pretrained LLAMA-2-7B model into 16 experts at each of the feedforward layers.

3.1 Pre-training Corpus

The pre-training corpus includes only single modality data, which are general text, nucleic acids sequences, protein amino acid sequences, and molecule SMILES (Simplified Molecular-Input Line-Entry System) strings. The details of the corpus are provided in Appendix A.

3.2 Tokenization

In previous work on cross-language modalities with nucleic acids, molecules, and proteins, the token set was often inherited from NLP methods such as SentencePiece[30]. However, given the different modalities and their unique next-token distributions, we have chosen to tokenize the sequences from nucleic acids, molecules, and proteins by characters, with different brackets used to distinguish characters in different modalities (Figure 2a).

3.3 Mixture-of-Experts

Based on the LLAMA-2-7B model, we have split 16 experts using restricted K-Means clustering according to the feedforward layer weights (Figure 2b). A routing layer has been added before the feedforward layer of the original model, and different modality data are fed to pretrain or fine-tune the routing layer to achieve the selection of different experts for different tokens. Considering the propensity to overfit on nucleic acids, protein sequences, and molecule SMILES strings, and our desire to preserve the original language capabilities,

Tasks	Entitytype	No.entities	EvaluationMetrics	BioLinkBERT -Large	GPT3.5 (few-shots)	SciMind
Name Entity Recognition						
BC5CDR Disease	Disease	19,665	F1entity-level	0.940	0.603	**0.957**
BC5CDR Chem	Chemical	12,694	F1entity-level	0.864	0.518	**0.881**
NCBI Disease	Disease	6881	F1entity-level	**0.888**	0.505	0.855
BC2GM	Chemical	79,842	F1entity-level	0.852	0.375	**0.898**
JNLPBA	Gene	20,703	MicroF1	0.801	0.413	**0.842**
Relation Extraction						
Chemprot	Protein-chemical	10,031	MicroF1	0.800	0.342	**0.861**
DDI	Chemical-chemical	4,920	MicroF1	0.834	0.516	**0.844**
GAD	Gene-disease	5330	MicroF1	**0.849**	0.524	0.805
Question Answering						
PubMedQA	Yes/No/Maybe	1000	Accuracy	0.722	0.765	**0.796**
BioASQ	Summary	885	Accuracy	0.948	0.886	**0.950**

Table 1: Performances on pharmaceutical sciences domain knowledge comprehension and extraction. The metrics of BioLinkBERT-Large and ChatGPT(few-shots) are taken from the original papers.

we adopted a selective expert activation strategy. For text tokens, we engaged 8 out of the 16 experts. Conversely, for tokens corresponding to other modalities, we restricted the activation to merely 2 out of the 16 experts.

3.4 Pretraining

We employed the Huawei MindSpore training framework for pre-training purposes on Huawei Ascend 910 AI chips. Prior to inputting the processed data into the model, an extra step was taken to expedite the training process. This involved converting the data format into the MindRecord format. The Ascend AI framework offers a variety of parallel training modes, efficient memory reuse, and features like automatic mixed precision. These capabilities significantly enhance the training of large-scale models. For further acceleration, we utilized the MindFormer operator during the training process.

4 Experiments and Results

4.1 Domain Knowledge comprehension

GPT3.5, when utilizing few-shot prompts, tends to struggle with understanding pharmaceutical domain knowledge, particularly in tasks such as name entity recognition and relation extraction. In light of previous research, we evaluated SciMind's performance on domain knowledge comprehension benchmarks. As illustrated in Table 1, across ten tasks encompassing name entity recognition, relation extraction, and question answering, SciMind surpassed the previous state-of-the-art model, BioLinkBert-Large, in eight tasks.

4.2 DNA promoter prediction

Predicting gene function is vital for comprehending intricate biological processes. This involves forecasting functional elements and interaction modalities in both coding regions and non-coding sequences that govern gene transcription. Promoters, integral elements in the non-coding regions of genes, regulate gene transcription by managing RNA polymerase binding and initiation. Therefore, the precise prediction of promoter sites is essential for understanding gene expression and genetic regulatory networks.

We evaluated the performance of SciMind using the benchmark data set by DeePromoter. The results presented in Table 2 indicate that SciMind's

Organism	Method	Precision	Recall	MCC
Human TATA	DeePromoter	**0.93**	**0.95**	**0.88**
	SciMind	0.92	0.91	0.84
Human non-TATA	DeePromoter	0.97	0.95	0.92
	SciMind	0.96	**0.97**	**0.94**
Mouse TATA	DeePromoter	**0.92**	0.95	**0.87**
	SciMind	0.90	0.96	0.83
Mouse non-TATA	DeePromoter	0.91	0.90	0.82
	SciMind	**0.92**	**0.96**	**0.87**

Table 2: Performances on prompt DNA promoter prediction.

Benchmark	Model	BLEU-2 ↑	BLEU-4 ↑	ROUGE-1 ↑	ROUGE-2 ↑	ROUGE-L ↑	METEOR ↑
ChEBI	MolT5-Large*	0.594	0.508	0.654	0.510	0.594	0.614
	Mistral-7B	0.604	0.521	0.658	0.522	0.597	0.634
	SciMind	**0.626**	**0.560**	**0.679**	**0.532**	**0.629**	**0.657**
L+M-24	MolT5-Large#	0.736	0.532	0.758	0.564	0.544	0.722
	Mistral-7B#	0.749	0.543	0.771	0.574	0.555	0.729
	Meditron-7B#	0.752	0.547	0.780	**0.588**	0.563	0.737
	SciMind#	**0.757**	**0.550**	**0.782**	0.584	0.563	**0.748**

Table 3: Performances on molecular captioning. The metrics value of methods annotated with * are taken from the original paper. And the metrics value of methods annotated with # are taken from the contest leaderboard (https://www.codabench.org/competitions/2914), where SciMind ranked No.1. Other metrics values are evaluated following the process of previous work.

predictive performance is on par with DeePromoter in this task. Moreover, SciMind exhibits a slight edge in predicting data with non-TATA promoters. These promoters are more prevalent in certain organisms and types of genes, and they can be involved in more complex regulatory processes.

4.3 Molecular captioning

The objective of the molecule captioning task is to provide a structural or biological functional description for a given molecule. In our approach, we represent molecules using SMILES strings, thereby transforming the task into a seq2seq translation problem. This problem is well-suited for processing by large language models. We have two benchmark datasets with varying sizes. The ChEBI dataset is annotated by humans, while the L+M-24 dataset is summarized by ChatGPT. A notable difference is that some ChEBI data includes descriptions identifying the core structures of molecules.

As shown in Table 3, our Mixture-of-Experts-based SciMind model achieves state-of-the-art (SOTA) performance on most of the metrics in both benchmark datasets.

4.4 Molecular generation

Molecular generation is the reverse task of molecule captioning. Given a natural language description of the desired molecule, the goal is to generate a molecule that matches the description. The results in Table 4 demonstrate that our Mixture-of-Experts-based SciMind achieves state-SOTA performance on most metrics across both benchmarks.

4.5 Protein-oriented prediction

We leverage the protein-oriented instruction dataset from Mol-Instruction to fine-tune SciMind. Figure 3 shows the Rouge-L metrics of five methods across four tasks: protein function, general description, catalytic activity, and domain/motif

Benchmark	Model	BLEU ↑	Exact ↑	Levenshtein ↓	MACCS FTS ↑	RDK FTS ↑	Morgan FTS ↑	Validity ↑
ChEBI	MolT5-large*	0.854	0.311	16.07	0.834	0.746	0.684	0.905
	Mistral-7B	0.850	0.380	18.00	**0.896**	**0.818**	0.757	0.935
	SciMind	**0.863**	**0.383**	**15.99**	0.885	0.813	**0.762**	**0.992**
L+M-24	MolT5-base#	0.664	0	46.51	0.746	0.637	0.463	0.999
	MolT5-large#	0.549	0	57.34	0.741	0.634	0.385	0.991
	Mistral-7B#	0.699	0	44.44	0.756	0.676	0.486	0.994
	Meditron-7B#	0.676	0.0001	48.03	0.756	0.677	0.487	0.995
	SciMind#	**0.707**	**0.0001**	**43.48**	**0.756**	**0.677**	**0.488**	**0.997**

Table 4: Molecular generation based on description. The metrics value of methods annotated with * are taken from the original paper. And the metrics value of methods annotated with # are taken from the contest leaderboard (https://www.codabench.org/competitions/3014), where SciMind ranked No.1. Other metrics values are evaluated following the process of previous work.

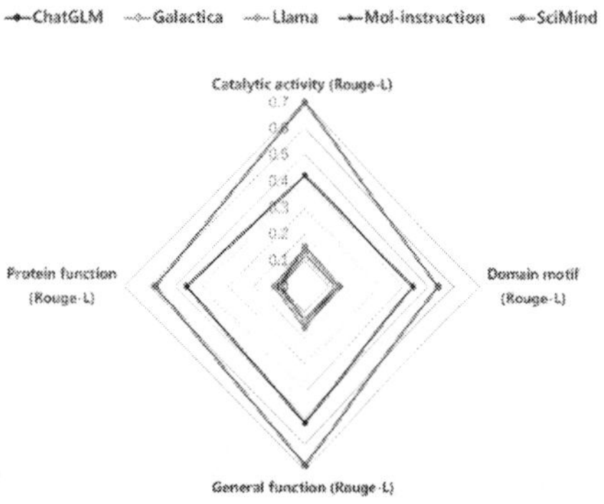

Figure 3: Performance on protein-oriented prediction

prediction. Compared to other single-modal language models, SciMind achieves the best performance on Rouge-L metrics across all four tasks.

5 Conclusions and discussion

In this paper, we introduced SciMind, a unified pre-training framework designed to include all the modalities in pharmaceutical sciences. we've designed a specialized token set and introduce a new pre-training and fine-tuning strategy that leverages the advantages of large-parameter models while minimizing their expenses. This strategy, supported by a prior expert allocation and selection mechanism, allows data of different modalities to choose the most suitable processing path. This method not only leads to a sparser model architecture, thus cutting down on inference costs, but also avoids modal alignment and the potential performance decrease due to model size reduction. We've created a multi-modal mixture-of-expert foundational large model for pharmaceutical sciences, named SciMind. This model has undergone extensive pre-training on publicly accessible datasets including nucleic acids, protein sequences, molecular structures strings, and biomedical texts, and could be fine-tuned for downstream tasks involving all modalities in pharmaceutical sciences. The experimental outcomes suggest that the SciMind model not only delivers outstanding performance but also shows high flexibility and interpretability in response to prompt words, offering a sturdy base for its use in pharmaceutical sciences.

Due to the lack of well-aligned multimodal data, our model has not fully demonstrated its advantages. In addition to molecular captioning and generation by description, the inclusion of the protein modality will make the interaction between the language and small molecule modalities more explainable and useful. This approach helps accumulate more information and is a promising direction to explore.

Acknowledgments

We acknowledge the support by the Huawei MindSpore team.

References

[1] OpenAI *et al.*, "GPT-4 Technical Report," *ArXiv E-Prints*, p. arXiv:2303.08774, Mar. 2023, doi: 10.48550/arXiv.2303.08774.

[2] Gemini Team *et al.*, "Gemini 1.5: Unlocking multimodal understanding across millions of tokens of context," *ArXiv E-Prints*, p. arXiv:2403.05530, Mar. 2024, doi: 10.48550/arXiv.2403.05530.

[3] H. Touvron *et al.*, "LLaMA: Open and Efficient Foundation Language Models," *ArXiv E-Prints*, p. arXiv:2302.13971, Feb. 2023, doi: 10.48550/arXiv.2302.13971.

[4] Gemini Team *et al.*, "Gemini: A Family of Highly Capable Multimodal Models," *ArXiv E-Prints*, p. arXiv:2312.11805, Dec. 2023, doi: 10.48550/arXiv.2312.11805.

[5] Y. Luo *et al.*, "BioMedGPT: Open Multimodal Generative Pre-trained Transformer for BioMedicine," *ArXiv E-Prints*, p. arXiv:2308.09442, Aug. 2023, doi: 10.48550/arXiv.2308.09442.

[6] J. Lee *et al.*, "BioBERT: a pre-trained biomedical language representation model for biomedical text mining," *Bioinformatics*, vol. 36, pp. 1234–1240, 2019.

[7] Z. Xiong *et al.*, "Pushing the Boundaries of Molecular Representation for Drug Discovery with the Graph Attention Mechanism," *J. Med. Chem.*, vol. 63, no. 16, pp. 8749–8760, Aug. 2020, doi: 10.1021/acs.jmedchem.9b00959.

[8] K. K. Yang, Z. Wu, C. N. Bedbrook, and F. H. Arnold, "Learned protein embeddings for machine learning," *Bioinformatics*, vol. 34, no. 15, pp. 2642–2648, Mar. 2018, doi: 10.1093/bioinformatics/bty178.

[9] Z. Wu *et al.*, "MoleculeNet: A Benchmark for Molecular Machine Learning," *Chem Sci*, vol. 9, no. 2, p. 513, 2018.

[10] X. Lin *et al.*, "PanGu Drug Model: learn a molecule like a human," *Sci. China Life Sci.*, vol. 66, pp. 879–882, 2022.

[11] X. Liu *et al.*, "MolFilterGAN: a progressively augmented generative adversarial network for triaging AI-designed molecules," *J. Cheminformatics*, vol. 15, 2023, [Online].

Available:
https://api.semanticscholar.org/CorpusID:258028901
[12] J. Dauparas *et al.*, "Robust deep learning–based protein sequence design using ProteinMPNN," *Science*, vol. 378, no. 6615, pp. 49–56, Oct. 2022, doi: 10.1126/science.add2187.
[13] L. Chen *et al.*, "TransformerCPI: improving compound-protein interaction prediction by sequence-based deep learning with self-attention mechanism and label reversal experiments," *Bioinformatics*, 2020, [Online]. Available: https://api.semanticscholar.org/CorpusID:218755832
[14] J. Abramson *et al.*, "Accurate structure prediction of biomolecular interactions with AlphaFold 3," *Nature*, May 2024, doi: 10.1038/s41586-024-07487-w.
[15] R. Krishna *et al.*, "Generalized biomolecular modeling and design with RoseTTAFold All-Atom," *Science*, vol. 384, no. 6693, p. eadl2528, doi: 10.1126/science.adl2528.
[16] A. Cooper and D. T. F. Dryden, "Allostery without conformational change," *Eur. Biophys. J.*, vol. 11, no. 2, pp. 103–109, Oct. 1984, doi: 10.1007/BF00276625.
[17] D. Christofidellis, G. Giannone, J. Born, O. Winther, T. Laino, and M. Manica, "Unifying Molecular and Textual Representations via Multi-task Language Modelling," in *International Conference on Machine Learning*, 2023. [Online]. Available: https://api.semanticscholar.org/CorpusID:256389950
[18] C. Edwards, T. Lai, K. Ros, G. Honke, K. Cho, and H. Ji, "Translation between Molecules and Natural Language," *ArXiv E-Prints*, p. arXiv:2204.11817, Apr. 2022, doi: 10.48550/arXiv.2204.11817.
[19] S. Liu *et al.*, "Multi-modal Molecule Structure-text Model for Text-based Retrieval and Editing," *Nat Mac Intell*, vol. 5, pp. 1447–1457, 2022.
[20] M. Xu, X. Yuan, S. Miret, and J. Tang, "ProtST: Multi-Modality Learning of Protein Sequences and Biomedical Texts," in *International Conference on Machine Learning*, 2023. [Online]. Available: https://api.semanticscholar.org/CorpusID:256390530
[21] Z. Zhang, Y. Lin, Z. Liu, P. Li, M. Sun, and J. Zhou, "MoEfication: Transformer Feed-forward Layers are Mixtures of Experts," in *Findings*, 2021. [Online]. Available: https://api.semanticscholar.org/CorpusID:247958465
[22] B. Su *et al.*, "A Molecular Multimodal Foundation Model Associating Molecule Graphs with Natural Language," *ArXiv E-Prints*, p. arXiv:2209.05481, Sep. 2022, doi: 10.48550/arXiv.2209.05481.
[23] Z. Liu *et al.*, "MolXPT: Wrapping Molecules with Text for Generative Pre-training," *ArXiv E-Prints*, p. arXiv:2305.10688, May 2023, doi: 10.48550/arXiv.2305.10688.
[24] Q. Pei *et al.*, "BioT5: Enriching Cross-modal Integration in Biology with Chemical Knowledge and Natural Language Associations," *ArXiv E-Prints*, p. arXiv:2310.07276, Oct. 2023, doi: 10.48550/arXiv.2310.07276.
[25] Y. Fang *et al.*, "Mol-Instructions: A Large-Scale Biomolecular Instruction Dataset for Large Language Models," *ArXiv E-Prints*, p. arXiv:2306.08018, Jun. 2023, doi: 10.48550/arXiv.2306.08018.
[26] C. Edwards, Q. Wang, L. Zhao, and H. Ji, "L+M-24: Building a Dataset for Language+ Molecules@ ACL 2024," *ArXiv Prepr. ArXiv240300791*, 2024.
[27] S. Liu *et al.*, "A Text-guided Protein Design Framework," *ArXiv*, vol. abs/2302.04611, 2023, [Online]. Available: https://api.semanticscholar.org/CorpusID:256697425
[28] H. Xu, A. Woicik, H. Poon, R. B. Altman, and S. Wang, "Multilingual translation for zero-shot biomedical classification using BioTranslator," *Nat. Commun.*, vol. 14, 2023, [Online]. Available: https://api.semanticscholar.org/CorpusID:256701737
[29] W. Xiang *et al.*, "FAPM: Functional Annotation of Proteins using Multi-Modal Models Beyond Structural Modeling," *bioRxiv*, 2024, [Online]. Available: https://api.semanticscholar.org/CorpusID:269762294
[30] T. Kudo and J. Richardson, "SentencePiece: A simple and language independent subword tokenizer and detokenizer for Neural Text Processing," in *Conference on Empirical Methods in Natural Language Processing*, 2018. [Online]. Available: https://api.semanticscholar.org/CorpusID:52051958

A Pre-training Corpus

DNA data

Our pretraining data for nucleic acid sequences is derived from DNABERT_S, which includes a human genome dataset containing 2.75 billion nucleotide bases. The multi-species genome dataset includes genomes from 135 different species, distributed across 6 categories and containing a total of 32.49 billion nucleotide bases, which is 12 times the size of the human genome dataset. We use *| |* to separate the characters in the nucleic acids, as shown in Figure 2a.

RNA data

This dataset is a subset of the RNAcentral active fasta file, available at https://ftp.ebi.ac.uk/pub/databases/RNAcentral/releases/24.0/sequences/rnacentral_active.fasta.gz, that has been converted to the parquet format. It represents approximately 10% of the overall dataset and contains 3,252,483 (3.2 million) sequences, comprising a total of 2,642,703,990 (2.6 billion) bases. We use *| |* to separate the characters in the nucleic acids, as shown in Figure 2a.

Protein data

Protein sequence databases, such as UniParc, contain a wide variety of sequences from different organisms. In our experiments, we follow the esm work and used the 250 million sequences from the UniParc database, which contains a total of 86 billion amino acids. These datasets are similar in size to large text corpora that are commonly used to train high-capacity neural network models for natural language processing tasks. We use <| |> to separate the characters in the protein sequences, as shown in Figure 2a.

Molecule data

The molecular data is taken from https://huggingface.co/datasets/kjappelbaum/chemnlp_iupac_smiles, which contains 30 million molecules' SMILES and their IUPAC names. We use {| |} to separate the characters in the molecule SMILES, as shown in Figure 2a.

B Finetuning corpus

All downstream tasks in this paper have been benchmarked against previous studies. Accordingly, we fine-tune and test our models using either the pre-split datasets or by splitting the data in the same manner as the original studies.

Knowledge Graph Extraction from Total Synthesis Documents

Andres M Bran[1,2] , Zlatko Joncev[1] ,
Philippe Schwaller[1,2],
[1] Laboratory of Artificial Chemical Intelligence (LIAC), Lausanne, Switzerland,
[2] National Centre of Competence in Research (NCCR) Catalysis, Lausanne, Switzerland

Correspondence: andres.marulandabran@epfl.ch

Abstract

Knowledge graphs (KGs) have emerged as a powerful tool for organizing and integrating complex information, making it a suitable format for scientific knowledge. However, translating scientific knowledge into KGs is challenging as a wide variety of styles and elements to present data and ideas is used. Although efforts for KG extraction (KGE) from scientific documents exist, evaluation remains challenging and field-dependent; and existing benchmarks do not focuse on scientific information. Furthermore, establishing a general benchmark for this task is challenging as not all scientific knowledge has a ground-truth KG representation, making any benchmark prone to ambiguity. Here we propose Graph of Organic Synthesis Benchmark (GOSyBench), a benchmark for KG extraction from scientific documents in chemistry, that leverages the native KG-like structure of synthetic routes in organic chemistry. We develop KG-extraction algorithms based on LLMs (GPT-4, Claude, Mistral) and VLMs (GPT-4o), the best of which reaches 73% recovery accuracy and 59% precision, leaving a lot of room for improvement. We expect GOSyBench can serve as a valuable resource for evaluating and advancing KGE methods in the scientific domain, ultimately facilitating better organization, integration, and discovery of scientific knowledge.

Knowledge graphs (KGs) have emerged as a powerful tool for representing and organizing complex information, enabling efficient storage, retrieval, and analysis of data across various domains (Hogan et al., 2021). The extraction of knowledge graphs from unstructured data sources, such as text documents, has gained significant attention in recent years due to its potential to unlock valuable insights and facilitate knowledge discovery. KGs have also recently been used in Retrieval-Augmented Generation (RAG) pipelines (Abu-Rasheed et al., 2024), as a strategy to ground text generation from large language models (LLMs) with domain-specific facts, thus improving performance across tasks (Khattab et al., 2023; Khattab and Zaharia, 2020).

0.1 Extraction of Knowledge Graphs

The field of Knowledge Graph Extraction (KGE) has witnessed substantial progress, with numerous approaches being developed to automatically construct KGs from textual data. These methods range from rule-based systems to machine learning-based techniques, and more recently, LLM-driven extraction (Meyer et al., 2023; Shu et al., 2024). Several benchmarks have been proposed to evaluate the performance of KGE systems, from open-domain ones like Open Graph Benchmark (Hu et al., 2020) and Text2KGBbench (Mihindukulasooriya et al., 2023), to more field specific ones like PharmaKG for biomedical data mining (Zheng et al., 2020). These benchmarks focus on evaluating algorithms on the extraction of specific facts from short sentences or paragraphs, while extraction from complete documents, and specially scientific ones, remains largely untested.

Scientific literature contains a wealth of knowledge that can be represented in KGs, the extraction of which would enable more efficient knowledge integration and facilitate discovery. Excellent efforts have been made to extract specific types of scientific information, such as entities and relations in chemical literature (Lowe and Sayle, 2013; Swain and Cole, 2016; Mavračić et al., 2021). While these advances have enabled the extraction of influential reaction datasets (Lowe, 2012), they are tailored to patents, which have a more standardized format and contain less scientific details as journal papers do. Moreover, these methods focus on extracting single reactions or short sequences, mostly ignoring the underlying network of objects and concepts originally expressed in the texts.

The lack of benchmarks specifically designed for

Proceedings of the 1st Workshop on Language + Molecules (L+M 2024), pages 75–85
August 15, 2024

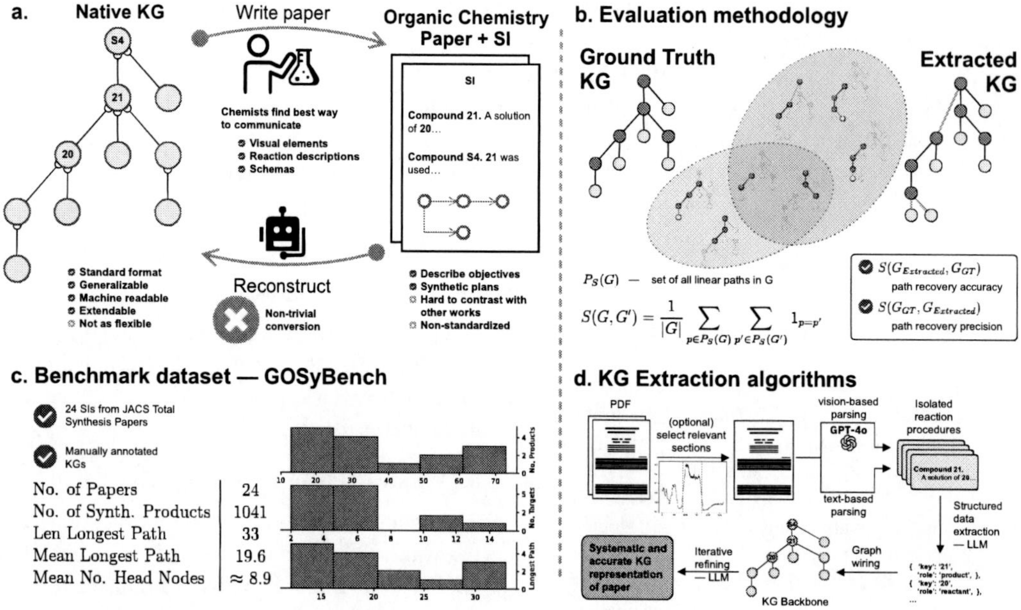

Figure 1: **Example Knowledge Graph and evaluation strategy. a.** Shows the data representation used for the task, where each node Si in the directed graph represents abstractly a substance, and each edge V (i → j) expresses that substance Sj is used in a reaction that has substance Si as a product. The goal of the KG is to accurately represent the information presented in the paper. **b.** Evaluation methodology followed in this work. **c.** Summary statistics of the resulting dataset. These highlight aspects critical to graph complexity, like number of substances (nodes), maximum path length, number of head nodes (indegree(Si) = 0), among others. **d.** Algorithm developed for KGE.

evaluating KGE in science poses a challenge, as the diverse nature of scientific knowledge and the absence of ground-truth KGs make it difficult to establish a standardized evaluation framework. The heterogeneity of scientific literature, with its wide range of domains, writing styles, and presentation formats, further complicates the development of a comprehensive benchmark.

0.2 KGs in Organic Chemistry

A knowledge graph is defined generally as a graph of data, intended to convey knowledge. Here, nodes represent entities of interest and edges represent relations between these entities (Hogan et al., 2021). As such, synthetic sequences in Organic Chemistry are susceptible of being represented under such a structure.

Research in synthetic organic chemistry (OC) focuses very generally on the synthesis of organic compounds through a suitable sequence of reactions. Under this conception, substances are *concepts* that are connected through reactions as *relationships*. Each substance may serve as product or reactant for a multitude of different reactions, leading to the natural definition of networks of chemical reactions. This has previously been studied under different models with different levels of depth (Fialkowski et al., 2005). This bare abstraction defines the backbone of a KG, and is this native KG-like structure makes OC an ideal domain for exploring KGE techniques.

But reactions –defined as an experimentally executed transformation that leads from one substance to another– are not the only type of relationships that may exist between substances. In research works in OC, substances are synthesized not only because they will be directly used as building blocks for the synthetic targets, but some are synthesized also to serve as model systems for more complex and valuable structures, some are synthesized but paths need to be abandoned due to unsuccessful reactions, and sometimes even substances are synthesized to facilitate structural elucidation of their precursors. Indeed, many more relationships are built on top of the reaction-graph backbone, that are of interest for organic chemists: these go beyond to inform about strategic aspects of synthesis and multi-level chemistry-driven decision processes.

This work focuses mainly on the extraction of the main backbone from research papers. These are typically given in papers' Supporting Information (SI) files, and contain detailed descriptions of synthetic routes and experimental procedures. These documents exhibit a wide variety of representations, designs, and conventions, making it challenging to extract consistent and comprehensive KGs, see Appendix A for examples. Despite the heterogeneity in the representation of OC knowledge, the underlying structure remains the same: a network of chemical reactions and synthetic plans. This property allows for the definition of a ground-truth KG, making OC a suitable domain for developing and evaluating KGE methods in science.

In this paper, we propose **GOSyBench**, a benchmark for KGE from scientific documents in the domain of organic chemistry. By leveraging the native KG-like structure of synthetic routes, we aim to provide a standardized evaluation framework for assessing the performance of KGE algorithms in extracting scientific knowledge. Our KG ontology defines substances as *entities*, with *reference_key* and *substance_name* as properties, that are connected by reactions as relationships. Furthermore, we develop novel KGE algorithms based on LLMs, and conduct extensive experiments and ablation studies to validate their effectiveness using our proposed benchmark.

1 Methods

1.1 Guidance / structured output generation

Despite their usefulness in various domains, one of the limitations of LLMs is their incapacity to generate consistent and controllable outputs that fit use-case specific guidelines. Recent research has focused in steering LLM generation through the enforcement of grammars in the resulting generations (Rebedea et al., 2023; Khattab et al., 2023). This not only helps steer models towards non-harmful outcomes, but also enables tool usage in agent-like scenarios (Boiko et al., 2023; Bran et al., 2024) and facilitates parsing of the results and integration in existing software (Liu, 2024).

1.2 Benchmark dataset curation

The dataset curation pipeline used involved a combination of automated knowledge extraction and expert human labeling. Initially, 24 Supplementary Information files (SIs) on total synthesis were manually selected from the Journal of the American Chemical Society (JACS), with the format and content of their SI used as a criterion. The SIs were selected such that the obtained sample represents a wide variety of text formatting, varying use of visual elements, order and location of relevant sections, among others, see Appendix A for examples.

The SIs were then processed using the KGE method presented in Section 1.3, resulting in a collection of 24 knowledge graphs, where each contains an approximation to the complete network of chemical reactions expressed in the SI. The process then continued with manual curation, which generally involved node relabeling, node creation/removal, and edge creation/removal. The resulting objects are directed graphs, with individual substances as nodes, and reactions as edges. Some statistics of the dataset are described in Figure 1, which highlights the size and overall complexity of the KGs being extracted.

1.3 KGE method

The Knowledge Graph Extraction method developed for this work has several steps, as shown in Figure 1d. Initially, the SI PDF is pre-processed to select the relevant sections describing the reaction procedures, as explained in more detail in Appendix B. This aims to lower the amount of text that needs to be processed in the steps following, and prevents errors by erroneous addition of spurious nodes to the graph. The PDF is then processed into text and split into single text segments describing chemical reactions. Two methods were tested for this: one based in rule-based text parsing from PDF, and one based in Vision-Language Models (VLMs), namely the recent GPT-4o by OpenAI. The latter method was implemented in view of the variability of representations and interleaved use of visual elements observed in SIs, as shown in Appendix A.

Resulting *reaction blocks* are then each processed individually by an LLM-powered generation pipeline, that detects and extracts all the substances declared in the input reaction. Each of these substances is represented as a structured object containing three main properties: *reference_key*, *substance_name*, and *role_in_reaction*. Each collection of substances is converted into a *reaction_unit*, a structured object resembling a node in a tree, where the head node is the product of the reaction and the children are all the substances with a role different than *product*.

Finally, a graph is constructed by connecting all the different *reaction_unit* objects, using each substance's *reference_key* as the node label.

The reported benchmark was used to perform ablations on 3 of the design choices for the algorithm, namely to test the effect of SI preprocessing to select relevant sections, the use of rule-based or vision-based PDF parsing, and the choice of LLM used for structured object generation. The results are shown in Figure 2.

1.4 PDF Parsing methods

Two parsing methods have been tested in this work. One is a simple, rule-based algorithm that is based on general observations from the structure of SIs in organic chemistry papers, while the other is fully driven by a Vision-Language Model (VLM), which aims to recover information by directly processing documents as humans would read it, without loss of visual elements.

1.4.1 Rule-based — Text

This approach consists of parsing the input PDF file using the PyMuPDF package (noa), which yields the complete text from the PDF, including titles and paragraphs, but also formatting details such as bold letters. Unfortunately it also includes spurious formatting details like page numbers and side notes from journals. Using this information, the text is split using "long sequences of bold letters" as a splitting criteria, which leads to a list of text segments. The idea behind this parsing is that most authors state products in bold font with the name of the product (*IUPAC*, or simply a reference name), followed by a reference key, and then proceed with the description of the reaction procedure in normal font (see Appendix A). This pattern is somewhat consistent and in some cases leads to very nicely parsed documents.

1.4.2 Image-based — Vision

The effectiveness of the rule-based method above is endangered by the variety of formats and representation styles that authors decide to use in their papers, as shown in the Appendix A. Understanding of these documents is heavily dependent on the reader's ability to interpret the visuals and contrast them and connect them with the text, thus the purely rule-based method falls short in some cases.

Leveraging the recent advances in VLM research, we propose directly using one such model for this task. In particular, we use the recently released GPT-4o, one of the most powerful end-to-end Large Multimodal Models (LMMs) from OpenAI.

The pipeline starts with the conversion of the input PDF into a suitable format, and for this we simply convert each page from the PDF into a png image using the pdf2image package (Belval, 2024). The images are then processed into overlapping batches of images, each batch in a single VLM call. This process ensures that the VLM sees a more global structure of the paper and thus has better context to give an appropriate response.

The VLM is then queried with all the images from a batch and a prompt with instructions (see Appendix C). The expected output of this is a summary of the relevant information for *each* reaction the VLM can identify in the image context; each reaction separated by a given separator token.

1.5 Evaluation metrics

A wealth of methods exist to compare graphs, each suitable for certain sets of use cases (Thompson et al., 2022; Shimada et al., 2016; Hartle et al., 2020). These include direct comparison of the node or edge sets, subgraph matching, spectral analysis, and the use of graph kernels, among others. In this work, we take an approach based on subgraph matching, that aims to capture the similarities relevant to synthetic routes in organic chemistry.

Appealing to the specific structure of the types of graphs used in this work, namely directed graphs with mostly a tree-like structure, we use 3 metrics based on the ratio of paths shared between the compared graphs, as shown in Equation 1.

$$S(G, G') = \frac{1}{|P_S(G)|} \sum_{p \in P_S(G)} \sum_{p' \in P_S(G')} 1_{p=p'} \tag{1}$$

Where $P_S(G)$ defines the set of all the linear paths p in G, and the $1_p = p'$ operator is defined as 1 if the condition $p = p'$ is met, 0 otherwise. The key difference between the methods used here is the definition of the equivalence operator $=$, which can take multiple forms depending on the property of interest. In particular, two options are defined: exact match and preservation of partial order. Exact match directly compares the two paths based on the exact sequence of nodes defined by each. This method thus directly measures to what extent the exact KG is reconstructed from documents.

The second method aims to capture a more nuanced structure in the retrieved KGs, through a slightly less strict comparison metric based on ordered sets. In this method, two paths are considered equivalent if the order relationships defined by each path are preserved in the other. Take for example the following two paths

$$p_0 = 6 \rightarrow S2 \rightarrow 7$$
$$p_1 = 6 \rightarrow 7$$

Where p_0 defines the order $6 \succ S2 \succ 7$. In this example, $p_0 \neq p_1$ under exact match, however they are under the PO equivalence as the order relationship $6 \succ 7$ exists in both paths. Such a less strict definition is particularly relevant in our case as it is typical in SIs to describe the formation of an intermediate and continue using it "without further purification". In these cases, the complete sequence p_0 with intermediate $S2$ may be reduced by the extraction models to p_1, which is not necessarily incorrect however missing some information.

A last method is used, which uses exact match as equivalence operator, but both G and G' are preprocessed to remove the leaves (nodes with $outdegree(n) = 0$), thus only comparing the backbone of the synthetic tree without considering reagents. Figure 1b shows such removed nodes in yellow, and the nodes belonging to the backbone in red.

2 Results

The proposed benchmark was used to perform ablations on 3 of the components of the KGE algorithm described in Section 1.3. Namely, we assess the effect of SI preprocessing (Appendix B), the parsing of PDFs using a rule-based approach, or directly through Vision-Language Models (VLMs), and the choice of LLM for parsing of reaction descriptions into formatted reaction units. In addition, we evaluate the performance of multiple LLMs from different providers on the latter task across multiple metrics using a more specific benchmark, aimed at selecting suitable LLMs for this task, without the need to execute the whole extraction pipeline.

2.1 KGE Benchmark

The aim of these experiments is to determine the effectivity of a given system at extracting a KG in the required format, not only at assessing the capabilities of LLMs, hence 2 binary variables are ablated that deal with document preprocessing, parsing and chunking. The latter is the LLM used, however here we have restricted ourselves to only testing models provided by OpenAI, mainly due to rate limit constraints from the other providers.

In Figure 2 we display the per-paper performance for each variation of the system in Figure 1d, across six metrics, all different forms of accuracy (left column=) and precision (right column) of synthetic path recovery. The upper row shows the results on exact path reconstruction, middle row a more relaxed version of this based on comparing the orders defined by each path, and bottom row compares the pruned graphs, assessing the similarity between the tree backbones; see Section 1.5 for details.

For each comparison method, $S(G_{EX}, G_{GT})$ measures the system's ability to reconstruct Ground Truth paths — highly important for organic chemistry as it defines the specific sequence of reactions, while $S(G_{GT}, G_{Extracted})$ measures the precision or "purity" of the resulting graphs, thus also accounting for erroneous introduction of nodes or edges in the extraction process.

The results show that the overall performance varies widely as a function of the paper, which is to be expected given the high variability in styles and formats used in these documents (see Appendix A). A systematic difference is found between the 2 models tested, with a clear advantage for GPT-4-turbo, the most advanced model, especially on reconstruction accuracy. The gap is nevertheless reduced in reconstruction precision which, as will be shown in the next section, can be attributed to the smaller model being better at detecting wrong inputs, thus introducing less noise into the extracted KG.

Interestingly, comparing the pruned graphs demonstrates GPT-3.5's poor performance on precision, with most values below 0.1, however the corresponding accuracy is relatively high, even surpassing GPT-4 based methods on the same metric. Such results imply that smaller models perform poorly in general conditions, however the information recovered by these is typically valid. More advanced models seem not to have a strong filter and generate valid structured outputs despite noisy filters, which in turns generate accurate but noisy KGs. These observations will be further elaborated in the following section.

From the results presented here it seems that using vision models like GPT-4o (columns in Figure

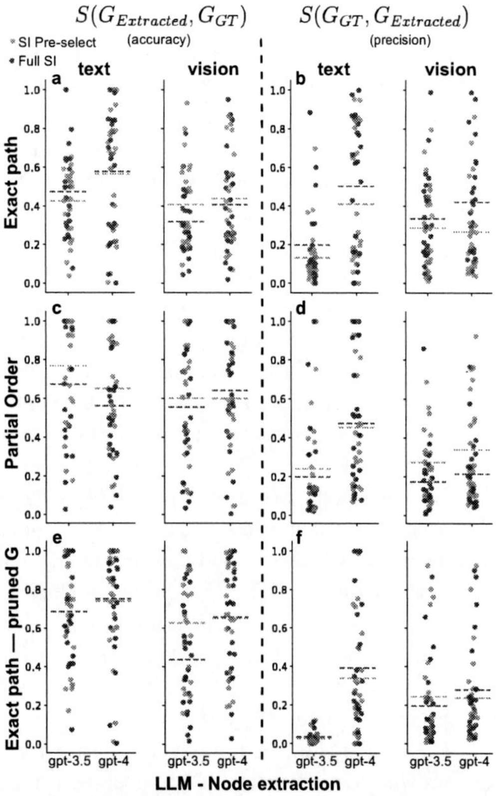

Figure 2: **Results from Knowledge Graph Extraction benchmark.** System performance on GOSyBench for multiple system ablations. The two main columns show accuracy (left) and precision (right). Each sub column shows the result for PDF parsing methods text-based (left) and vision-based (right). Rows present different metrics used for graph comparison, and the color distinguishes between SI pre-processing methods.

2), or preprocessing the document before to select the most relevant parts of the SI (colors in Figure) do not improve the system's performance. Vision only helps slightly improve the accuracy of the system when a smaller model is used, however such system still underperforms relative to the larger GPT-4.

A more in-depth exploration of the results is needed to determine how to best leverage vision models for this task.

2.2 LLM Performance across tasks

To assess the effect of the choice of LLM in the KGE method developed in this work, another benchmark with a narrower scope was produced. The benchmark aims to assess LLM's abilities to recover specific information from reaction description text samples. This involved the creation of 3 smaller datasets, each designed to test the models at specific tasks, namely ability to recognize and retrieve the correct product and reactant sets, ability to produce empty responses whenever a non-reaction text is given, and the ability to correctly retrieve the *reference_key* of substances.

All of these are elements of utmost importance for the algorithm's success at reconstructing a paper's KG, as failure to correctly perform these contaminates the resulting KG with spurious nodes and edges, and leads to the loss of real nodes and edges.

For the sake of completeness and ease of implementation, we have tested LLMs from 3 API providers, namely OpenAI, Anthropic and Mistral. Moreover, the models tested span a wide range of sizes and scores on standard benchmarks. As shown in Figure 3, the top-performing model in terms of product and reactants retrieval accuracy is *gpt-4-turbo*, on of the most advanced models as shown by benchmarks, in terms of reasoning capabilities. Nevertheless, other models, some smaller and far cheaper, perform almost on-par with gpt-4 on this metric (mistral small and medium, mixtral 8x7b, all claude models).

Surprisingly, the "smarter" models do not perform as good on other tasks, particularly "Wrong inp" and "Key exact". Smaller, less poweful models, like *mistral-small*, *mixtral-8x7b* and *gpt-3.5-turbo* do better in rejecting wrong inputs than their more advanced counterparts despite their less developed reasoning capabilities. An important observation is that, when given a non-reaction text, smaller models give an error as they fail to find the requested information and fail to produce an answer in the requested format, thus being caught as exception during model validation. In counterpart, larger models tend to give a response, despite the input text not containing the desired information, typically through hallucinations.

In spite of these observations, the ablations in Section 2.1 have been performed only with OpenAI models as we had higher rate limits, allowing us to perform multiple experiments concurrently.

3 Conclusions

We have proposed a novel benchmark for knowledge graph extraction in science from full papers. We exploit the native KG-like structure of synthetic

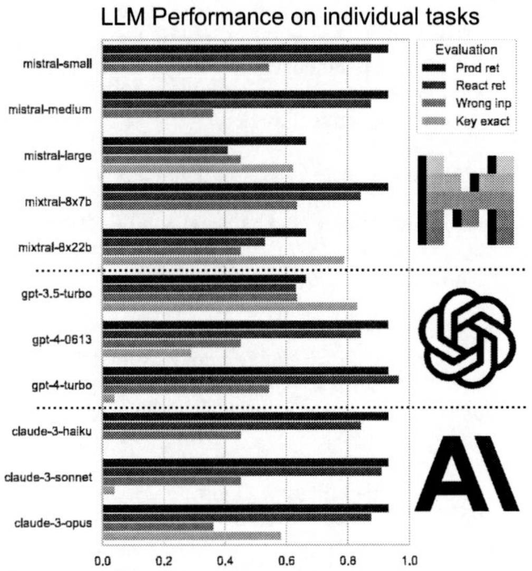

Figure 3: **Capability-specific benchmark for LLMs.** The performance of multiple LLM across multiple scales and providers is shown. Models are evaluated on 4 metrics: **Prod ret** evaluates the accuracy of retrieving the correct product name from an input paragraph (which involves separating product name from its reference key), **React ret** evaluates the same, for retrieval of reactants used in the described reaction, **Wrong inp** assesses how good the models are at rejecting inputs that do not describe a chemical reaction, and **Key exact** evaluates the ability of models to output the exact reference key for products.

organic chemistry and propose a benchmark with 24 manually curated papers. This benchmark is continuously growing to incorporate more high quality samples of challenging papers. We developed an LLM-based algorithm for KGE and evaluate each individual part using a small, handcrafted benchmark to test the capabilities of LLMs for each specific task, and find that advanced models have better recall of input context, however smaller models are advantageous to detect text that can not be identified as a reaction, thus not contaminating the generated KG with spurious nodes. Finally, we perform ablations on our algorithm and show that the usage of Language-Vision Models (LVMs) does not directly improve the system's performance, despite having empirical reasons to believe so. Overall, there is still a lot of room for improvement as our algorithms reach a maximum of 73% average in accuracy, and 59.7% in precision. More work needs to go into desiging and optimizing algorithms for this task, however we believe the release of GOSyBench sets the field into the right direction by providing a challenging, diverse and high-quality dataset for benchmarking.

4 Future work and outlook

The efforts presented here deal with the extraction and evaluation of the reaction networks from chemistry papers, which is only the backbone structure of a much richer KG for organic chemistry. However as discussed in Section 0.2, additional relationship types between substances are implicitly reported in papers, such as failed reactions and abandoned synthetic plans, use of substances as model systems, among others. All these are important details that describe not only a successful route to a target substance, but encode also the difficulties, lessons, and other valuable insights that are reported in chemistry papers. From early experiments, we have found that extracting such new connections is possible with LLMs thanks to their summarizing and reasoning capabilities. Achieving such a milestone has the potential to unlock promising advances in reaction search and chemical knowledge retrieval in general.

In addition to this, the currently presented ontology can further be enhanced with additional substance properties reported in papers. Starting with extraction of the SMILES strings for each molecule (Mavračić et al., 2021; Rajan et al., 2021, 2023), along with yields, scalability, and analytical results, the resulting KGs can continuously be populated with more substance-specific details to better represent the knowledge in papers.

Additionally, papers report multiple visualizations that display different views, or highlight different aspects of the molecules and reactions in question. The interplay between text and image modalities is strong in papers, and leveraging VLMs will be an essential step towards better KGE in chemistry, as has been shown in this work.

References

pymupdf/PyMuPDF: PyMuPDF is a high performance Python library for data extraction, analysis, conversion & manipulation of PDF (and other) documents.

Hasan Abu-Rasheed, Christian Weber, and Madjid Fathi. 2024. Knowledge graphs as context sources for llm-based explanations of learning recommendations. *ArXiv*, abs/2403.03008.

Edouard Belval. 2024. Belval/pdf2image. Original-date: 2017-05-28T19:00:59Z.

Daniil A Boiko, Robert MacKnight, Ben Kline, and Gabe Gomes. 2023. Autonomous chemical research with large language models. *Nature*, 624(7992):570–578.

Andres M. Bran, Sam Cox, Oliver Schilter, Carlo Baldassari, Andrew D. White, and Philippe Schwaller. 2024. Augmenting large language models with chemistry tools. *Nature Machine Intelligence*, 6(5):525–535. Publisher: Nature Publishing Group.

Marcin Fialkowski, Kyle J. M. Bishop, Victor A. Chubukov, Christopher J. Campbell, and Bartosz A. Grzybowski. 2005. Architecture and Evolution of Organic Chemistry. *Angewandte Chemie International Edition*, 44(44):7263–7269. _eprint: https://onlinelibrary.wiley.com/doi/pdf/10.1002/anie.200502272.

Harrison Hartle, Brennan Klein, Stefan McCabe, Alexander Daniels, Guillaume St-Onge, Charles Murphy, and Laurent Hébert-Dufresne. 2020. Network comparison and the within-ensemble graph distance. *Proceedings of the Royal Society A: Mathematical, Physical and Engineering Sciences*, 476(2243):20190744.

Aidan Hogan, Eva Blomqvist, Michael Cochez, Claudia D'amato, Gerard De Melo, Claudio Gutierrez, Sabrina Kirrane, José Emilio Labra Gayo, Roberto Navigli, Sebastian Neumaier, Axel-Cyrille Ngonga Ngomo, Axel Polleres, Sabbir M. Rashid, Anisa Rula, Lukas Schmelzeisen, Juan Sequeda, Steffen Staab, and Antoine Zimmermann. 2021. Knowledge Graphs. *ACM Computing Surveys*, 54(4):71:1–71:37.

Weihua Hu, Matthias Fey, M. Zitnik, Yuxiao Dong, Hongyu Ren, Bowen Liu, Michele Catasta, and J. Leskovec. 2020. Open Graph Benchmark: Datasets for Machine Learning on Graphs. *ArXiv*.

O. Khattab, Arnav Singhvi, Paridhi Maheshwari, Zhiyuan Zhang, Keshav Santhanam, Sri Vardhamanan, Saiful Haq, Ashutosh Sharma, Thomas T. Joshi, Hanna Moazam, Heather Miller, Matei Zaharia, and Christopher Potts. 2023. Dspy: Compiling declarative language model calls into self-improving pipelines. *ArXiv*, abs/2310.03714.

O. Khattab and Matei A. Zaharia. 2020. Colbert: Efficient and effective passage search via contextualized late interaction over bert. *Proceedings of the 43rd International ACM SIGIR Conference on Research and Development in Information Retrieval.*

Jason Liu. 2024. jxnl/instructor. Original-date: 2023-06-14T10:42:23Z.

Daniel M. Lowe and Roger A. Sayle. 2013. Leadmine : A grammar and dictionary driven approach to chemical entity recognition.

Daniel Mark Lowe. 2012. *Extraction of chemical structures and reactions from the literature*. Ph.D. thesis, University of Cambridge.

Juraj Mavračić, Callum J. Court, Taketomo Isazawa, Stephen R. Elliott, and Jacqueline M. Cole. 2021. ChemDataExtractor 2.0: Autopopulated Ontologies for Materials Science. *Journal of Chemical Information and Modeling*, 61(9):4280–4289. Publisher: American Chemical Society.

Lars Meyer, Claus Stadler, Johannes Frey, Norman Radtke, Kurt Junghanns, Roy Meissner, Gordian Dziwis, Kirill Bulert, and Michael Martin. 2023. Llm-assisted knowledge graph engineering: Experiments with chatgpt. *ArXiv*, abs/2307.06917.

Nandana Mihindukulasooriya, Sanju Mishra Tiwari, Carlos F. Enguix, and Kusum Lata. 2023. Text2kgbench: A benchmark for ontology-driven knowledge graph generation from text. *ArXiv*, abs/2308.02357.

Luc Patiny and Guillaume Godin. 2023. Automatic extraction of FAIR data from publications using LLM.

Kohulan Rajan, Henning Otto Brinkhaus, M. Isabel Agea, Achim Zielesny, and Christoph Steinbeck. 2023. DECIMER.ai: an open platform for automated optical chemical structure identification, segmentation and recognition in scientific publications. *Nature Communications*, 14(1):5045. Publisher: Nature Publishing Group.

Kohulan Rajan, Achim Zielesny, and Christoph Steinbeck. 2021. DECIMER 1.0: deep learning for chemical image recognition using transformers. *Journal of Cheminformatics*, 13(1):61.

Traian Rebedea, Razvan Laurentiu Dinu, Makesh Narsimhan Sreedhar, Christopher Parisien, and Jonathan Cohen. 2023. Nemo guardrails: A toolkit for controllable and safe llm applications with programmable rails. In *Conference on Empirical Methods in Natural Language Processing*.

Yutaka Shimada, Yoshito Hirata, Tohru Ikeguchi, and Kazuyuki Aihara. 2016. Graph distance for complex networks. *Scientific Reports*, 6(1):34944.

Dong Shu, Tianle Chen, Mingyu Jin, Yiting Zhang, Chong Zhang, Mengnan Du, and Yongfeng Zhang. 2024. Knowledge graph large language model (kg-llm) for link prediction. *ArXiv*, abs/2403.07311.

Matthew C. Swain and Jacqueline M. Cole. 2016. ChemDataExtractor: A Toolkit for Automated Extraction of Chemical Information from the Scientific Literature. *Journal of Chemical Information and Modeling*, 56(10):1894–1904. Publisher: American Chemical Society.

Rylee Thompson, Boris Knyazev, Elahe Ghalebi, Jungtaek Kim, and Graham W. Taylor. 2022. On Evaluation Metrics for Graph Generative Models. *arXiv preprint*. ArXiv:2201.09871 [cs].

Shuangjia Zheng, Jiahua Rao, Ying Song, Jixian Zhang, Xianglu Xiao, Evandro Fei Fang, Yuedong Yang, and

Zhangming Niu. 2020. Pharmkg: a dedicated knowledge graph benchmark for bomedical data mining. *Briefings in bioinformatics*.

A Supplementary Information Files

A typical practice in organic chemistry publishing is having Supplementary Information files (SIs) where all information regarding experimental procedures, analytical results, and sometimes computational and theoretical predictions, are reported. In these documents, which all share a general *underlying* structure, reactions are described with references to other substances in the same document, with a notation shared between the SI and the main manuscript. Hence, a numeration scheme exists for the substances in each paper that can be followed to find the experimental procedure for the preparation of any compound synthesized as part of the research work. Despite of this homogeneity, large differences are noticeable, as is evident from figures 4, 5 and 6.

As these examples show, representations and formats are far from standardized. The SI displayed in Figure 4 shows a common format: compound name and reference in bold, accompanied by the molecular structure of the product substance, and followed by the reaction procedure. Notice however that a subsequent reaction is described directly in the same paragraph, without *announcing* the next product.

Figure 5 shows an SI with a heavier use of visual elements, where colored marbles are used to reference individual steps in a short reaction sequence. The marbles are then used throughout to refer to specific intermediates, with no reference in text to the products' reference keys. Lastly, Figure 6 shows another example where the product is not directly announced in the text, but rather a new reaction procedure is presented after a graphical depiction of the reaction in question, making it impossible for a text parser to grasp this information.

B SI Preprocessing

SIs in chemistry research papers contain many sections, however the one of interest for this work is the part on Experimental Methods. For our purposes, it may make sense to extract the most relevant parts of the document and process only that, however no naming convention or guidelines exist for this, making it difficult to identify and isolate the specific sections.

To address this, we develop a simple rule-based method to identify the relevant sections, partially inspired by Patiny and Godin (2023). For this, we rely on the observation that reaction descriptions

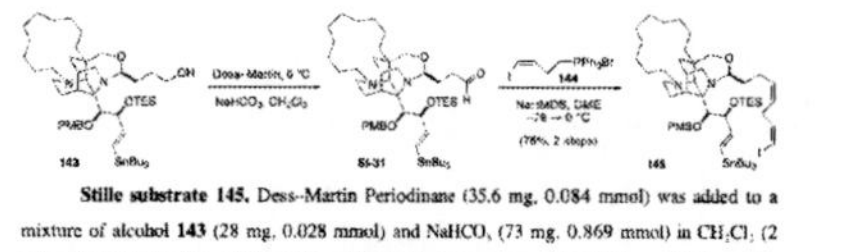

Stille substrate 145. Dess–Martin Periodinane (35.6 mg, 0.084 mmol) was added to a mixture of alcohol **143** (28 mg, 0.028 mmol) and $NaHCO_3$ (73 mg, 0.869 mmol) in CH_2Cl_2 (2 mL) at 0 °C. After 1 h, additional Dess–Martin Periodinane was added (5.0 mg, 0.012 mmol). After 30 min, the reaction mixture was quenched with saturated aqueous $NaHCO_3$ (1 mL) and saturated aqueous sodium metabisulfite (1 mL). The resulting cloudy mixture was stirred vigorously for 5 min at 0 °C, then for 30 min at rt. The layers were separated and the aqueous layer was extracted with EtOAc (5 x 1 mL). The combined organic layers were washed with brine (1 x 1 mL), dried by passage over a plug of silica gel (EtOAc eluent), and evaporated under reduced pressure. The residue was purified by flash chromatography (19:1 hexanes:EtOAc containing 2% Et_3N; then 9:1 hexanes:EtOAc containing 2% Et_3N) to afford aldehyde **SI-31** (24.0 mg, 86%) as a colorless foam which was used directly in the subsequent transformation.

NaHMDS (288 μL, 0.288 mmol, 1 M in THF) was added dropwise over 1 min to a mixture of phosphonium salt **144**[9] (251.5 mg, 0.481 mmol) in DME (4.3 mL) at –78 °C. After stirring 1 h 10 min, aldehyde **SI-31** (24.0 mg, 0.0.024 mmol, dried under vacuum over $CaSO_4$) in DME (1 mL) was added. The mixture was maintained at –78 °C for 25 min, then placed in a 0 °C bath for 15 min. The reaction mixture was diluted with H_2O (2 mL), brine (2 mL), and EtOAc (2 mL). The mixture was warmed to rt and the layers were separated. The aqueous layer was further extracted with EtOAc (4 x 2 mL). The combined organic layers were dried by passage over a plug of silica gel (EtOAc eluent) and evaporated under reduced pressure. The residue was first purified by passage over a second plug of silica gel (4:1 hexanes:EtOAc containing 2%

Figure 4: Example of an SI. Taken from https://pubs.acs.org/doi/10.1021/ja074300t. This example shows

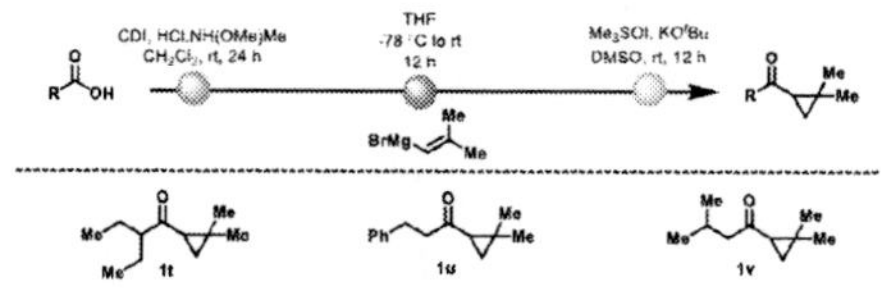

Synthesis of **1t-v**:

To a solution of carboxylic acid (20 mmol, 1eq.) in CH_2Cl_2 (60 mL) was added carbonyldiimidazole (23 mmol, 1.15 eq.) portion wise and the solution stirred at room temperature for 1 h. After this time, N_2 was bubbled through the solution for 30 min. Then, *N,O*-dimethylhydroxylamine hydrochloride (26 mmol, 1.3 eq.) was added and the reaction mixture was stirred at room temperature for 24 h. Subsequently, the reaction mixture was quenched with saturated aqueous NH_4Cl and extracted with CH_2Cl_2 (3 × 70 mL). The combined organic layer was dried over $MgSO_4$ and concentrated in vacuo to afford the product.

The corresponding amide (1 eq.) was placed in a round bottom flask under N_2. The flask was cooled to -78 °C and dry THF (5 mL/mmol) was added. 2-Methyl-1-propenylmagnesium bromide solution (1.2 eq.) was added dropwise at -78 °C and the reaction mixture was stirred at -78 °C for 15 min. The reaction mixture was then stirred at room temperature for 12 h. Subsequently, the reaction mixture was quenched with saturated aqueous NH_4Cl and extracted with CH_2Cl_2 (3 × 30 mL). The organic layers were collected, dried over $MgSO_4$ and concentrated in vacuo. The desired compound

Figure 5: Example of an SI. Taken from https://pubs.acs.org/doi/10.1021/jacs.1c01356. This example shows

typically follow the pattern "reaction setup → workup → analytics", as the example below. As can be seen, the analytics section has a higher ratio of certain special and numeric characters relative to other parts of the text.

Example of a typical synthesis paragraph obtained from an SI file:

> To a solution of alkene **5** (266 mg, 0.92 mmol, 1.0 equiv.) in DCM (30 mL) was bubbled ozone (40% in air) at -78 °C until the starting material disappeared (TLC analysis, about 1 min), and the mixture was purged with air at -78 °C followed by addition of PPh3 (250 mg, 0.95 mmol, 1.0 equiv.). The mixture was warmed up to room temperature slowly, and stirred at the same temperature for 12 h. After removal of the solvent, the residue was purified by a flash column chromatography on silica gel (hexane/EtOAc = 5 : 1 to 3 : 1) to give compound 6 as a colorless oil (173 mg, 65%), which is an inconsequential 1.05: 1 mixture.
> Rf = 0.25 (hexane/EtOAc = 8:1, PMA); [α]21
> D = - 4.44 (c 1.31, CHCl3); 1H NMR (400 MHz, CDCl3) δ 9.77 – 9.70 (m, 1.69H, overlap), 2.63 – 2.48 (m, 2.21H, overlap), 2.42 – 2.18 (m, 9.27H, overlap), 2.18 – 2.06 (m, 3.58H, overlap), 2.00 – 1.82 (m, 5.93H, overlap), 1.82 – 1.72 (m, 4.72H, overlap), 1.71 – 1.60 (m, 3.95H, overlap), 1.58 – 1.49

To leverage this, we split the complete document into sentences, and then calculate the ratio of special characters to normal letters for each. Plotting the values of these ratio with the line index in the x-axis, patterns like those in Figure 7 are apparent. An alogrithm is also applied for smoothing and performing selection by selecting the longest region with a prominent signal as the "relevant" SI. We find that this strategy generally leads to an accurate selection of the relevant parts.

C Vision-Language Models

The following prompt was used as a template to pass the images to GPT-4o for the vision-based parsing method exposed in Figure 1.

> These are some pages from the SI of an organic chemistry paper. Describe all the reactions shown there, if any. Separate each reaction with {SEPARATOR}, describe products and reactants for each reaction. Ignore all characterization data. Consider work-up and purification as part of the same reaction. Use the following format to represent the products and main reactants: {SUBSTANCE_FORMAT}. Do not rewrite

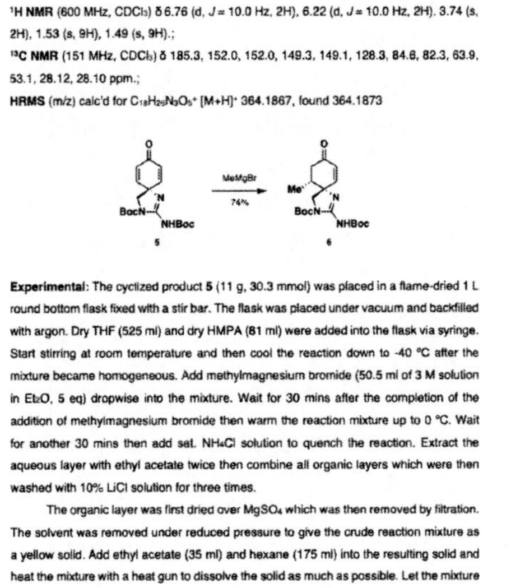
^{1}H NMR (600 MHz, $CDCl_3$) δ 6.76 (d, J = 10.0 Hz, 2H), 6.22 (d, J = 10.0 Hz, 2H), 3.74 (s, 2H), 1.53 (s, 9H), 1.49 (s, 9H).;
^{13}C NMR (151 MHz, $CDCl_3$) δ 185.3, 152.0, 152.0, 149.3, 149.1, 128.3, 84.6, 82.3, 63.9, 53.1, 28.12, 28.10 ppm.;
HRMS (m/z) calc'd for $C_{18}H_{26}N_3O_5^+$ [M+H]$^+$ 364.1867, found 364.1873

Experimental: The cyclized product **5** (11 g, 30.3 mmol) was placed in a flame-dried 1 L round bottom flask fixed with a stir bar. The flask was placed under vacuum and backfilled with argon. Dry THF (525 ml) and dry HMPA (81 ml) were added into the flask via syringe. Start stirring at room temperature and then cool the reaction down to -40 °C after the mixture became homogeneous. Add methylmagnesium bromide (50.5 ml of 3 M solution in Et_2O, 5 eq) dropwise into the mixture. Wait for 30 mins after the completion of the addition of methylmagnesium bromide then warm the reaction mixture up to 0 °C. Wait for another 30 mins then add sat. NH_4Cl solution to quench the reaction. Extract the aqueous layer with ethyl acetate twice then combine all organic layers which were then washed with 10% LiCl solution for three times.

The organic layer was first dried over $MgSO_4$ which was then removed by filtration. The solvent was removed under reduced pressure to give the crude reaction mixture as a yellow solid. Add ethyl acetate (35 ml) and hexane (175 ml) into the resulting solid and heat the mixture with a heat gun to dissolve the solid as much as possible. Let the mixture

Figure 6: Example of an SI. Taken from `https://pubs.acs.org/doi/10.1021/jacs.3c01991`. This example shows

the reaction procedures, just describe the substances involved.

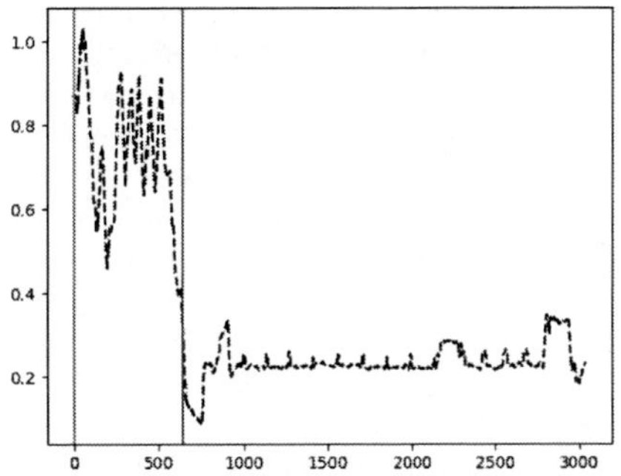

Figure 7: SIs were processed like this. Based on the frequency of special characters etc. Based on the observation that, most commonly, text-summaries of analytical data are given after the end of each reaction, giving a distinctive signal to each line in the document, producing more or less a spectrum that can then be analysed and processed.

NLPeople at *L+M-24* Shared Task: An Ensembled Approach for Molecule Captioning from SMILES

Shinnosuke Tanaka[1], **Carol Mak**[1], **Flaviu Cipcigan**[1], **James Barry**[1],
Mohab Elkaref[1], **Movina Moses**[2], **Vishnudev Kuruvanthodi**[1], **Geeth De Mel**[1]
IBM Research Europe[1] and IBM Research[2]
{shinnosuke.tanaka, carol.mak, flaviu.cipcigan, vishnudev.k, james.barry, mohab.elkaref, movina.moses, vishnudev.k }@ibm.com, geeth.demel@uk.ibm.com

Abstract

This paper presents our approach submitted to the Language + Molecules 2024 (*L+M-24*) Shared Task in the Molecular Captioning track. The task involves generating captions that describe the properties of molecules that are provided in SMILES format. We propose a method for the task that decomposes the challenge of generating captions from SMILES into a classification problem, where we first predict the molecule's properties. The molecules whose properties can be predicted with high accuracy show high translation metric scores in the caption generation by LLMs, while others produce low scores. Then we use the predicted properties to select the captions generated by different types of LLMs, and use that prediction as the final output. Our submission achieved an overall increase score of 15.21 on the dev set and 12.30 on the evaluation set, based on translation metrics and property metrics from the baseline.

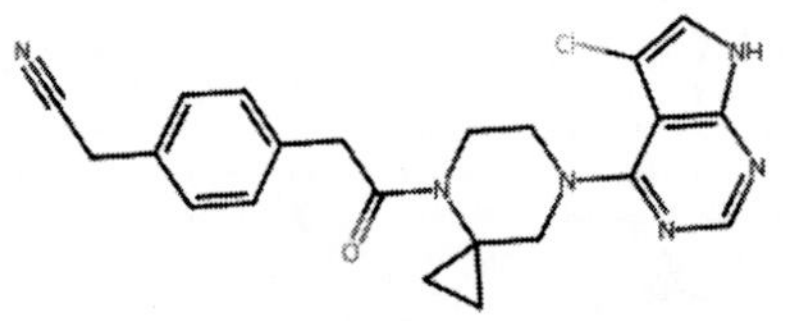

SMILES
N#CCc1ccc(CC(=O)N2CCN(c3ncnc4[nH]cc(Cl)c34)CC23CC3)cc1

Figure 1: A sample molecule depicted using RDKit (Landrum et al., 2024) and its caption from the training data. **Caption:** The molecule is a jak inhibitor, immunomodulator, protein tyrosine kinase inhibitor, protein kinase inhibitor and belongs to the autoimmune disease treatment class of molecules.

1 Introduction

Molecular design is the process of devising molecules with desired properties and functions. While this is widely practiced in fields such as drug discovery, new materials, and chemical processes, predicting the properties of designed molecules remains a challenging problem. To tackle this problem, language models trained on molecular information have gained attention (Ahmad et al., 2022). The *L+M-24* shared task (Edwards et al., 2024) involves translation between SMILES (Weininger, 1988), a string-encoded molecular format, and descriptive captions of the molecule's properties. The dataset covers four high-impact areas of molecular science: Biomedical, Human Interaction, Light and Electricity, and Agriculture and Industry, providing pairs of molecules and their corresponding captions for these properties.

An example of the data is shown in Figure 1. In this sample, specific diseases and protein properties are described, yet the ways of describing molecular properties are highly diverse. For instance, while drug discovery seeks to generate specific information related to diseases, industrial chemistry researchers prefer to include functions of molecules such as absorption wavelengths of light. Given this variability in the desired captions, the task of generating desired captions is highly challenging.

In this paper, we describe our submission to the Molecular Captioning track. We first address the properties of SMILES as a multi-label classification problem. Predicting properties is essential for molecule captioning and offers the following advantage: a lightweight model can be built that predicts the properties of the molecules compared to fine-tuning existing large transformer-based models. Such an approach can get classification accuracy of 80% against experimental measurements with as little as 100 datapoints (McDonagh et al., 2024, 2023).

We also fine-tune $\text{LlaSMol}_{\text{Mistral}}$ and Multitask Text Chemistry T5 (Christofidellis et al., 2023) models for the end-to-end molecular captioning. We obtain the system's output by selecting the generated captions from these models based on the predicted properties. We achieve an overall increase

Proceedings of the 1st Workshop on Language + Molecules (L+M 2024), pages 86–91
August 15, 2024 ©2024 Association for Computational Linguistics

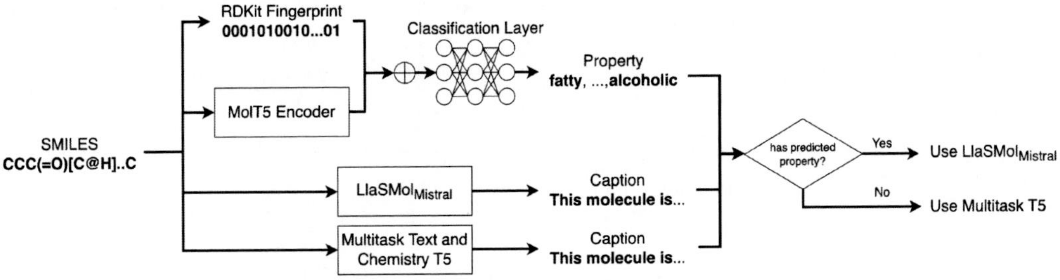

Figure 2: Overview of the submission system

score from the MolT5-Small[1] baseline of 15.21 on the dev set and 12.30 on the eval set. In the next section, we discuss some related work that inspired our contributions to this shared task.

2 Related Work

Text2Mol (Edwards et al., 2021) stands out as a pioneering study integrating modalities between text and molecules. This task involves retrieving molecules using natural language descriptions as queries. They employ the SciBERT (Beltagy et al., 2019) model to encode the text information and a Graph Convolutional Network for the molecular information. The model is based on a cross-modal attention structure and successfully integrates the two modalities.

MolT5 (Edwards et al., 2022) is a T5 (Raffel et al., 2020) based model that enables both molecule captioning and molecule generation, which generates SMILES from natural language. The model is first trained using an objective that replaces corrupted spans. This task is performed on general text data in the form of the C4 Corpus (Colossal Clean Crawled Corpus) as well as on SMILES from the ZINC-15 dataset (Sterling and Irwin, 2015). This pre-training procedure encourages the model to learn textual and chemical information. The model is then fine-tuned for molecule captioning and molecule generation using ChEBI-20 (Edwards et al., 2021), which comprises approximately 33k text-molecule pairs.

Another T5 based model, Text+Chem T5 (Christofidellis et al., 2023), aims at improving multitasking and multi-domain capabilities. This model is trained not only on SMILES and caption pairs such as ChEBI-20 but also on reaction-products pairs such as Pistachio dataset used in (Toniato et al., 2021), and experimental procedures dataset (Vaucher et al., 2019) for chemical synthesis actions. It can perform multiple tasks beyond text2molecule and molecule2text translation, including mol2mol and text2text tasks. The mol2mol tasks contain forward reaction prediction, which predicts products from given reactants, and retrosynthesis, which predicts the necessary substances for synthesis from a given chemical compound. The text2text task consists of paragraph to action, which generates sequential steps to execute a described chemical reaction. A notable aspect of this model is its ability to perform all these tasks without additional fine-tuning, using a single model instead of individual specialised models for each task. This eliminates the need to develop tailored models for each domain, achieving a unified representation of the chemical domain with one model.

3 System Description

Figure 2 shows an overview of the submission system. First, we develop a classifier to predict properties from a given SMILES string. The molecular properties are extracted using the evaluation script for the property metrics[2] by determining whether a predefined string is included in the tokenised captions using `scibert_scivocab_uncased`[3]. Based on our analysis of the extracted properties, there are 1,084 unique properties present in the training data. Since properties are extracted using string-matching, some occur together. Some co-occurances are correct biochemically, like "Biomedical disease – Heart disease" and "Biomedical disease – Diabetic heart disease". Others are not, like "Biomedical disease – Non-alcoholic

[1] https://huggingface.co/language-plus-molecules/molt5-small-smiles2caption-LPM24

[2] https://github.com/language-plus-molecules/LPM-24-Dataset/blob/main/evaluation/text_property_metrics.py

[3] https://huggingface.co/allenai/scibert_scivocab_uncased

Molecule Type	Model	BLEU-2	BLEU-4	ROUGE-1	ROUGE-2	ROUGE-L	METEOR
Has Predicted Props.	Multitask T5	82.15	59.49	91.64	**69.74**	60.20	87.05
	$\text{LlaSMol}_{\text{Mistral}}$	**82.66**	**59.81**	**92.27**	69.53	**60.54**	**87.70**
No Props. Predicted	Multitask T5	**43.12**	**30.58**	**52.35**	**38.51**	**50.67**	**51.87**
	$\text{LlaSMol}_{\text{Mistral}}$	35.24	24.27	48.99	35.45	47.95	45.50

Table 1: Translation metrics by molecular type on dev set.

fatty liver disease" and "Human Interaction and Organoleptics – organoleptic effect relations – fatty". This leads to chemically incorrect labelling for some molecules. A molecule whose description is "This molecule impacts non-alcoholic fatty liver disease" is not necessarily fatty in the sense of organoleptic effects, yet it is always labelled as so.

3.1 Property Classification

We build multi-label classifiers for each molecular property in the dataset. The SMILES string is converted to a binary fingerprint using the fingerprinter in RDKit 2023.9.6 (Landrum et al., 2024) with a minimum path length of 1, maximum path length of 7 and 2048 bits. SMILES strings are also provided to the encoder part of MolT5-Small, and the embedding representation is obtained by mean pooling the last hidden layer. The obtained fingerprint and embedding are concatenated and passed through a classifier consisting of three linear layers to predict the classes.

We only train the classifier on labels with over 1,500 positive examples. Because of this limitation, the *predictable subset* of the labels contains 53 properties. The classifier outputs multiple labels for each molecule that exceeds a threshold based on the Sigmoid function of the activation layer. Labels not meeting the threshold are not output; hence, some molecules may have no predicted properties.

3.2 LLMs for Caption Generation

Following the classification task, we use the SMILES string as inputs to experiment with the following methods.

Fine-Tuning LLMs We also utilise models that predict the captions directly using only the SMILES as input. In initial experiments, we found that included properties harmed performance for the Multitask T5 model[4] and as a result we did not include them. For the $\text{LlaSMol}_{\text{Mistral}}$ model, we loaded pretrained LoRA modules into the model and followed the prompt pattern in their work, which did not include properties.

Multitask T5 model is trained with a learning rate of 5e-4 and a batch size of 8 for 10 epochs on the extra training set provided by the task organiser. For fine-tuning and caption generation, we use a prompt template in Appendix A.1 Table 5, which is presented in (Christofidellis et al., 2023). $\text{LlaSMol}_{\text{Mistral}}$ is a Mistral-7b model trained on the SMolInstruct dataset by Yu et al. (2024), which covers 14 chemistry tasks including a molecular captioning task derived from the ChEBI-20 dataset. Here, the base model is frozen and additional modules are trained using LoRA (Hu et al., 2022). The LoRA component only comprises 0.58% of the full model parameters. We further fine-tuned $\text{LlaSMol}_{\text{Mistral}}$ on the *L+M-24* dataset. The prompt used is shown in Appendix A.1 Table 6. First we trained on the concatenation of train and the extra training data for 3 epochs. We then further finetuned the LoRA modules for 10 epochs on the training set.

3.3 Ensembling

We perform an ensemble by selecting generated captions from Multitask T5 and $\text{LlaSMol}_{\text{Mistral}}$ based on the result of the property classification model. If the model predicts at least one label for the target SMILES, we choose the caption from the $\text{LlaSMol}_{\text{Mistral}}$ model; otherwise, we choose from the Multitask T5 model.

4 Results and Discussion

In this section, we present the results of our classification models and generated captions using Multitask T5 and $\text{LlaSMol}_{\text{Mistral}}$.

4.1 Property Classification

When evaluated on the dev set using *only the predictable subset*, an F1 score of 97.86% was achieved. Thus, on the predictable subset, we have classifiers with a high percentage of true positives

[4]`https://huggingface.co/GT4SD/multitask-text-and-chemistry-t5-base-augm`

Model	Overall Increase	Translation Metric Increase	BLEU-2	BLEU-4	ROUGE-1	ROUGE-2	ROUGE-L	METEOR
baselines								
MolT5-Small	0.00	0.00	70.90	51.20	74.50	55.80	54.40	70.10
Meditron-7b	13.15	5.50	**79.20**	**57.60**	79.70	**60.20**	57.50	75.70
ours								
Multitask T5	**15.31**	5.23	78.22	56.73	57.28	60.17	57.28	76.27
$\text{LlaSMol}_{\text{Mistral}}$	10.59	4.68	78.84	57.17	78.82	58.79	56.50	74.87
Ensembled	15.21	**5.52**	78.70	57.04	**80.04**	60.03	**57.51**	**76.72**

Table 2: Overall increase from MolT5-Small baseline and translation metrics results on dev set.

Model	Prop. Metric Increase	Overall Prop. F1	Biomedical	Human Interaction	Agr. + Industry	Light + Electro	X-icides	Toxins	Light	Electricity
baselines										
MolT5-Small	0.00	7.88	23.33	0.56	4.36	3.27	0.00	0.00	6.54	0.00
Meditron-7b	15.70	8.93	11.94	6.51	3.04	14.22	0.00	11.05	14.10	14.34
ours										
Multitask T5	**18.67**	**19.10**	**36.97**	7.27	7.40	**24.76**	0.00	11.36	**25.26**	**24.26**
$\text{LlaSMol}_{\text{Mistral}}$	12.56	15.35	32.28	7.30	6.58	15.22	0.00	11.20	18.69	11.77
Ensembled	18.44	19.09	36.75	**7.73**	**7.65**	24.24	0.00	**12.28**	25.21	23.28

Model	Inhibitors	anti-X	Modulators	Antagonists	Treatments	Agonists	Cancer	Disease	Combos
baselines									
MolT5-Small	0.09	0.00	0.00	0.00	1.70	0.00	24.27	49.94	0.00
Meditron-7b	22.65	8.98	24.98	21.15	15.13	26.35	72.62	**82.02**	0.56
ours									
Multitask T5	**26.04**	**10.35**	**31.11**	26.54	**19.37**	**31.71**	**73.59**	81.89	**0.93**
$\text{LlaSMol}_{\text{Mistral}}$	14.57	5.33	15.69	12.95	9.11	19.06	70.76	81.76	0.38
Ensembled	25.86	10.11	30.81	**26.80**	19.14	31.69	70.42	81.87	**0.93**

Table 3: Property metric increase from MolT5-Small baseline and F1 scores of each property on dev set.

and a low percentage of false positives. When considering *all* properties in the dev set, at least one property was predicted for 69% in dev set, while no properties were predicted for the remaining 31%.

4.2 Caption Generation

Table 1 shows the translation metrics for each model, both when the classifier predicts at least one property (**Has Predicted Props.**) and when it does not (**No Props. Predicted**). When at least one property was predicted, $\text{LlaSMol}_{\text{Mistral}}$ model exceeded Multitask T5 model in 5 out of 6 metrics, excluding ROUGE-2. Conversely, when no properties were predicted, Multitask T5 significantly outperformed the $\text{LlaSMol}_{\text{Mistral}}$. Hence, based on these results, we adopted an ensemble approach where we used the captions generated by the $\text{LlaSMol}_{\text{Mistral}}$ model when at least one property was predicted, and those generated by Multitask T5 model when no properties were predicted.

Table 2 shows the overall increase, translation metric Increase and the scores of each translation metric on dev set of the two baseline models, $\text{LlaSMol}_{\text{Mistral}}$, Multitask T5 and ensembled model of $\text{LlaSMol}_{\text{Mistral}}$ and Multitask T5. Table 3 shows the property metric increase and F1 scores of each property metric. Each Increase is calculated as the average improvement from the baseline results of MolT5-Small. In the translation metrics, the Ensembled model achieved the best performance in four metrics, including the translation metric increase, indicating it has the highest performance among all models. On the other hand, in the property metrics, the Multitask T5 model showed the best performance in 13 metrics, including the property metric increase. Despite the baseline Meditron-7b model exhibiting the highest BLEU-2 score of 79.2%, our models outperformed the baseline for the property-specific F1 score. As a result, the Overall Increase was highest for the Multitask T5 model, with a score of 15.31.

Even though these predictions show higher F1 scores, the BLEU-2 score remains lower because there are numerous ways to describe molecules in natural language. This points to some features of the description which are not features of the molecule but features of the particular distribution of the dataset:

1. The order of words or phrases in a sentence, which is not essentially important, can still significantly influence these translation metric scores.

2. The `scibert_scivocab_uncased` tokeniser includes punctuation, thus mis-predicting the location of a comma or a full stop will break a correct bigram and lead to a lower BLEU score.

Team	Overall Increase	Translation Metric Increase	Prop. Metric Increase	BLEU-2	BLEU-4	Overall Prop. F1	Rank
avaliev	**27.08**	<u>6.37</u>	**33.99**	73.81	53.04	**26.99**	1
qizhipei	<u>14.66</u>	**6.45**	<u>17.39</u>	<u>75.58</u>	54.77	<u>13.76</u>	2
protonunfold	12.39	5.77	14.60	**75.66**	**54.98**	11.51	3
NLPeople (ours)	12.30	5.68	14.50	75.54	<u>54.83</u>	11.63	4
langmolecules[†]	10.34	5.47	11.96	75.16	54.72	9.70	8
langmolecules[‡]	0.00	0.00	0.00	66.82	48.29	3.23	18

Table 4: Top four results and two baseline results on the eval set. [†] represents the results from the baseline model, Meditron-7b, and [‡] represents the results from MolT5-Small respectively. Best results are in **Bold**, and second-best results are <u>underlined</u>.

3. Mis-predicting the number of properties will also reduce the BLEU score. Some of these properties are very general, such as the organoleptics, and may be correctly predicted for a molecule even if they do not exist in the ground truth caption. For example, molecules with long carbon tails will all likely taste fatty, but only the subset of those who were actually tasted by humans have the fatty caption.

Given all these features of the data, it would be interesting to create realistic performance bounds for a molecule to text model evaluated using BLEU scores, similar to the ones Crusius et al. (2024) used for regression and classification datasets by randomising over the features of the caption that *cannot* be predicted from a molecule. For example in our testing, using the *ground truth labels* in a zero-shot prompted Meditron-7b gave a BLEU-2 score of 76.36. Thus, our intuition is that we are close to saturating this benchmark, with some models achieving performance *higher* than this value.

Finally, Table 4 shows the results of the evaluation set. It includes the increases in overall, translation, and property metrics, as well as BLEU scores and property F1 scores, from the official leaderboard. Our team NLPeople's submission results from ensembling Multitask T5 and $\text{LlaSMol}_{\text{Mistral}}$. Based on the results of the property classification, out of 21,942 data points, approximately 35% used cations generated by Multitask T5, while the remaining 65% are from $\text{LlaSMol}_{\text{Mistral}}$.The team avaliev significantly outperformed other teams in the property metric, resulting in the highest overall score of 27.08. Our submission showed an increase of 12.30 overall from the MolT5-Small baseline, ranking fourth and achieving the second-highest BLEU-4 score of 54.83 among all teams.

5 Conclusion

In this work, we present our approach to the molecular captioning task. We propose combining a property classification model, LLMs for caption generation, and an ensemble method. Our results show that molecules distinguished by property classification exhibit varying strengths and weaknesses depending on the model used. This approach achieved a translation increase score of 5.52 on the dev set and 5.68 on the eval set. For property metrics, we recorded an increase score of 18.44 on the dev set and 14.50 on the eval set. The overall increase score was 15.21 on the dev set and 12.30 on the eval set, ranking 4th in this shared task.

References

Walid Ahmad, Elana Simon, Seyone Chithrananda, Gabriel Grand, and Bharath Ramsundar. 2022. Chemberta-2: Towards chemical foundation models. *Preprint*, arXiv:2209.01712.

Iz Beltagy, Kyle Lo, and Arman Cohan. 2019. SciBERT: A pretrained language model for scientific text. In *Proceedings of the 2019 Conference on Empirical Methods in Natural Language Processing and the 9th International Joint Conference on Natural Language Processing (EMNLP-IJCNLP)*, pages 3615–3620, Hong Kong, China. Association for Computational Linguistics.

Dimitrios Christofidellis, Giorgio Giannone, Jannis Born, Ole Winther, Teodoro Laino, and Matteo Manica. 2023. Unifying molecular and textual representations via multi-task language modelling. In *Proceedings of the 40th International Conference on Machine Learning*, ICML'23. JMLR.org.

Daniel Crusius, Flaviu Cipcigan, and Philip Biggin. 2024. Are we fitting data or noise? analysing the predictive power of commonly used datasets in drug-, materials-, and molecular-discovery.

Carl Edwards, Tuan Lai, Kevin Ros, Garrett Honke, Kyunghyun Cho, and Heng Ji. 2022. Translation between molecules and natural language. In *Proceedings of the 2022 Conference on Empirical Methods in Natural Language Processing*, pages 375–413, Abu Dhabi, United Arab Emirates. Association for Computational Linguistics.

Carl Edwards, Qingyun Wang, Lawrence Zhao, and Heng Ji. 2024. L+M-24: Building a dataset for language + molecules @ acl 2024. *Preprint*, arXiv:2403.00791.

Carl Edwards, ChengXiang Zhai, and Heng Ji. 2021. Text2Mol: Cross-modal molecule retrieval with natural language queries. In *Proceedings of the 2021 Conference on Empirical Methods in Natural Language Processing*, pages 595–607, Online and Punta Cana, Dominican Republic. Association for Computational Linguistics.

Edward J Hu, Yelong Shen, Phillip Wallis, Zeyuan Allen-Zhu, Yuanzhi Li, Shean Wang, Lu Wang, and Weizhu Chen. 2022. LoRA: Low-rank adaptation of large language models. In *International Conference on Learning Representations*.

Greg Landrum, Paolo Tosco, Brian Kelley, Ric, David Cosgrove, sriniker, Riccardo Vianello, gedeck, NadineSchneider, Gareth Jones, Eisuke Kawashima, Dan Nealschneider, Andrew Dalke, Brian Cole, Matt Swain, Samo Turk, Aleksandr Savelev, Alain Vaucher, Maciej Wójcikowski, Ichiru Take, Vincent F. Scalfani, Daniel Probst, Kazuya Ujihara, Rachel Walker, guillaume godin, Axel Pahl, Juuso Lehtivarjo, Francois Berenger, strets123, and jasondbiggs. 2024. rdkit/rdkit: 2023_09_6 (q3 2023) release.

James L. McDonagh, Benjamin H. Wunsch, Stamatia Zavitsanou, Alexander Harrison, Bruce Elmegreen, Stacey Gifford, Theodore van Kessel, and Flaviu Cipcigan. 2023. Machine guided discovery of novel carbon capture solvents. *Preprint*, arXiv:2303.14223.

James L. McDonagh, Stamatia Zavitsanou, Alexander Harrison, Dimitry Zubarev, Theordore van Kessel, Benjamin H. Wunsch, and Flaviu Cipcigan. 2024. Chemical space analysis and property prediction for carbon capture solvent molecules. *Digital Discovery*, 3(3):528–543.

Colin Raffel, Noam Shazeer, Adam Roberts, Katherine Lee, Sharan Narang, Michael Matena, Yanqi Zhou, Wei Li, and Peter J. Liu. 2020. Exploring the limits of transfer learning with a unified text-to-text transformer. *J. Mach. Learn. Res.*, 21(1).

T. Sterling and J. J. Irwin. 2015. Zinc 15 – ligand discovery for everyone. *Journal of Chemical Information and Modeling*, 55:2324–2337.

Alessandra Toniato, Philippe Schwaller, Antonio Cardinale, Joppe Geluykens, and Teodoro Laino. 2021. Unassisted noise reduction of chemical reaction data sets. *Preprint*, arXiv:2102.01399.

Alain Vaucher, Federico Zipoli, Joppe Geluykens, Vishnu Nair, Philippe Schwaller, and Teodoro Laino. 2019. Automated extraction of chemical synthesis actions from experimental procedures.

David Weininger. 1988. Smiles, a chemical language and information system. 1. introduction to methodology and encoding rules. *J. Chem. Inf. Comput. Sci.*, 28:31–36.

Botao Yu, Frazier N. Baker, Ziqi Chen, Xia Ning, and Huan Sun. 2024. Llasmol: Advancing large language models for chemistry with a large-scale, comprehensive, high-quality instruction tuning dataset. *arXiv preprint arXiv:2402.09391*.

A Appendix

A.1 Prompt Templates

We present the prompt templates in Tables 5 and 6.

```
Caption the following SMILES: {SMILES}
```

Table 5: Multitask Text+Chem T5 Prompt with Molecule

```
Query: Describe this molecule: <SMILES> {SMILES}
</SMILES>

Response: The molecule is an imidazole derivative
with short-acting sedative, hypnotic, and general
anesthetic properties.  Etomidate appears to
have gamma-aminobutyric acid (GABA) like effects,
mediated through GABA-A receptor.  The action
enhances the inhibitory effect of GABA on
the central nervous system by causing chloride
channel opening events which leads to membrane
hyperpolarization.
```

Table 6: Prompt with SMILES and Caption for the Mistral-7b LlaSMol model.

Knowlab's Submission to L+M Shared Task: All you need is continued pretraining of chemistry texts even for molecule captioning

Yunsoo Kim
University College London
yunsoo.kim.23@ucl.ac.uk

Honghan Wu
University College London
honghan.wu@ucl.ac.uk

Abstract

This paper presents our submission to the L+M-24 shared task, focused on translating molecular structures into natural language descriptions, known as the molecule captioning task. We selected a small language model (SLM), Phi-3-mini-4k, to evaluate the impact of continued pretraining and instruction tuning for domain-specific chemical knowledge. The Phi-3 model was continued pretrained with 90M chemistry textbooks and abstracts, followed by instruction tuning on 150K question answering sets of SMILES and general chemistry knowledge. Despite the continued pretraining phase not including direct exposure to SMILES representations, it significantly enhanced the Phi-3 model's performance, a 300% increase for the BLEU scores, in the molecule captioning task. The code and model are released at `https://github.com/bluesky333/Phi3KnowChem` to facilitate research in chemical small language modeling.

1 Introduction

The intersection of natural language processing (NLP) and chemistry began with drug discovery and biochemistry but recently moved to the other fields of chemistry such as electrochemistry for battery and rheology for chemical property prediction (Krallinger et al., 2015; Li et al., 2016; Huang and Cole, 2022; Kim et al., 2023). With the recent advancement of large language models (LLMs), the language model for chemistry domain knowledge started to cover molecule representation such as the simplified molecular-input line-entry system (SMILES) and 3D structure of molecules (Edwards et al., 2022; Taylor et al., 2022; Fang et al., 2023; Zhang et al., 2024a,b). As the research in LLMs has been facilitated by the benchmark datasets for evaluating the model's understanding of domain knowledge, there has been a pressing need for a benchmark specifically for molecule and language models (Hendrycks et al., 2020).

To address this gap, the L+M-24 shared task was introduced as one of the first competitions focused on translating between language and molecule representations (Edwards et al., 2024). This task involves generating captions based on input molecules represented in SMILES, pushing the boundaries of molecule captioning by leveraging language models. The task covers four key applications within chemical knowledge: biochemistry, electrochemistry, organoleptics, and agricultural chemistry. Progress in these specific is essential for building foundational models applicable to small molecule applications.

Traditionally, models designed for such tasks require extensive domain-specific pretraining and fine-tuning with molecule representation to understand and generate chemistry-related text effectively (Edwards et al., 2022; Taylor et al., 2022; Fang et al., 2023; Zhang et al., 2024a). This process is often resource-intensive and requires large, specialized datasets.

In this work, we explore the efficacy of continued pretraining and instruction tuning on a small language model (SLM), specifically the 3.8B parameter model, Phi-3-mini-4k, for the molecule captioning task.

Our approach involves two primary stages:

1. Continued Pretraining: We further pretrain the Phi-3-mini-4k model using a corpus of 90 million chemistry textbooks and abstracts. This step aimed to infuse the model with a broad and deep understanding of chemical language and concepts.

2. Instruction Tuning: We further refined the model with 150,000 instruction tuning tasks focused on SMILES question answering and general chemistry knowledge question answering. This step was designed to enhance the model's ability to handle SMILES representation and chemical queries.

Proceedings of the 1st Workshop on Language + Molecules (L+M 2024), pages 92–97
August 15, 2024

The resulting models underwent fine-tuning with the shared task's training data for 1 epoch, and our best-performing model surpassed the performance of the MolT5-base model, which was trained with 100 million SMILES strings (Edwards et al., 2022).

The contributions of this paper are as follows:

1. **Pretraining without molecule still helps.** Our study demonstrates that continued pretraining using a chemical text corpus significantly enhances performance in molecule captioning tasks, even without direct exposure to molecular representations. We saw an almost 300% increase for BLEU scores, about a 67% increase for the ROUGE score, and a 19% increase for Meteor with the continued pretraining.

2. **Phi-3KnowChem model.** We introduce the Phi-3KnowChem model, a small language model (SLM) based on the Phi-3 architecture, pretrained with a chemical corpus and instruction-tuning datasets. To the best of our knowledge, this is the first Phi-3 model specifically trained for the chemical domain.

3. **Open source.** To foster research in chemical small language modeling, we will release the model weights and codes to prompote reproducibility and collaboration in the field.

2 Methods

2.1 Language Model

Phi-3 (Abdin et al., 2024) We use Phi-3-mini-4K model, which we refer to as Phi-3 model throughout our paper. Phi-3 has 3.8B parameters and is trained on an augmented textbook corpus and high-quality web data consisting of 3.3 trillion tokens. While specific training details are not disclosed, Phi-3 building blocks are reported to be a similar structure to the Llama-2 model (Touvron et al., 2023). Phi-3 showed an outstanding performance in MMLU which includes high school chemistry and college chemistry subjects (Hendrycks et al., 2020).

2.2 Pretrain Data

The pretraining corpus comprised 8 million tokens sourced from chemistry textbooks and an additional 82 million tokens extracted from chemical journal abstracts published by the Royal Society of Chemistry (Chen et al., 2020). The textbook data was acquired from the HuggingFace repository [1]. This diverse corpus provides a rich source of chemical language and concepts, enabling the model to develop a comprehensive understanding of the domain. Examples of the pretraining corpus are provided in Table 1.

Textbook
To discuss the electronic states of atoms we need a system of notation for multi-electron wavefunctions. As we saw in Chapter 8, the assignment of electrons to orbitals is called the electron configuration of the atom. One creates an electronic configuration representing the electronic structure of a multi-electron atom or ion in its ground or lowest-energy state as follows.
RSC Abstract
Rhenium, the non - noble metal with an acceptable price, was found to be a good additive that largely improved Pt / WO3 / ZrO2 catalysis for glycerol hydrogenolysis. Compared with conventionally employed Pt / WO3 / ZrO2, the Re - promoted catalyst led to almost quantitative glycerol conversion (> 99% vs. 57.7%), giving useful C3 alcohols in excellent total selectivity (> 95%) under reduced reaction pressure (2.5 MPa). The addition of Re led to such an impressive enhancement of the catalyst activity that even the reaction performed under atmospheric H2 pressure (0.1 MPa) afforded 96.8% glycerol conversion and a good selectivity of C3 compounds at 95.2%. Further XRD, Raman, BET, CO chemisorption, TEM, H2-TPR, XPS, NH3-TPD, 1H MAS NMR and Py-IR studies indicated that introduction of Re greatly improved the dispersion of Pt and catalyst acidity, and resulted in this largely enhanced catalyst activity.

Table 1: Examples of Pretrain Corpus.

2.3 Instruction Tuning Data

The instruction tuning phase utilized two primary datasets:

1. **SMILES Question Answering Pairs:** Consisting of 129,699 question-answer pairs from ChEMBL, this dataset contains 3,892 unique

[1] Hack90/libre_chem_textbooks

SMILES representations. The dataset was acquired from the HuggingFace repository. [2] Each pair involves a question related to the chemical properties of the molecule, along with the corresponding answer.

2. **CAMEL-AI Chemistry Dataset:** Chemistry instruction tuning dataset which was generated using GPT-4 was used to cover a broad range of chemical queries and tasks (Li et al., 2024). The dataset is made up of 20,000 instruction pairs in 25 topics and 25 subtopics for each topic. By incorporating this diverse dataset into the instruction tuning process, we aimed to further refine the model's ability to comprehend and respond to various chemical queries beyond SMILES representation.

The examples of the instruction tuning data are shown in Table 2.

SMILES QA
SMILES: CC(=O)/N=c1/sc(S(N)(=O)=O)nn1C Question: How many rotatable bonds does this compound have? Answer: 1
CAMEL-AI Chemistry QA
What are the expected products of the reaction between sodium chloride (NaCl) and silver nitrate (AgNO3)? Provide the balanced chemical equation and identify the type of reaction that occurs. Answer: When sodium chloride (NaCl) reacts with silver nitrate (AgNO3), a double displacement reaction occurs, also known as a metathesis reaction. The expected products of this reaction are silver chloride (AgCl) and sodium nitrate (NaNO3). The balanced chemical equation for this reaction is: NaCl (aq) + AgNO3 (aq) → AgCl (s) + NaNO3 (aq) In this reaction, the sodium (Na) and silver (Ag) ions switch places, forming new compounds. Silver chloride (AgCl) is an insoluble solid that precipitates out of the solution, while sodium nitrate (NaNO3) remains dissolved in the solution.

Table 2: Examples of instruction tuning dataset.

3 Experiment and Results

3.1 SLM Training

We conducted continued pretraining and instruction tuning using 8 A6000 GPUs, each with 48 GB GPU memory. We used LLaMaFactory[3] and used Deep3 for efficient training (Rasley et al., 2020). Continued pretraining was done with an epoch of 3 and a learning rate of 1e-5. The instruction tuning was done with the same learning rate as the continued pretraining but only for 1 epoch. The total training took less than a day. We named the resulting model as Phi-3-KnowChem.

For the shared task fine-tuning, we used a different computational resource, 2 A5000 GPUs with a total GPU memory of 48 GB. The finetuning for the shared task was done using low-rank adaptation (LoRA) and deepSpeed zero redundancy optimizer to reduce the GPU memory requirement (Rasley et al., 2020; Hu et al., 2021). We trained the model for the captioning task with a learning rate of 1e-3 and epoch 1. Hyperparameters for LoRA were as follows: rank - 128, alpha 256, and projector learning rate 2e-5. We used a simple prompt for the training and the evaluation: 'Describe the input molecule represented in SMILES. SMILES string'. The whole train dataset for the task was used for the fine-tuning.

3.2 Evaluation

For the evaluation, we used 1 A5000 GPU and used temperature of 1. For the baseline performance, we used the greedy search as the decoding strategy. We change this strategy with the beam search using multinomial sampling. The number of beams was 3. For the evaluation metrics scoring, we submitted the text output to the codabench. The evaluation metrics used include BLEU-2, BLEU-4, Meteor, ROUGE-1, ROUGE-2, and ROUGE-L.

3.3 Evaluation Results

The results in Table 3 for the chemical language training provide several notable trends. Firstly, the baseline Phi-3 model perform very poorly on the task even after 1 epoch of finetuning. This suggests that the model has a limited understanding of chemistry-specific language, as indicated by lowest scores across all metrics (Meteor: 0.5582, ROUGE-1: 0.4225, ROUGE-2: 0.3186, ROUGE-L: 0.3016). These baseline scores highlight the challenges of molecule captioning when using a general language

[2] alxfgh/ChEMBL_Drug_Instruction_Tuning

[3] https://github.com/hiyouga/LLaMA-Factory

Model	BLEU-2	BLEU-4	Meteor	ROUGE-1	ROUGE-2	ROUGE-L
Phi-3	0.2299	0.1678	0.5582	0.4225	0.3186	0.3016
Phi-3+PT	0.6804	0.4922	0.6644	0.7074	0.5308	0.5142
Phi-3+PT+IT	0.6959	0.5023	0.6750	0.7232	0.5373	0.5193
Phi-3+PT+IT+Beam	0.7056	0.5083	0.6901	0.7261	0.5361	0.5201

Table 3: Molecule Captioning Evaluation Results. The result is sorted by the ROUGE-L. PT stands for continued pretrained model. IT stands for instruction-tuned model. Beam stands for the beam search decoding strategy.

Prompt
Describe the input molecule represented in SMILES. CSc1ccc(C(C)N(C)C)cn1
Phi-3
The molecule is a anti viral. The molecule is a hiv inhibitor and is anti viral compound. The molecule is a hiv integrase inhibitor and is anti viral agent. The molecule is a hiv replication inhibitor and is anti viral agent compound. The molecule is a hiv protease inhibitor and is anti viral agent, belonging to the anti viral class of molecules. The molecule is a hiv treatment and is anti viral compound, anti viral activity, and anti viral. The molecule is a hiv integrase inhibitor and is anti viral compound, anti viral activity, and anti viral. The molecule is a hiv inhibitor and aids treatment, belonging to the anti viral compound class of molecules. The molecule is a hiv treatment and aids treatment, impacting both hiv treatment and aids. The molecule is a hiv inhibitor and aids treatment, impacting both hiv replication and cancer
Phi-3+PT
The molecule is a anti inflammatory.
Phi-3+PT+IT
The molecule is a anti inflammatory.
Phi-3+PT+IT+Beam
The molecule is a anti viral and belongs to the anti viral agent class of molecules, with the characteristic of being anti viral.

Table 4: Response comparison between baseline Phi-3 and trained models. The example was randomly sampled.

model that lacks specialized training in the chemical domain.

Additionally, the effect of continued training is observed. Continued pretraining (PT) on a large corpus of chemistry texts resulted in significant improvements across all evaluation metrics. The continued pretraining effectively infused the model with domain-specific knowledge, enhancing its performance by a substantial margin even without exposure to SMILES string. The performance boost with the continued pretraining was almost 300% increase for BLEU scores, about 67% increase for the ROUGE score, and 19% increase for Meteor. Adding an instruction tuning (IT) phase which contained about 4K unique SMILES representations further improved the model's performance in the molecule captioning task for all the evaluation metrics. This shows that prior exposure to SMILES representation can improve the performance of the related downstream task.

Beam search with multinomial sampling also increased the performance in all the evaluation metrics except ROUGE-2. This suggests that while continued pretraining and instruction tuning lay a strong foundation for chemical language understanding, advanced decoding techniques like beam search can further refine the output quality.

The model responses were compared as shown in Table 4. Rather than giving the right caption for the molecule, the Phi-3 model repeated sentences describing an anti-viral agent. Also, we see grammatical mistakes, using 'a' instead of 'an'. The continued pretrained model and instruction-tuned model both gave the same response, while the beam search strategy yielded a different response that was slightly longer than the other two models.

4 Conclusion

In this paper, we have presented our approach and findings from experimenting with the Phi-3-mini-4k model on the molecule captioning task as part of the L+M-24 shared task. Our experiment focused on evaluating the efficacy of continued pretraining and instruction tuning for enhancing the model's domain-specific chemical knowledge and its ability to generate accurate molecular descriptions.

The results demonstrated that both continued pre-training and instruction tuning play critical roles in enhancing the performance of the Phi-3 model on molecule captioning tasks. Continued pretraining with a chemistry-specific corpus provides a substantial boost by enriching the model's knowledge base, while instruction tuning with targeted question-answer pairs refines its ability to handle specific queries related to chemical structures. The addition of beam search decoding, though providing marginal gains, contributes to producing higher-quality and more accurate descriptions. These findings highlight the importance of domain-specific training and advanced decoding strategies in improving the capabilities of language models for specialized tasks like molecule captioning. In fact, on the leaderboard, our Phi-3-KnowChem outperformed the MolT5-base model.

Nevertheless, while these findings provide valuable insights, further in-depth analysis is warranted to explore the nuances of model performance in the chemical domain fully. The exploration of other tasks such as chemical property prediction can contribute to more accurate and comprehensive assessments of LM performance in real-world chemical applications.

Limitation

The computational constraints restricted the size and complexity of the models that could be feasibly trained and evaluated. There are larger versions of the Phi-3 model, 7B, and 14B models which can potentially perform much better than the version we used in this study.

Broader Impacts and Ethics Statement

Our work does not raise any major ethical concerns regarding the usage of the Phi-3 model as it was used for research purposes only. However, our Phi-3-KnowChem is not rigorously tested for use in real-world chemical applications or scenarios. Thus, they may not be suitable for use in the decision-making process for the chemical industry.

References

Marah Abdin, Sam Ade Jacobs, Ammar Ahmad Awan, Jyoti Aneja, Ahmed Awadallah, Hany Awadalla, Nguyen Bach, Amit Bahree, Arash Bakhtiari, Harkirat Behl, et al. 2024. Phi-3 technical report: A highly capable language model locally on your phone. *arXiv preprint arXiv:2404.14219*.

Yifan Chen, Tamara Polajnar, Colin Batchelor, and Simone Teufel. 2020. A corpus of very short scientific summaries. In *Proceedings of the 24th Conference on Computational Natural Language Learning*, pages 153–164.

Carl Edwards, Tuan Lai, Kevin Ros, Garrett Honke, Kyunghyun Cho, and Heng Ji. 2022. Translation between molecules and natural language. *arXiv preprint arXiv:2204.11817*.

Carl Edwards, Qingyun Wang, Lawrence Zhao, and Heng Ji. 2024. L+m-24: Building a dataset for language+ molecules@ acl 2024. *arXiv preprint arXiv:2403.00791*.

Yin Fang, Xiaozhuan Liang, Ningyu Zhang, Kangwei Liu, Rui Huang, Zhuo Chen, Xiaohui Fan, and Huajun Chen. 2023. Mol-instructions: A large-scale biomolecular instruction dataset for large language models. *arXiv preprint arXiv:2306.08018*.

Dan Hendrycks, Collin Burns, Steven Basart, Andy Zou, Mantas Mazeika, Dawn Song, and Jacob Steinhardt. 2020. Measuring massive multitask language understanding. *arXiv preprint arXiv:2009.03300*.

Edward J Hu, Yelong Shen, Phillip Wallis, Zeyuan Allen-Zhu, Yuanzhi Li, Shean Wang, Lu Wang, and Weizhu Chen. 2021. Lora: Low-rank adaptation of large language models. *arXiv preprint arXiv:2106.09685*.

Shu Huang and Jacqueline M Cole. 2022. Batterybert: A pretrained language model for battery database enhancement. *Journal of chemical information and modeling*, 62(24):6365–6377.

Yunsoo Kim, Hyuk Ko, Jane Lee, Hyun Young Heo, Jinyoung Yang, Sungsoo Lee, and Kyu-hwang Lee. 2023. Chemical language understanding benchmark. In *Proceedings of the 61st Annual Meeting of the Association for Computational Linguistics (Volume 5: Industry Track)*, pages 404–411.

Martin Krallinger, Obdulia Rabal, Florian Leitner, Miguel Vazquez, David Salgado, Zhiyong Lu, Robert Leaman, Yanan Lu, Donghong Ji, Daniel M Lowe, et al. 2015. The chemdner corpus of chemicals and drugs and its annotation principles. *Journal of cheminformatics*, 7:1–17.

Guohao Li, Hasan Hammoud, Hani Itani, Dmitrii Khizbullin, and Bernard Ghanem. 2024. Camel: Communicative agents for" mind" exploration of large language model society. *Advances in Neural Information Processing Systems*, 36.

Jiao Li, Yueping Sun, Robin J Johnson, Daniela Sciaky, Chih-Hsuan Wei, Robert Leaman, Allan Peter Davis, Carolyn J Mattingly, Thomas C Wiegers, and Zhiyong Lu. 2016. Biocreative v cdr task corpus: a resource for chemical disease relation extraction. *Database*, 2016.

Jeff Rasley, Samyam Rajbhandari, Olatunji Ruwase, and Yuxiong He. 2020. Deepspeed: System optimizations enable training deep learning models with over 100 billion parameters. In *Proceedings of the 26th ACM SIGKDD International Conference on Knowledge Discovery & Data Mining*, pages 3505–3506.

Ross Taylor, Marcin Kardas, Guillem Cucurull, Thomas Scialom, Anthony Hartshorn, Elvis Saravia, Andrew Poulton, Viktor Kerkez, and Robert Stojnic. 2022. Galactica: A large language model for science. *arXiv preprint arXiv:2211.09085*.

Hugo Touvron, Louis Martin, Kevin Stone, Peter Albert, Amjad Almahairi, Yasmine Babaei, Nikolay Bashlykov, Soumya Batra, Prajjwal Bhargava, Shruti Bhosale, et al. 2023. Llama 2: Open foundation and fine-tuned chat models. *arXiv preprint arXiv:2307.09288*.

Di Zhang, Wei Liu, Qian Tan, Jingdan Chen, Hang Yan, Yuliang Yan, Jiatong Li, Weiran Huang, Xiangyu Yue, Dongzhan Zhou, et al. 2024a. Chemllm: A chemical large language model. *arXiv preprint arXiv:2402.06852*.

Kaiwei Zhang, Yange Lin, Guangcheng Wu, Yuxiang Ren, Xuecang Zhang, Xiaoyu Zhang, Weitao Du, et al. 2024b. Sculpting molecules in 3d: A flexible substructure aware framework for text-oriented molecular optimization. *arXiv preprint arXiv:2403.03425*.

Mol2Lang-VLM: Vision- and Text-Guided Generative Pre-trained Language Models for Advancing Molecule Captioning through Multimodal Fusion

Duong Thanh Tran†**, Nhat Truong Pham**†**, Nguyen Doan Hieu Nguyen, Balachandran Manavalan***

Department of Integrative Biotechnology, Sungkyunkwan University, Republic of Korea
{duongtt, truongpham96, ndhieunguyen, bala2022}@skku.edu
†Equal contribution
***Correspondence:** bala2022@skku.edu

Abstract

This paper introduces Mol2Lang-VLM, an enhanced method for refining generative pre-trained language models for molecule captioning using multimodal features to achieve more accurate caption generation. Our approach leverages the encoder and decoder blocks of the Transformer-based architecture by introducing third sub-layers into both. Specifically, we insert sub-layers in the encoder to fuse features from SELFIES strings and molecular images, while the decoder fuses features from SMILES strings and their corresponding descriptions. Moreover, cross multi-head attention is employed instead of common multi-head attention to enable the decoder to attend to the encoder's output, thereby integrating the encoded contextual information for better and more accurate caption generation. Performance evaluation on the CheBI-20 and L+M-24 benchmark datasets demonstrates Mol2Lang-VLM's superiority, achieving higher accuracy and quality in caption generation compared to existing methods. Our code and pre-processed data are available at https://github.com/nhattruongpham/mol-lang-bridge/tree/mol2lang/.

1 Introduction

In the field of cheminformatics, molecule captioning plays a crucial role in helping researchers by automatically generating captions for molecular structures. The accuracy and quality of these captions are vital as they directly impact the understanding of chemical information and scientific discoveries. Traditional techniques primarily rely on unimodal data, often focusing only on textual representations like SMILES (Simplified Molecular Input Line Entry System) (Weininger, 1988) strings or SELFIES (Self-referencing Embedded Strings) (Krenn et al., 2020) strings. Although these methods have shown satisfactory results, their dependence on a single modality limits the richness and accuracy of the generated captions.

The rise of multimodal data, which uses information from different sources, presents an opportunity for significant advancements in molecule captioning. Multimodal approaches integrate various forms of molecule, enabling a more comprehensive understanding of molecular characteristics. However, effectively utilizing multimodal data in generative models is challenging and requires advanced techniques to integrate and improve the models effectively.

In this paper, we introduce an enhanced methodology, named Mol2Lang-VLM, to improve generative models in molecule captioning by utilizing multimodal features. Our approach integrates SELFIES strings and high-level features from molecular images in the encoder, while incorporating SMILES features and corresponding descriptions in the decoder. This multimodal integration allows the model to have a deeper understanding of chemical structures within the generative model, which is further refined during the decoder stage.

2 Related Work

2.1 Unimodal Language Models

MolT5 (Edwards et al., 2022) involves translating molecular structures into natural language using a text-to-text transfer transformer (T5) (Raffel et al., 2020) model. This model leverages the robust linguistic capabilities of T5 to understand and generate descriptions of molecular structures accurately. BioT5 (Pei et al., 2023) extends the capabilities of T5 to integrate chemical knowledge and natural language associations into biological contexts. BioT5 employs SELFIES for representing small molecules, as it offers considerable advantages over SMILES. Specifically, SELFIES ensures a more reliable and error-resistant molecular representation, thereby avoiding the problem of invalid structures that frequently occur with SMILES. This

Proceedings of the 1st Workshop on Language + Molecules (L+M 2024), pages 98–103
August 15, 2024 ©2024 Association for Computational Linguistics

model improves the cross-modal understanding between biological texts and chemical data. While MolT5 and BioT5 are encoder-decoder language models, MolXPT (Liu et al., 2023) utilizes a generative pre-trained Transformer (GPT) (Radford and Narasimhan, 2018) which is a decoder-only language model by introducing a generative pre-training approach by wrapping molecular structures within descriptive texts. MolXPT leverages both text and SMILES sequences for molecular modeling. It wraps SMILES sequences with text, allowing them to influence each other. Specifically, it detects molecule names in text sequences and replaces them with corresponding SMILES representations. ChemBERTa (Chithrananda et al., 2020) is an encoder-only language model that utilizes the RoBERTa (Liu et al., 2019) model that focuses on molecular representation learning and property prediction.

SwinOCSR (Xu et al., 2022) uses Swin Transformer (Liu et al., 2021) architecture for end-to-end optical chemical structure recognition of molecular images. This model can effectively recognize and describe chemical structures from images, providing a significant improvement in the accuracy of vision-language tasks in cheminformatics.

While the aforementioned models have made significant contributions to molecule captioning, their reliance on unimodal data restricts their potential for advancements. By not harnessing the power of multimodal data, these models encounter limitations in terms of information richness, completeness, contextual understanding, generalization, and interpretability.

2.2 Multimodal Language Models

GIT-Mol (Liu et al., 2024) introduces a multimodal large language model that integrates graph, image, and text data to enhance molecular science applications. This model leverages the strengths of different data modalities to provide comprehensive and accurate molecular descriptions. Besides that, MoMu (Su et al., 2022) associates molecular graphs with natural language, providing a sophisticated multimodal foundation model. This model enhances the interpretability and accuracy of molecular captions by integrating graph representations of molecules with their textual descriptions.

While the use of multimodal data is feasible, the aforementioned models face certain issues. These models necessitate significant computational resources and large dataset training. Additionally, scaling up multimodal models can pose challenges.

3 Methodology

3.1 Generative Language Model

We use the T5 (Raffel et al., 2020) architecture as our generative language model. The process begins with the tokenization of the SELFIES string, resulting in token embeddings $X_t \in \mathbb{R}^{L_{\text{enc}} \times d_t}$. Here, L_{enc} represents the length of the encoder input, while d_t denotes the dimensionality of the feature vectors. The encoder comprises a sequence of N encoding layers, with each layer consisting of a Multi-head Self-Attention (MSA) (Vaswani et al., 2017) mechanism (Eq. 1) and a Feed-Forward Network (FFN) (Eq. 2). Following each sub-layer, there is a residual connection that precedes layer normalization (LN). Unlike the original Transformer (Vaswani et al., 2017), T5 incorporates relative position embeddings (Shaw et al., 2018), which are added to the respective logits during the computation of attention weights and shared across all layers in the model.

$$Z_l^{\text{enc}'} = \text{LN}(\text{MSA}(Z_{l-1}^{\text{enc}}) + Z_{l-1}^{\text{enc}}) \quad (1)$$

$$Z_l^{\text{enc}} = \text{LN}(\text{FFN}(Z_l^{\text{enc}'}) + Z_l^{\text{enc}'}) \quad (2)$$

In parallel with the encoder, the decoder similarly consists of N layers. It exhibits three distinctive aspects compared to the encoder: First, target sequences, which are molecular captions, are tokenized into embeddings $Y_t \in \mathbb{R}^{L_{\text{dec}} \times d_t}$, where L_{dec} is the length of the target sequence. They are shifted right by one token to ensure that the ground-truth token is used as the input to predict the next token. Second, a Masked Multi-head Self-Attention (MMSA) (Vaswani et al., 2017) is utilized to ensure auto-regressive generation, maintaining a strict left-to-right processing order (Eq. 3). Third, a Cross Multi-head Attention (CMA) (Vaswani et al., 2017) layer is employed, which enables the decoder to attend to the encoder's output, thereby integrating the encoded contextual information (Eq. 4). Analogous to the encoder, the decoder includes a FFN in each layer (Eq. 5).

$$Z_l^{\text{dec}'} = \text{LN}(\text{MMSA}(Z_{l-1}^{\text{dec}}) + Z_{l-1}^{\text{dec}}) \quad (3)$$

$$Z_l^{\text{dec}''} = \text{LN}(\text{CMA}(Z_l^{\text{dec}'}, Z_N^{\text{enc}}, Z_N^{\text{enc}}) + Z_l^{\text{dec}'}) \quad (4)$$

$$Z_l^{\text{dec}} = \text{LN}(\text{FFN}(Z_l^{\text{dec}''}) + Z_l^{\text{dec}''}) \quad (5)$$

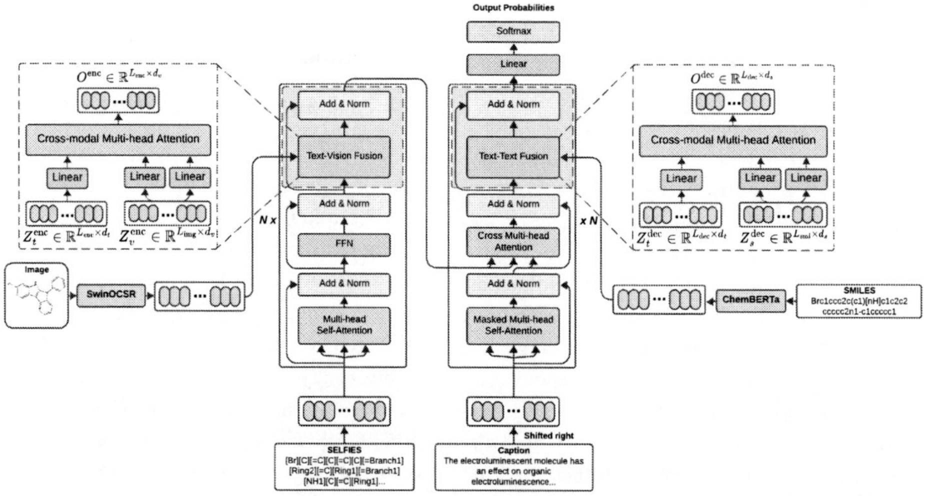

Figure 1: Overview of Mol2Lang-VLM's architecture. The green areas represent the two inserted sub-layers used to fuse the features. The T5 architecture uses relative position embeddings, which are integrated into the Multi-head Attention mechanism and, therefore, are not shown in the figure. Additionally, Cross Multi-head Attention is employed in the decoder instead of Multi-head Attention.

3.2 Vision- and Text-Guided Fusion

Inspired by VG-GPLMs (Yu et al., 2021), we integrate a third sub-layer into both the encoder and decoder of the language model. In the encoder, we insert text-vision fusion at the end of the encoder to learn the cross-modality between the SELFIES string and the molecular image. In the decoder, we replace the last FFN with text-text fusion to capture the relationship between the corresponding caption and the SMILES string. In both fusion processes, we utilize the CMA mechanism to learn the correlation between the two sets of features. The overview of the architecture is exhibited in Figure 1.

In the fusion process of the encoder, the embeddings of SELFIES, denoted as Z_t^{enc}, are linearly projected to the query Q^{enc} (Eq. 6), while the embeddings of the image, denoted as Z_v^{enc}, are linearly projected to the key K^{enc} (Eq. 7) and the value V^{enc} (Eq. 8). These projections are performed before feeding them to the CMA mechanism, which generates the output O^{enc} (Eq. 9).

$$Q^{\text{enc}} = Z_t^{\text{enc}} W_q^{\text{enc}} \tag{6}$$

$$K^{\text{enc}} = Z_v^{\text{enc}} W_k^{\text{enc}} \tag{7}$$

$$V^{\text{enc}} = Z_v^{\text{enc}} W_v^{\text{enc}} \tag{8}$$

$$O^{\text{enc}} = \text{CMA}(Q^{\text{enc}}, K^{\text{enc}}, V^{\text{enc}}) \tag{9}$$

The fusion process of the decoder occurs after the CMA between the decoder's embeddings and the output embeddings of the encoder, resulting in Z_t^{dec}. In this fusion process, Z_t^{dec} are linearly projected to the query Q^{dec} (Eq. 10), while the embeddings of SMILES, denoted as Z_s^{dec}, are also projected to the key K^{dec} (Eq. 11) and the value V^{dec} (Eq. 12). Subsequently, CMA is applied to generate O^{dec} (Eq. 13). The features of SMILES help enhance the overall effectiveness of the features, enabling more effective generation of the desired output.

$$Q^{\text{dec}} = Z_t^{\text{dec}} W_q^{\text{dec}} \tag{10}$$

$$K^{\text{dec}} = Z_s^{\text{dec}} W_k^{\text{dec}} \tag{11}$$

$$V^{\text{dec}} = Z_s^{\text{dec}} W_v^{\text{dec}} \tag{12}$$

$$O^{\text{dec}} = \text{CMA}(Q^{\text{dec}}, K^{\text{dec}}, V^{\text{dec}}) \tag{13}$$

At each fusion, the output is concatenated with the initial embeddings to produce $Z_t^{\text{enc}'}$ and $Z_t^{\text{dec}'}$ (Eq. 14 and 15).

$$Z_t^{\text{enc}'} = (Z_t^{\text{enc}} \oplus O^{\text{enc}}) W_c^{\text{enc}} \tag{14}$$

$$Z_t^{\text{dec}'} = (Z_t^{\text{dec}} \oplus O^{\text{dec}}) W_c^{\text{dec}} \tag{15}$$

Finally, forget gates, denoted as F^{enc} and F^{dec}, are applied to filter out noisy and redundant information introduced during the interactions (Eq. 16 and 17), then point-wise multiplication is applied on O^{enc} and O^{dec} to produce $O^{\text{enc}'}$ and $O^{\text{dec}'}$ (Eq. 18).

$$F^{\text{enc}} = \sigma((Z_t^{\text{enc}} \oplus O^{\text{enc}}) W_f^{\text{enc}}) \tag{16}$$

$$F^{\text{dec}} = \sigma((Z_t^{\text{dec}} \oplus O^{\text{dec}})W_f^{\text{dec}}) \quad (17)$$

$$O^{\text{enc}'} = F^{\text{enc}} \otimes O^{\text{enc}}, O^{\text{dec}'} = F^{\text{dec}} \otimes O^{\text{dec}} \quad (18)$$

4 Implementation Details

4.1 Architectures

We employ BioT5 (Pei et al., 2023) as our generative language model, which uses the *T5-base* version. The model consists of 252 million parameters and has a configuration that includes an embedding dimensionality of 768. It is composed of 12 layers in both the encoder and decoder. The input tokens and output tokens are limited to a maximum length of 512.

To extract visual features from molecular images, we utilize the encoder of SwinOCSR (Xu et al., 2022) which employs the Swin Transformer (Liu et al., 2021) architecture, uses *Swin-L* version. The encoder has a total of 194 million parameters. By inputting images with the size of 224×224, the encoder generates feature embeddings with a length of 49 and a hidden dimensionality of 1536.

To extract features from SMILES representations, we use ChemBERTa (Chithrananda et al., 2020), which is built upon the *RoBERTa-base* architecture with a total of 44 million parameters. The input tokens for ChemBERTa are also limited to a length of 512.

To compute the cross-modality attention in text-vision fusion of the encoder, as well as text-text fusion of the decoder, all features are linearly projected to a gated dimensionality of 256. The text-vision fusion is then integrated at the last two layers of the encoder (the 11th and 12th layers). Concurrently, text-text fusion is incorporated into the initial two layers of the decoder (the 1st and 2nd layers).

4.2 Datasets

L+M-24: The L+M-24 dataset, first introduced from *Language + Molecules Workshop @ ACL 2024* (Edwards et al., 2024), is designed to highlight three key benefits of natural language in molecule design: compositionality, functionality, and abstraction. It contains over $160,560$ molecule-description pairs, which are divided into 80%/20% for train/validation splits.

CheBI-20: The CheBI-20 dataset is widely used in molecular description tasks. It was first introduced in the Text2Mol (Edwards et al., 2021). This dataset contains $33,010$ molecule-description pairs, which are split into 80%/10%/10% for train/validation/test sets.

Since the aforementioned datasets currently lack SELFIES strings and molecular images, we employ *selfies* [1] and *RDKit* [2] package to generate this additional data. We use the prompting template of the molecule captioning task from BioT5 (Pei et al., 2023) to fine-tune the model.

4.3 Configurations

Training: During the training process, we utilize a batch size of 64. To optimize the model, we employ the AdamW (Loshchilov and Hutter, 2019) optimizer. The learning rate scheduler follows a cosine annealing strategy, with a base learning rate of $3e-5$. The warming-up steps for the learning rate scheduler are set to 1 epoch to gradually adjust the learning rate.

Inference: To ensure a fair comparison when evaluating the model, we employ greedy decoding for generating molecular captions by setting the number of beam search to 1, with the decoder starting token as *<pad>*, and the end of sentence token as *</s>*. Furthermore, post-processing is also applied to skip all special tokens.

5 Results and Discussion

Table 1 presents the performance comparison of Mol2Lang-VLM with all baseline models, such as MolT5-Small, MolT5-Base, MolT5-Large, and BioT5 on the L+M-24 dataset. We used several performance evaluation metrics to evaluate these models, including BLEU-2, BLEU-4, ROUGE-1, ROUGE-2, ROUGE-L, and METEOR. Notably, Mol2Lang-VLM outperforms all three baseline models in almost all metrics, with BLEU-2, BLEU-4, ROUGE-1, ROUGE-2, ROUGE-L, and METEOR values of 77.7, 56.3, 78.6, 59.1, 56.5, and 74.1, respectively. Although Mol2Lang-VLM achieves a lower METEOR of 0.2 compared to MolT5-Large, its number of parameters is approximately 1.5 times lower than MolT5-Large, indicating that the model can learn more efficiently. Compared to BioT5, Mol2Lang-VLM achieves better performance in terms of BLEU-2, BLEU-4, ROUGE-1, and METEOR, with slightly lower scores in ROUGE-2 and ROUGE-L, demonstrating that it generally outperforms BioT5.

We also evaluate our proposed method, along

[1] https://github.com/aspuru-guzik-group/selfies

[2] https://github.com/rdkit/rdkit

Model	#Params	BLEU-2	BLEU-4	ROUGE-1	ROUGE-2	ROUGE-L	METEOR
MolT5-Small	77M	70.9	51.2	74.5	55.8	54.4	70.1
MolT5-Base	248M	73.8	53.5	75.0	55.9	53.9	71.8
MolT5-Large	783M	<u>76.9</u>	<u>55.6</u>	77.7	58.0	55.7	**74.3**
BioT5	252M	74.6	54.1	<u>78.5</u>	**59.3**	**56.9**	72.7
Ours	496M	**77.7**	**56.3**	**78.6**	<u>59.1</u>	<u>56.5</u>	<u>74.1</u>

Table 1: Molecule captioning results on the validation split of L+M-24 dataset (**Best**, <u>Second Best</u>). The baseline results are derived from *Language + Molecules Workshop @ ACL 2024* (Edwards et al., 2024). The Text2Mol metric is excluded from the table because Text2Mol is trained on a different distribution of data compared to the L+M-24 dataset.

Model	#Params	BLEU-2	BLEU-4	ROUGE-1	ROUGE-2	ROUGE-L	METEOR	Text2Mol
MolT5-Small	77M	51.9	43.6	62.0	46.9	56.3	55.1	54.0
MolT5-Base	248M	54.0	45.7	63.4	48.5	57.8	56.9	54.7
MolT5-Large	783M	59.4	50.8	65.4	51.0	59.4	61.4	58.2
BioT5	252M	**63.5**	**55.6**	**69.2**	**55.9**	**63.3**	**65.6**	**60.3**
Ours	496M	<u>61.2</u>	<u>52.7</u>	<u>67.4</u>	<u>53.2</u>	<u>61.4</u>	<u>63.3</u>	<u>59.8</u>

Table 2: Molecule captioning results on the test split of CheBI-20 dataset (**Best**, <u>Second Best</u>). The baseline results are derived from MolT5 (Edwards et al., 2022) and BioT5 (Pei et al., 2023).

Model	BLEU-2	BLEU-4	ROUGE-1	ROUGE-2	ROUGE-L	METEOR
Our model w/o forget gate	<u>75.7</u>	<u>54.7</u>	**78.7**	<u>59.0</u>	**56.7**	<u>73.0</u>
Our model w/ forget gate	**77.7**	**56.3**	<u>78.6</u>	**59.1**	<u>56.5</u>	**74.1**

Table 3: Molecule captioning results on the validation split of the L+M-24 dataset to compare between the model with and without a forget gate (**Best**, <u>Second Best</u>).

with all three baseline models and BioT5, on the CheBI-20 dataset. Table 2 displays the performance comparison in terms of BLEU-2, BLEU-4, ROUGE-1, ROUGE-2, ROUGE-L, METEOR, and Text2Mol metrics. Interestingly, Mol2Lang-VLM achieves the second-best performance in all metrics, while BioT5 excels on this dataset. This might be acceptable because, in some cases, the fused information may not provide significant additional context or may even introduce noise, making it challenging for the model to effectively utilize the fused embeddings.

Moreover, we conduct an ablation analysis to evaluate Mol2Lang-VLM with and without employing the forget gate. Table 3 compares the performance of these two strategies. Mol2Lang-VLM with the forget gate outperforms the version without it across most metrics, including BLEU-2, BLEU-4, ROUGE-2, and METEOR. The presence of the forget gate mechanism contributes to enhanced caption quality in terms of accuracy and relevance, showcasing the effectiveness of incorporating this mechanism in the model architecture for improved captioning outcomes.

6 Conclusion

This paper introduced Mol2Lang-VLM, a vision- and text-guided generative pre-trained language model designed to enhance molecule captioning performance through multimodal fusion. Our proposed approach achieved comparative results in terms of BLEU, ROUGE, METEOR, and Text2Mol metrics, demonstrating its effectiveness in generating accurate and meaningful captions for molecular structures. The findings highlight the potential of Mol2Lang-VLM in advancing molecule captioning tasks. Future research can explore alternative fusion methods, fine-tuning strategies, and the generalization of the model to other tasks. Additionally, integrating Mol2Lang-VLM with downstream applications and enhancing interpretability can further enhance its practical utility in the field of cheminformatics.

Acknowledgements

This work was supported by the National Research Foundation of Korea (NRF) funded by the Ministry of Science and ICT (RS-2024-00344752). This research was supported by the Department of Integrative Biotechnology, Sungkyunkwan University (SKKU) and the BK21 FOUR Project. This work was supported by the Korea Bio Data Station (K-BDS) with computing resources including technical support.

References

Seyone Chithrananda, Gabriel Grand, and Bharath Ramsundar. 2020. Chemberta: Large-scale self-supervised pretraining for molecular property prediction. *ArXiv*, abs/2010.09885.

Carl Edwards, Tuan Lai, Kevin Ros, Garrett Honke, Kyunghyun Cho, and Heng Ji. 2022. Translation between molecules and natural language. In *Proceedings of the 2022 Conference on Empirical Methods in Natural Language Processing*, pages 375–413, Abu Dhabi, United Arab Emirates. Association for Computational Linguistics.

Carl Edwards, Qingyun Wang, Lawrence Zhao, and Heng Ji. 2024. L+M-24: Building a dataset for Language + Molecules @ ACL 2024. *arXiv preprint arXiv:2403.00791*.

Carl Edwards, ChengXiang Zhai, and Heng Ji. 2021. Text2Mol: Cross-modal molecule retrieval with natural language queries. In *Proceedings of the 2021 Conference on Empirical Methods in Natural Language Processing*, pages 595–607, Online and Punta Cana, Dominican Republic. Association for Computational Linguistics.

Mario Krenn, Florian Häse, AkshatKumar Nigam, Pascal Friederich, and Alan Aspuru-Guzik. 2020. Self-referencing embedded strings (selfies): A 100% robust molecular string representation. *Machine Learning: Science and Technology*, 1(4):045024.

Pengfei Liu, Yiming Ren, Jun Tao, and Zhixiang Ren. 2024. Git-mol: A multi-modal large language model for molecular science with graph, image, and text. *Computers in Biology and Medicine*, page 108073.

Yinhan Liu, Myle Ott, Naman Goyal, Jingfei Du, Mandar Joshi, Danqi Chen, Omer Levy, Mike Lewis, Luke Zettlemoyer, and Veselin Stoyanov. 2019. Roberta: A robustly optimized bert pretraining approach. *Preprint*, arXiv:1907.11692.

Ze Liu, Yutong Lin, Yue Cao, Han Hu, Yixuan Wei, Zheng Zhang, Stephen Lin, and Baining Guo. 2021. Swin transformer: Hierarchical vision transformer using shifted windows. In *Proceedings of the IEEE/CVF International Conference on Computer Vision (ICCV)*.

Zequn Liu, Wei Zhang, Yingce Xia, Lijun Wu, Shufang Xie, Tao Qin, Ming Zhang, and Tie-Yan Liu. 2023. MolXPT: Wrapping molecules with text for generative pre-training. In *Proceedings of the 61st Annual Meeting of the Association for Computational Linguistics (Volume 2: Short Papers)*, pages 1606–1616, Toronto, Canada. Association for Computational Linguistics.

Ilya Loshchilov and Frank Hutter. 2019. Decoupled weight decay regularization. *Preprint*, arXiv:1711.05101.

Qizhi Pei, Wei Zhang, Jinhua Zhu, Kehan Wu, Kaiyuan Gao, Lijun Wu, Yingce Xia, and Rui Yan. 2023. BioT5: Enriching cross-modal integration in biology with chemical knowledge and natural language associations. In *Proceedings of the 2023 Conference on Empirical Methods in Natural Language Processing*, pages 1102–1123, Singapore. Association for Computational Linguistics.

Alec Radford and Karthik Narasimhan. 2018. Improving language understanding by generative pre-training.

Colin Raffel, Noam Shazeer, Adam Roberts, Katherine Lee, Sharan Narang, Michael Matena, Yanqi Zhou, Wei Li, and Peter J. Liu. 2020. Exploring the limits of transfer learning with a unified text-to-text transformer. *Journal of Machine Learning Research*, 21(140):1–67.

Peter Shaw, Jakob Uszkoreit, and Ashish Vaswani. 2018. Self-attention with relative position representations. In *Proceedings of the 2018 Conference of the North American Chapter of the Association for Computational Linguistics: Human Language Technologies, Volume 2 (Short Papers)*, pages 464–468, New Orleans, Louisiana. Association for Computational Linguistics.

Bing Su, Dazhao Du, Zhao Yang, Yujie Zhou, Jiangmeng Li, Anyi Rao, Hao Sun, Zhiwu Lu, and Ji-Rong Wen. 2022. A molecular multimodal foundation model associating molecule graphs with natural language. *Preprint*, arXiv:2209.05481.

Ashish Vaswani, Noam Shazeer, Niki Parmar, Jakob Uszkoreit, Llion Jones, Aidan N Gomez, Ł ukasz Kaiser, and Illia Polosukhin. 2017. Attention is all you need. In *Advances in Neural Information Processing Systems*, volume 30. Curran Associates, Inc.

David Weininger. 1988. Smiles, a chemical language and information system. 1. introduction to methodology and encoding rules. *Journal of chemical information and computer sciences*, 28(1):31–36.

Zhanpeng Xu, Jianhua Li, Zhaopeng Yang, Shiliang Li, and Honglin Li. 2022. Swinocsr: end-to-end optical chemical structure recognition using a swin transformer. *Journal of Cheminformatics*, 14(1):41.

Tiezheng Yu, Wenliang Dai, Zihan Liu, and Pascale Fung. 2021. Vision guided generative pre-trained language models for multimodal abstractive summarization. In *Proceedings of the 2021 Conference on Empirical Methods in Natural Language Processing*, pages 3995–4007, Online and Punta Cana, Dominican Republic. Association for Computational Linguistics.

DNA Language Model and Interpretable Graph Neural Network Identify Genes and Pathways Involved in Rare Diseases

Ali Saadat, Jacques Fellay
School of Life Sciences
Ecole Polytechnique Fédérale de Lausanne
Lausanne, Switzerland
{ali.saadat, jacques.fellay}@epfl.ch

Abstract

Identification of causal genes and pathways is a critical step for understanding the genetic underpinnings of rare diseases. We propose novel approaches to gene prioritization and pathway identification using DNA language model, graph neural networks, and genetic algorithm. Using HyenaDNA, a long-range genomic foundation model, we generated dynamic gene embeddings that reflect changes caused by deleterious variants. These gene embeddings were then utilized to identify candidate genes and pathways. We validated our method on a cohort of rare disease patients with partially known genetic diagnosis, demonstrating the re-identification of known causal genes and pathways and the detection of novel candidates. These findings have implications for the prevention and treatment of rare diseases by enabling targeted identification of new drug targets and therapeutic pathways.

1 Introduction

The landscape of genomics research has undergone a profound transformation with the advent of high-throughput sequencing technologies (Metzker, 2009). The generation of a vast amount of genomics data offers unprecedented insights into human genetic diversity (Auton et al., 2015; Chen et al., 2023). However, this wealth of data brings significant challenges in terms of data analysis and interpretation. A main challenge in deciphering the underlying mechanisms of diseases is establishing a link between genotype and phenotype (Gallagher and Chen-Plotkin, 2018). This task becomes even harder in the context of rare diseases, where the scarcity of data reduces statistical power (Seaby and Ennis, 2020).

Traditional methods for finding disease-associated genes/pathways have predominantly relied on statistical approaches, such as correlating specific genetic variants with disease occurrence (Auer and Lettre, 2015; Uffelmann et al., 2021). These approaches show decent performance if the cohort size is large, which is often a big obstacle in rare disease studies. Moreover, these methods usually utilize basic variant statistics (such as number of variant carriers), and might not take into account the gene-specific impact of variants on the gene sequence (MacArthur et al., 2014).

Another family of computational approaches for gene/pathway prioritization rely on the concept of guilt-by-association, where genes/pathways are considered potentially relevant based on their similarity to known disease genes (Lee et al., 2011; Guala and Sonnhammer, 2017). These methods work well in scenarios where some underlying genetic factors of the phenotype are well-studied, which is not the case for many diseases (Amberger et al., 2018). Moreover, these methods might introduce bias since they look for similar genes, thereby missing novel disease-causing genes (Gillis and Pavlidis, 2012).

Recent years have seen a remarkable rise in the performance of language models, particularly in the field of natural language processing (NLP) (Devlin et al., 2018; Radford et al., 2019). These models 'learn' language by processing vast amounts of text data, enabling them to perform a wide range of downstream tasks such as translation, summarization, and question-answering with unprecedented accuracy and fluency (Zhao et al., 2023). Parallel to this development, the concept of language models has been applied to genomics, giving rise to DNA language models (DNA-LMs) (Zhou et al., 2023; Dalla-Torre et al., 2023; Benegas et al., 2023; Nguyen et al., 2023). Genomic sequences, much like textual data, comprise long chains of information, in this case nucleotides instead of words. DNA-LMs apply the principles of NLP to interpret and analyze these sequences, translating the 'language' of DNA into meaningful biological insights. By learning from extensive genomic data, these

Proceedings of the 1st Workshop on Language + Molecules (L+M 2024), pages 104–116
August 15, 2024 ©2024 Association for Computational Linguistics

models can provide new perspectives on downstream biological processes (Consens et al., 2023; Marin et al., 2023).

HyenaDNA (Nguyen et al., 2023) is a long-range genomic foundation model pre-trained on the human reference genome at single nucleotide resolution. It can process long-range DNA sequences and represent them as embeddings in a high-dimensional space. For any genomic region such as a gene, HyenaDNA generates embeddings that capture the inherent information of the DNA sequence. These embeddings dynamically change in response to genetic variants, offering insights into how genetic alterations impact biological processes.

We hypothesize that variants with strong deleterious effects have a detectable impact on gene embeddings. We designed complementary methods to identify genes and pathways that contain such deleterious variants and could therefore play a causal role in the pathogenesis of rare diseases. For gene prioritization, we propose two approaches (case-vs-control and case-only) to quantitatively rank candidate genes (Figure 1a). For pathway identification, we propose a method that combines DNA-LM, interpretable graph neural networks (GNN) (Wu et al., 2021; Ying et al., 2019) and Genetic Algorithm (Katoch et al., 2020) (Figure 1b). We validate our methods on a cohort of rare disease patients with partially known genetic diagnosis, demonstrating the re-identification of known causal genes and the detection of novel candidates.

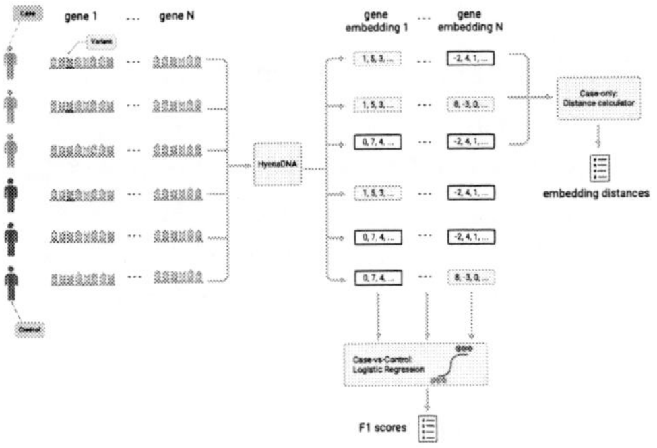

(a) Gene prioritization workflow: DNA sequences of candidate genes are passed to HyenaDNA for gene embedding generation. The embeddings are used to calculate a gene specific score (F_1 score for case-vs-control, distance score for case-only), which is used to rank and select top candidate genes.

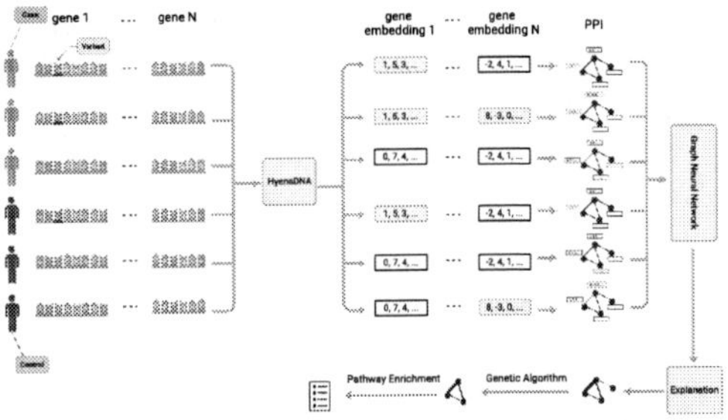

(b) Pathway identification workflow: for each individual, a protein-protein interaction network is constructed with gene embeddings as node features. A GNN is trained to classify cases graphs from controls, and GNNExplainer is applied to score the importance of nodes and edges for graph classification. Afterwards, a Genetics Algorithm is used to find the most explainable subnetwork, and a pathway enrichment analysis is performed on that subnetowrk to find the over-represented biological pathways.

Figure 1: Overall summary of of the methods. Figures created with `BioRender.com`.

2 Methods

2.1 Study participants

We selected two cohorts from our in-house database of exome-sequenced individuals. The first cohort consists of 120 previously healthy children who were admitted to pediatric intensive care units (PICUs) with respiratory failure due to a common viral respiratory infection. This cohort serves as the "rare disease" patient group for this study. As control group, we selected a total of 172 healthy individuals. The studies were approved by the relevant ethics commissions and all study participants provided a signed informed consent for research including human genetic testing.

2.2 Short-read alignment and variant calling

Adapter sequences were trimmed from sequencing reads using fastp (Chen et al., 2018) and the reads were subsequently aligned against the human reference genome (hg38) using the maximum exact matches algorithm in Burrows-Wheeler Aligner (Li and Durbin, 2009). The Genome Analysis Software Kit (GATK4) best-practice pipeline was used to call variants in the multi-sample mode (DePristo et al., 2011). In summary, PCR duplicates were removed and base quality scores were recalibrated to correct for sequencing artifacts. We called individual-level variants with GATK HaplotypeCaller before combining single-sample callsets for joint genotyping. To exclude low quality variants, we applied variant quality score recalibration and manual filtering (depth ≥ 20, genotype quality $\geq$

20, and $0.2 \leq$ heterozygous allele balance ≤ 0.8).

2.3 Variant annotation and filtering

To predict the potential impact of each variant, we used Variant Effect Predictor (VEP) (McLaren et al., 2016). To identify loss-of-function variants, we used Loss-of-Function Transcript Effect Estimator (LOFTEE) as a VEP plugin (Karczewski et al., 2020).

To classify the variant into putative pathogenicity groups, we implemented the ACMG/AMP guidelines (Richards et al., 2015) in R (`https://www.r-project.org`) (see full description Appendix A). A probability of pathogenicity (PoP) was assigned to each variant according to the ACMG/AMP Bayesian classification framework (Tavtigian et al., 2018). Variants with PoP ≥ 0.9 were considered as damaging. Genes with at least one pathogenic variant were included in the downstream analysis.

2.4 Gene embedding calculation

For candidate gene selection, we kept the genes that passed the following criteria: 1) At least one patient carries ≥ 1 pathogenic variant in the gene. 2) The length of the gene (including exons, introns, 3'-UTR, and 5'-UTR) is less than 450,000 nucleotides, which is the maximum input size of the medium-size HyenaDNA.

For each candidate gene, we obtained the reference gene sequence using biomaRt (Kinsella et al., 2011). Then for each study participant, we altered the reference alleles based on the position of the variants in the gene. The resulting DNA sequence was then fed into the medium-size HyenaDNA to get embeddings for each nucleotide. To construct a gene embedding, we extracted the nucleotide embeddings from positions of pathogenic variants, then we averaged them. All the gene embeddings were stored in a database to be used for the next steps. For loading pre-trained weights, we used the HuggingFace (Wolf et al., 2019) interface in Python (`https://www.python.org`). For model inference and embedding calculation, we used one Nvidia A100 (40GB) GPU.

2.5 Case-vs-control analysis

To assess the impact of pathogenic variants on the gene embeddings, we implemented a case-vs-control approach. For each gene, we trained a logistic regression (with L1 and L2 regularization) using the gene embeddings to classify patients from healthy controls. We used scikit-learn (Pedregosa et al., 2011) to train the model on 75% of the data and evaluate it with the remaining 25% resulting in a F_1 score for each gene. We compared the gene-specific F_1 scores and ranked genes based on this metric (Figure 1a).

For top candidate gene selection, we used Density-Based Spatial Clustering of Applications with Noise (DBSCAN) (Ester et al., 1996) as an outlier detector. We applied DBSCAN on the calculated F_1 scores to find outliers and selected corresponding genes as top candidates.

Finally, to validate the results, we implemented a permutation test. We randomly shuffled the labels (case or control) for N=1000 times. Then we trained a logistic regression on 75% of the data and calculated a F_1 score on the other 25%. We counted the number of times that the random F_1 score was more than or equal than the observed F_1 score. We calculated a p-value as follow (with $\epsilon = 0.001$):

$$p = \frac{\text{count(random } F_1 \geq \text{Observed } F_1) + \epsilon}{N + \epsilon}$$

2.6 Case-only analysis

We also developed a case-only method to prioritize candidate genes if healthy controls are not available. In this approach, for each gene we divided the gene embeddings into mutant (if the patient carried a pathogenic variant) and non-mutant (if the patient was not a carrier). Then we calculated a distance score as the average Euclidean distance between mutant and non-mutant gene embeddings. We utilized these gene-specific distance scores to rank candidate genes (Figure 1a).

For top candidate gene selection, similar to the case-vs-control approach, we applied DBSCAN on the distance scores and selected outliers as the top candidate genes.

To validate the results, we implemented a statistical test as follow : For N=1000 times we generated random reference and alternative embeddings and calculated the distance score. We counted the number of times that the random distance score was more than or equal than the observed distance score. We calculated a p-value as follow (with $\epsilon = 0.001$):

$$p = \frac{\text{count(random distance score} \geq \text{Observed distance score)} + \epsilon}{N + \epsilon}$$

2.7 Graph neural network training

To understand the underlying mechanism of the disease, we designed an explainable approach based on graph neural network (GNN). A summary of the method can be found in figure 1b. First, we created a protein-protein interaction (PPI) network that indicates interactions between genes carrying pathogenic variants. We used the STRING database (Szklarczyk et al., 2023) and included interactions with confidence score ≥ 0.6.

Afterwards, we created individual-specific graphs, which include gene embeddings as node features. We trained a GNN to classify patients' graphs from controls. GNN architecture consists of two hidden graph convolution layers (Zhang et al., 2019) with 16 nodes for message passing and a global sort pooling (Zhang et al., 2018) for node feature aggregation. Pooling is essential because the model is trained for graph classification, therefore with pooling we can generate graph representations from node features. We used AdamW (Loshchilov and Hutter, 2019) optimizer with learning rate = 0.001 and weight decay = 0.001 for training. We used batch size = 32 and trained the model for 1000 epochs. We used PyTorch geometric (Fey and Lenssen, 2019) for implementing and training the GNN.

2.8 Subnetwork identification and pathway enrichment analysis

After training the GNN, we used GNNExplainer (Ying et al., 2019) to assign an explainability score to each node, showing how important they are for graph classification . We applied GNNExplainer for all the samples and averaged the explainability scores for each node across samples.

After obtaining the explainability scores, we used the Genetic Algorithm (GA) (Katoch et al., 2020) to identify the "best" subnetwork with maximum fitness, defined as the average of explainability scores of its nodes. GA is a bio-inspired algorithm that mimics evolution by implementing natural selection, chromosomal crossover, and mutation. Previous studies have successfully utilized GA for subnetwork identification (Ulgen et al., 2019; Wu et al., 2011). To summarize the GA, we start with a population of random subnetworks, then we select 50% of subnetworks with probabilities proportional to their fitness scores (roulette wheel selection). Afterwards, we create new subnetworks by mutating them (adding or removing edges) and crossovering them (connecting two subnetworks, if possible). We started with an initial population of 100 subnetworks and repeated the GA for 10 generations with a mutation rate of 0.5. At the end, we chose the "most fit" subnetwork at the last generation.

Finally, to gain biological insights into the selected subnetwork, we performed pathway enrichment analysis, a method for identifying biological functions that are over-represented in a group of genes (Chicco and Agapito, 2022). We used the GSEApy package (Fang et al., 2022), which uses Enrichr (Kuleshov et al., 2016) for over-representation analysis and the Reactome database (Milacic et al., 2023) as reference. We kept significantly enriched pathways with false discovery rate (FDR) ≤ 0.05.

3 Results

3.1 Study participants

As patient cohort (rare disease cases), we used exome data from 120 previously healthy children admitted to PICUs with respiratory failure due to a common viral respiratory infection. Their median age was 78 days, 50 (42%) were female, and 90 (78%) were of European ancestry. Respiratory Syncytial Virus (RSV) and Human Rhinovirus (HRV) were the most common detected pathogens, in 67 (56%) and 31 (26%) of the cases, respectively. As controls, we selected 172 healthy individuals from our in-house database of exome-sequenced individuals, representing a random subset of the general population. Since the phenotype we are studying is rare, we assume that the controls are not enriched in individuals with genetic risk factors for infectious disease susceptibility.

3.2 Variant classification

In the patient group, 55,300 variants were mapped to coding and splicing regions and were scored with the ACMG/AMP Bayesian classification framework. 48,875 variants had a PoP ≤ 0.1 and were considered benign. 5,838 variants had an intermediate PoP (between 0.1 and 0.9), resulting in their classification as variants of unknown significance (VUS). 587 variants (in 508 genes) exceeded the pathogenicity threshold (≥ 0.9) and were considered as damaging.

3.3 Gene prioritization

A total of 498 (98%) candidate genes passed the selection criteria (Methods, Gene embedding cal-

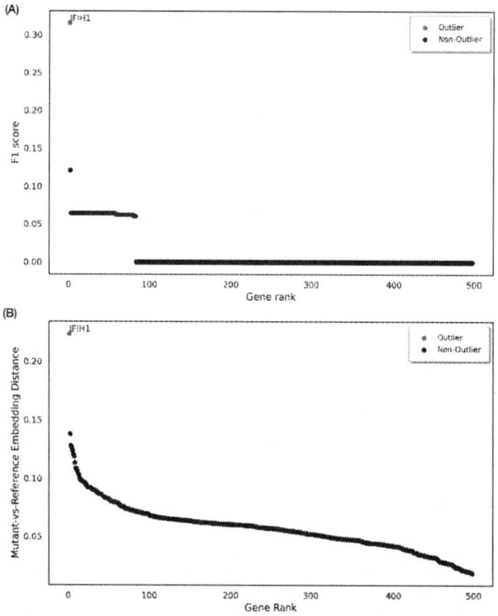

Figure 2: Gene prioritization results. (A) Genes ranked according to their corresponding F_1 score calculated based on case-vs-control workflow. (B) Gene ranking based on average distance of mutants and non-mutant embeddings, computed according to the case-only workflow.

culation). For each candidate gene, we calculated gene embeddings using the pre-trained HyenaDNA for all 292 study participants (120 cases and 172 controls), resulting in gene-specific embeddings in the embedding space. We then ranked candidate genes using two approaches:

1) Case-vs-control: We trained a logistic regression for each gene and calculated a gene-specific F_1 scores. We used these scores to rank the genes and find top candidates by applying DBSCAN for outlier detection. The top candidate gene with the highest F_1 score was *IFIH1* (Figure 2.A). We performed a permutation test which resulted in p-value=0.009 (Supplementary figure S1).

2) Case-only: in this scenario we used the gene-specific distance score (calculated based on the average Euclidean distance of mutant and non-mutant embeddings) for gene prioritization and top-candidate selection. *IFIH1* ranked first and was selected as an outlier using the DBSCAN method (Figure 2.B) and was significantly different from the expected distribution (p-value=10^{-6}, Supplementary figure S2).

3.4 PPI construction and graph neural network training

We constructed a high-quality PPI based on the interactions between the protein products of all candidate genes, resulting in a PPI with 138 nodes and 176 edges. For each participant, we initialized the same PPI structure, but used their personalized gene-embeddings as node features, resulting in 292 (120 cases and 172 controls) unique graphs. We used these graphs to train a GNN for classifying cases from controls. GNN structure consisted of 2 graph convolution layers with 16 nodes, and global sort pooling to generate graph representations from node features. We trained the GNN for 1000 epochs.

3.5 Subnetwork identification and pathway enrichment analysis

After training the GNN, we used GNNExplainer to assign an explainability score to each node, showing how important they are for graph classification. We applied GNNExplainer for all the samples and averaged the explainability scores for each node across samples. Figure 3.A shows the PPI with explainability scores reflected on the edges' widths. After obtaining the explainability scores, we used the Genetic Algorithm to identify the "best" subnetwork with maximum fitness. The fitness of a subnetwork was defined as the average of explainability scores of its nodes . This resulted in a subnetwork with 10 genes including *IFIH1*, *OAS1*, *OAS3*, *MX1*, *IFNAR1*, *IL10RB*, *ZNFX1*, *NLRC5*, *TRIM40*, and *ABCE1* (Figure 3.B). Finally, we performed pathway enrichment analysis using the Reactome database as reference and kept significantly enriched pathways with FDR $\leq$ 0.05. Top 10 resulting pathways are shown in figure 4.

4 Discussion

In this study we aim to harness the potential of DNA foundation models to translate the intricate 'language' of DNA into meaningful and actionable information. We propose a framework to utilize DNA-LMs for gene prioritization and pathway identification in rare disease studies. Based on the hypothesis that variants with strong deleterious effects alter the gene embeddings significantly in the embedding space, we demonstrate that it is possible to prioritize disease-associated genes/pathways in a cohort of 120 children requiring intensive care support because of a severe illness caused by a

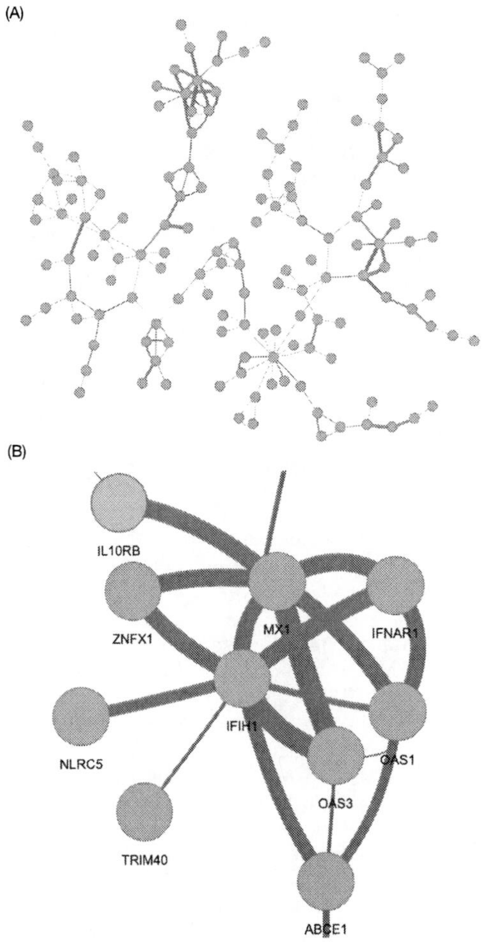

Figure 3: Subnetwork identification results. (A) PPI of candidate genes scored using GNNExplainer. The thickness of edges reflects the importance of nodes connected to it. (B) Selected subnetwork with maximum fitness, defined as the average nodes' importance scores. This subnetwork is identified via the Genetic Algorithm.

respiratory virus.

For gene prioritization, we propose two approaches to analyze the gene embeddings (Figure 1a): case-vs-control and case-only. The case-only approach is particularly promising for rare disease research, where finding a well-matched control group is often challenging. The ability of the method to differentiate between mutant and non-mutant gene embeddings within the same patient cohort is a novel and practical solution to this long-standing issue. By applying the gene prioritization workflow, we successfully re-identified *IFIH1* - which encodes an RIG-I-like receptor involved in the sensing of viral RNA (Rehwinkel and Gack, 2020) - as the top candidate gene in our patient cohort.

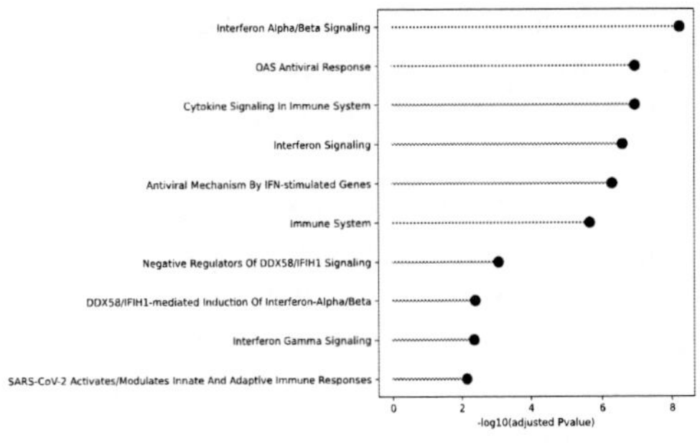

Figure 4: Top 10 significantly enriched pathways using the Reactome database. Genes in the selected subnetwork were used as input.

For pathway identification, we propose an integrative method, combining DNA-LM with interpretable GNN and Genetic Algorithm (Figure 1b). This approach takes into account various information such as PPI, number of variant carriers, and context-specific impact of variants on gene sequences. By applying this method, we were able to identify potentially relevant genes (*IFIH1*, *OAS1*, *OAS3*, *MX1*, *IFNAR1*, *IL10RB*, *ZNFX1*, *NLRC5*, *TRIM40*, and *ABCE1*) that can explain the disease pathogenesis.

All the identified genes are coding for molecules that play an important role in antiviral defense. *IFIH1* encodes MDA5, which is a cytoplasmic viral RNA sensor that recognizes single- or double-strand RNA to launch a type 1 interferon response (Rehwinkel and Gack, 2020). *OAS1* and *OAS3* encode enzymes that activate host RNase L to degrade viral RNA (Hornung et al., 2014). *ABCE1* encodes a protein that is involved in the regulation of OAS/RNase L pathway (Martinand et al., 1998). *MX1* encodes a guanosine-triphosphate-metabolizing protein that antagonizes the replication process of viruses (Haller and Kochs, 2019). *IFNAR1* and *IL10RB* encode cytokine receptors that mediate the antiviral immunity (Zanin et al., 2021; Moore et al., 2001). *ZNFX1* encodes a protein that binds to viral RNA and interacts with mitochondrial antiviral signaling (MAVS) protein, promoting the expression of interferon-stimulated genes (Vavassori et al., 2021). *NLRC5* and *TRIM40* encode regulators of antiviral signaling pathways (Kuenzel et al., 2010; Zhao et al., 2017). Deficiencies in some of these genes have been previously studied and shown to impair immunity against specific human viruses (Lamborn et al., 2017; Asgari et al., 2017; Chen et al., 2021; Abolhassani et al., 2022; Korol et al., 2023; Saadat et al., 2023; Lee et al., 2023).

In this study we focused on DNA-LMs, although protein language models (pLMs) such as ESM-1b (Brandes et al., 2023) have demonstrated state-of-the-art performance in scoring missense variants. The reason we used a DNA-LM instead of pLM is that DNA-LMs can model various variant types (e.g., splicing, stop-gained, etc.) while pLMs focus only on missense variants. Moreover, by using DNA-LMs, our method can be extended to other variant types such as those mapping to introns, branchpoint motives, or untranslated regions (UTRs).

While our method shows promise, there are inherent challenges and limitations. Our proposed workflow identifies genes with significant changes in their embeddings, yet a careful analysis is required to quantify the minimum embedding distortion to be detectable by the model. Moreover, the interpretation of gene embeddings requires careful consideration, since not all genetic variations captured in the embeddings might be clinically relevant.

The potential for integrating DNA-LMs with other techniques, such as multi-omics, could further enhance our understanding of genetic diseases. This has significant implications for the identification of disease-causing genes/pathways, potentially leading to more targeted and effective treatments in personalized medicine. The demonstration that DNA-LMs can accurately identify genes and pathways involved in rare diseases paves the way for further research and application of artificial intelligence in various genomics research domains.

Code Availability

The code for this study is available here.

References

Hassan Abolhassani, Nils Landegren, Paul Bastard, Marie Materna, Mohammadreza Modaresi, Likun Du, Maribel Aranda-Guillén, Fabian Sardh, Fanglei Zuo, Peng Zhang, Harold Marcotte, Nico Marr, Taushif Khan, Manar Ata, Fatima Al-Ali, Remi Pescarmona, Alexandre Belot, Vivien Béziat, Qian Zhang, Jean-Laurent Casanova, Olle Kämpe, Shen-Ying Zhang, Lennart Hammarström, and Qiang Pan-Hammarström. 2022. Inherited IFNAR1 deficiency in a child with both critical COVID-19 pneumonia and multisystem inflammatory syndrome. *J. Clin. Immunol.*, 42(3):471–483.

Joanna S Amberger, Carol A Bocchini, Alan F Scott, and Ada Hamosh. 2018. Omim.org: leveraging knowledge across phenotype–gene relationships. *Nucleic Acids Research*, 47(D1):D1038–D1043.

Samira Asgari, Luregn J. Schlapbach, Stéphanie Anchisi, Christian Hammer, Istvan Bartha, Thomas Junier, Geneviève Mottet-Osman, Klara M. Posfay-Barbe, David Longchamp, Martin Stocker, Samuel Cordey, Laurent Kaiser, Thomas Riedel, Tony Kenna, Deborah Long, Andreas Schibler, Amalio Telenti, Caroline Tapparel, Paul J. McLaren, Dominique Garcin, and Jacques Fellay. 2017. Severe viral respiratory infections in children with ifih1 loss-of-function mutations. *Proceedings of the National Academy of Sciences*, 114(31):8342–8347.

Paul L Auer and Guillaume Lettre. 2015. Rare variant association studies: considerations, challenges and opportunities. *Genome Medicine*, 7(1):16.

Adam Auton, 1000 Genomes Project Consortium, Shane McCarthy, Gil A. McVean, and Goncalo R. Abecasis. 2015. A global reference for human genetic variation. *Nature*, 526(7571):68–74.

Gonzalo Benegas, Sanjit Singh Batra, and Yun S. Song. 2023. Dna language models are powerful predictors of genome-wide variant effects. *Proceedings of the National Academy of Sciences*, 120(44).

Nadav Brandes, Grant Goldman, Charlotte H. Wang, Chun Jimmie Ye, and Vasilis Ntranos. 2023. Genome-wide prediction of disease variant effects with a deep protein language model. *Nature Genetics*, 55(9):1512–1522.

Shifu Chen, Yanqing Zhou, Yaru Chen, and Jia Gu. 2018. fastp: an ultra-fast all-in-one fastq preprocessor. *Bioinformatics*, 34(17):i884–i890.

Siwei Chen, Laurent C. Francioli, Genome Aggregation Database (gnomAD) Consortium, Grace Tiao, Benjamin M. Neale, Daniel G. MacArthur, and Konrad J. Karczewski. 2023. A genomic mutational constraint map using variation in 76, 156 human genomes. *Nature*, 625(7993):92–100.

Yongkun Chen, Laura Graf, Tao Chen, Qijun Liao, Tian Bai, Philipp P Petric, Wenfei Zhu, Lei Yang, Jie Dong, Jian Lu, Ying Chen, Juan Shen, Otto Haller, Peter Staeheli, Georg Kochs, Dayan Wang, Martin Schwemmle, and Yuelong Shu. 2021. Rare variant MX1 alleles increase human susceptibility to zoonotic H7N9 influenza virus. *Science*, 373(6557):918–922.

Davide Chicco and Giuseppe Agapito. 2022. Nine quick tips for pathway enrichment analysis. *PLOS Computational Biology*, 18(8):e1010348.

Micaela E. Consens, Cameron Dufault, Michael Wainberg, Duncan Forster, Mehran Karimzadeh, Hani Goodarzi, Fabian J. Theis, Alan Moses, and Bo Wang. 2023. To transformers and beyond: Large language models for the genome. *arXiv preprint*.

Hugo Dalla-Torre, Liam Gonzalez, Javier Mendoza-Revilla, Nicolas Lopez Carranza, Adam Henryk Grzywaczewski, Francesco Oteri, Christian Dallago, Evan Trop, Bernardo P. de Almeida, Hassan Sirelkhatim, Guillaume Richard, Marcin Skwark, Karim Beguir, Marie Lopez, and Thomas Pierrot. 2023. The nucleotide transformer: Building and evaluating robust foundation models for human genomics.

Mark A DePristo, Eric Banks, Ryan Poplin, Kiran V Garimella, Jared R Maguire, Christopher Hartl, Anthony A Philippakis, Guillermo del Angel, Manuel A Rivas, Matt Hanna, Aaron McKenna, Tim J Fennell, Andrew M Kernytsky, Andrey Y Sivachenko, Kristian Cibulskis, Stacey B Gabriel, David Altshuler, and Mark J Daly. 2011. A framework for variation discovery and genotyping using next-generation dna sequencing data. *Nature Genetics*, 43(5):491–498.

Jacob Devlin, Ming-Wei Chang, Kenton Lee, and Kristina Toutanova. 2018. Bert: Pre-training of deep bidirectional transformers for language understanding. *arXiv preprint*.

Martin Ester, Hans-Peter Kriegel, Jörg Sander, and Xiaowei Xu. 1996. A density-based algorithm for discovering clusters in large spatial databases with noise. In *Proceedings of the Second International Conference on Knowledge Discovery and Data Mining*, KDD'96, page 226–231. AAAI Press.

Zhuoqing Fang, Xinyuan Liu, and Gary Peltz. 2022. Gseapy: a comprehensive package for performing gene set enrichment analysis in python. *Bioinformatics*, 39(1).

Matthias Fey and Jan Eric Lenssen. 2019. Fast graph representation learning with pytorch geometric. *Preprint*, arXiv:1903.02428.

Michael D. Gallagher and Alice S. Chen-Plotkin. 2018. The post-gwas era: From association to function. *The American Journal of Human Genetics*, 102(5):717–730.

Jesse Gillis and Paul Pavlidis. 2012. "guilt by association" is the exception rather than the rule in gene networks. *PLoS Computational Biology*, 8(3):e1002444.

Dimitri Guala and Erik L. L. Sonnhammer. 2017. A large-scale benchmark of gene prioritization methods. *Scientific Reports*, 7(1).

Otto Haller and Georg Kochs. 2019. Mx genes: host determinants controlling influenza virus infection and trans-species transmission. *Human Genetics*, 139(6–7):695–705.

Veit Hornung, Rune Hartmann, Andrea Ablasser, and Karl-Peter Hopfner. 2014. Oas proteins and cgas: unifying concepts in sensing and responding to cytosolic nucleic acids. *Nature Reviews Immunology*, 14(8):521–528.

Konrad J. Karczewski, FGenome Aggregation Database (gnomAD) Consortium, and Daniel G. MacArthur. 2020. The mutational constraint spectrum quantified from variation in 141, 456 humans. *Nature*, 581(7809):434–443.

Sourabh Katoch, Sumit Singh Chauhan, and Vijay Kumar. 2020. A review on genetic algorithm: past, present, and future. *Multimedia Tools and Applications*, 80(5):8091–8126.

R. J. Kinsella, A. Kahari, S. Haider, J. Zamora, G. Proctor, G. Spudich, J. Almeida-King, D. Staines, P. Derwent, A. Kerhornou, P. Kersey, and P. Flicek. 2011. Ensembl biomarts: a hub for data retrieval across taxonomic space. *Database*, 2011(0):bar030–bar030.

Cecilia B Korol, Serkan Belkaya, Fahad Alsohime, Lazaro Lorenzo, Stéphanie Boisson-Dupuis, Joseph Brancale, Anna-Lena Neehus, Silvia Vilarinho, Alsum Zobaida, Rabih Halwani, Saleh Al-Muhsen, Jean-Laurent Casanova, and Emmanuelle Jouanguy. 2023. Fulminant viral hepatitis in two siblings with inherited IL-10RB deficiency. *J. Clin. Immunol.*, 43(2):406–420.

Sven Kuenzel, Andreas Till, Michael Winkler, Robert Häsler, Simone Lipinski, Sascha Jung, Joachim Grötzinger, Helmut Fickenscher, Stefan Schreiber, and Philip Rosenstiel. 2010. The nucleotide-binding oligomerization domain-like receptor nlrc5 is involved in ifn-dependent antiviral immune responses. *The Journal of Immunology*, 184(4):1990–2000.

Maxim V. Kuleshov, Matthew R. Jones, Andrew D. Rouillard, Nicolas F. Fernandez, Qiaonan Duan, Zichen Wang, Simon Koplev, Sherry L. Jenkins, Kathleen M. Jagodnik, Alexander Lachmann, Michael G. McDermott, Caroline D. Monteiro, Gregory W. Gundersen, and Avi Ma'ayan. 2016. Enrichr: a comprehensive gene set enrichment analysis web server 2016 update. *Nucleic Acids Research*, 44(W1):W90–W97.

Ian T. Lamborn, Huie Jing, Yu Zhang, Scott B. Drutman, Jordan K. Abbott, Shirin Munir, Sangeeta Bade, Heardley M. Murdock, Celia P. Santos, Linda G. Brock, Evan Masutani, Emmanuel Y. Fordjour, Joshua J. McElwee, Jason D. Hughes, Dave P. Nichols, Aziz Belkadi, Andrew J. Oler, Corinne S. Happel, Helen F. Matthews, Laurent Abel, Peter L. Collins, Kanta Subbarao, Erwin W. Gelfand, Michael J. Ciancanelli, Jean-Laurent Casanova, and Helen C. Su. 2017. Recurrent rhinovirus infections in a child with inherited mda5 deficiency. *Journal of Experimental Medicine*, 214(7):1949–1972.

Danyel Lee, Jérémie Le Pen, Ahmad Yatim, Beihua Dong, Yann Aquino, Masato Ogishi, Rémi

Pescarmona, Estelle Talouarn, Darawan Rinchai, Peng Zhang, Magali Perret, Zhiyong Liu, Iolanda Jordan, Sefika Elmas Bozdemir, Gulsum Iclal Bayhan, Camille Beaufils, Lucy Bizien, Aurelie Bisiaux, Weite Lei, Milena Hasan, Jie Chen, Christina Gaughan, Abhishek Asthana, Valentina Libri, Joseph M Luna, Fabrice Jaffré, H-Heinrich Hoffmann, Eleftherios Michailidis, Marion Moreews, Yoann Seeleuthner, Kaya Bilguvar, Shrikant Mane, Carlos Flores, Yu Zhang, Andrés A Arias, Rasheed Bailey, Agatha Schlüter, Baptiste Milisavljevic, Benedetta Bigio, Tom Le Voyer, Marie Materna, Adrian Gervais, Marcela Moncada-Velez, Francesca Pala, Tomi Lazarov, Romain Levy, Anna-Lena Neehus, Jérémie Rosain, Jessica Peel, Yi-Hao Chan, Marie-Paule Morin, Rosa Maria Pino-Ramirez, Serkan Belkaya, Lazaro Lorenzo, Jordi Anton, Selket Delafontaine, Julie Toubiana, Fanny Bajolle, Victoria Fumadó, Marta L DeDiego, Nadhira Fidouh, Flore Rozenberg, Jordi Pérez-Tur, Shuibing Chen, Todd Evans, Frédéric Geissmann, Pierre Lebon, Susan R Weiss, Damien Bonnet, Xavier Duval, CoV-Contact Cohort§, COVID Human Genetic Effort¶, Qiang Pan-Hammarström, Anna M Planas, Isabelle Meyts, Filomeen Haerynck, Aurora Pujol, Vanessa Sancho-Shimizu, Clifford L Dalgard, Jacinta Bustamante, Anne Puel, Stéphanie Boisson-Dupuis, Bertrand Boisson, Tom Maniatis, Qian Zhang, Paul Bastard, Luigi Notarangelo, Vivien Béziat, Rebeca Perez de Diego, Carlos Rodriguez-Gallego, Helen C Su, Richard P Lifton, Emmanuelle Jouanguy, Aurélie Cobat, Laia Alsina, Sevgi Keles, Elie Haddad, Laurent Abel, Alexandre Belot, Lluis Quintana-Murci, Charles M Rice, Robert H Silverman, Shen-Ying Zhang, and Jean-Laurent Casanova. 2023. Inborn errors of OAS-RNase L in SARS-CoV-2-related multisystem inflammatory syndrome in children. *Science*, 379(6632):eabo3627.

Insuk Lee, U. Martin Blom, Peggy I. Wang, Jung Eun Shim, and Edward M. Marcotte. 2011. Prioritizing candidate disease genes by network-based boosting of genome-wide association data. *Genome Research*, 21(7):1109–1121.

Heng Li and Richard Durbin. 2009. Fast and accurate short read alignment with burrows–wheeler transform. *Bioinformatics*, 25(14):1754–1760.

Ilya Loshchilov and Frank Hutter. 2019. Decoupled weight decay regularization. *Preprint*, arXiv:1711.05101.

D. G. MacArthur, T. A. Manolio, D. P. Dimmock, H. L. Rehm, J. Shendure, G. R. Abecasis, D. R. Adams, R. B. Altman, S. E. Antonarakis, E. A. Ashley, J. C. Barrett, L. G. Biesecker, D. F. Conrad, G. M. Cooper, N. J. Cox, M. J. Daly, M. B. Gerstein, D. B. Goldstein, J. N. Hirschhorn, S. M. Leal, L. A. Pennacchio, J. A. Stamatoyannopoulos, S. R. Sunyaev, D. Valle, B. F. Voight, W. Winckler, and C. Gunter. 2014. Guidelines for investigating causality of sequence variants in human disease. *Nature*, 508(7497):469–476.

Frederikke Isa Marin, Felix Teufel, Marc Horlacher, Dennis Madsen, Dennis Pultz, Ole Winther, and Wouter Boomsma. 2023. Bend: Benchmarking dna language models on biologically meaningful tasks. *arXiv preprint*.

Camille Martinand, Tamim Salehzada, Michelle Silhol, Bernard Lebleu, and Catherine Bisbal. 1998. Rnase l inhibitor (rli) antisense constructions block partially the down regulation of the 2-5a/rnase l pathway in encephalomyocarditis-virus-(emcv)-infected cells. *European Journal of Biochemistry*, 254(2):248–255.

William McLaren, Laurent Gil, Sarah E. Hunt, Harpreet Singh Riat, Graham R. S. Ritchie, Anja Thormann, Paul Flicek, and Fiona Cunningham. 2016. The ensembl variant effect predictor. *Genome Biology*, 17(1).

Michael L. Metzker. 2009. Sequencing technologies — the next generation. *Nature Reviews Genetics*, 11(1):31–46.

Marija Milacic, Deidre Beavers, Patrick Conley, Chuqiao Gong, Marc Gillespie, Johannes Griss, Robin Haw, Bijay Jassal, Lisa Matthews, Bruce May, Robert Petryszak, Eliot Ragueneau, Karen Rothfels, Cristoffer Sevilla, Veronica Shamovsky, Ralf Stephan, Krishna Tiwari, Thawfeek Varusai, Joel Weiser, Adam Wright, Guanming Wu, Lincoln Stein, Henning Hermjakob, and Peter D'Eustachio. 2023. The reactome pathway knowledgebase 2024. *Nucleic Acids Research*, 52(D1):D672–D678.

Kevin W. Moore, Rene de Waal Malefyt, Robert L. Coffman, and Anne O'Garra. 2001. Interleukin-10 and the interleukin-10 receptor. *Annual Review of Immunology*, 19(1):683–765.

Eric Nguyen, Michael Poli, Marjan Faizi, Armin Thomas, Callum Birch-Sykes, Michael Wornow, Aman Patel, Clayton Rabideau, Stefano Massaroli, Yoshua Bengio, Stefano Ermon, Stephen A. Baccus, and Chris Ré. 2023. Hyenadna: Long-range genomic sequence modeling at single nucleotide resolution. *arXiv preprint*.

F. Pedregosa, G. Varoquaux, A. Gramfort, V. Michel, B. Thirion, O. Grisel, M. Blondel, P. Prettenhofer, R. Weiss, V. Dubourg, J. Vanderplas, A. Passos, D. Cournapeau, M. Brucher, M. Perrot, and E. Duchesnay. 2011. Scikit-learn: Machine learning in Python. *Journal of Machine Learning Research*, 12:2825–2830.

Alec Radford, Jeff Wu, Rewon Child, David Luan, Dario Amodei, and Ilya Sutskever. 2019. Language models are unsupervised multitask learners.

Jan Rehwinkel and Michaela U. Gack. 2020. Rig-i-like receptors: their regulation and roles in rna sensing. *Nature Reviews Immunology*, 20(9):537–551.

Sue Richards, Nazneen Aziz, Sherri Bale, David Bick, Soma Das, Julie Gastier-Foster, Wayne W. Grody, Madhuri Hegde, Elaine Lyon, Elaine Spector, Karl

Voelkerding, and Heidi L. Rehm. 2015. Standards and guidelines for the interpretation of sequence variants: a joint consensus recommendation of the american college of medical genetics and genomics and the association for molecular pathology. *Genetics in Medicine*, 17(5):405–424.

Ali Saadat and Jacques Fellay. 2024. Fine-tuning the ESM2 protein language model to understand the functional impact of missense variants. In *ICML 2024 Workshop on Efficient and Accessible Foundation Models for Biological Discovery*.

Ali Saadat, Jérôme Gouttenoire, Paolo Ripellino, David Semela, Soraya Amar, Beat M. Frey, Stefano Fontana, Elise Mdawar-Bailly, Darius Moradpour, Jacques Fellay, and Montserrat Fraga. 2023. Inborn errors of type i interferon immunity in patients with symptomatic acute hepatitis e. *Hepatology*, 79(6):1421–1431.

Eleanor G Seaby and Sarah Ennis. 2020. Challenges in the diagnosis and discovery of rare genetic disorders using contemporary sequencing technologies. *Briefings in Functional Genomics*, 19(4):243–258.

Damian Szklarczyk, Rebecca Kirsch, Mikaela Koutrouli, Katerina Nastou, Farrokh Mehryary, Radja Hachilif, Annika L Gable, Tao Fang, Nadezhda T Doncheva, Sampo Pyysalo, Peer Bork, Lars J Jensen, and Christian von Mering. 2023. The STRING database in 2023: protein-protein association networks and functional enrichment analyses for any sequenced genome of interest. *Nucleic Acids Res.*, 51(D1):D638–D646.

Sean V. Tavtigian, Marc S. Greenblatt, Steven M. Harrison, Robert L. Nussbaum, Snehit A. Prabhu, Kenneth M. Boucher, and Leslie G. Biesecker. 2018. Modeling the acmg/amp variant classification guidelines as a bayesian classification framework. *Genetics in Medicine*, 20(9):1054–1060.

Emil Uffelmann, Qin Qin Huang, Nchangwi Syntia Munung, Jantina de Vries, Yukinori Okada, Alicia R. Martin, Hilary C. Martin, Tuuli Lappalainen, and Danielle Posthuma. 2021. Genome-wide association studies. *Nature Reviews Methods Primers*, 1(1).

Ege Ulgen, Ozan Ozisik, and Osman Ugur Sezerman. 2019. pathfindr: An r package for comprehensive identification of enriched pathways in omics data through active subnetworks. *Frontiers in Genetics*, 10.

Stefano Vavassori, Janet Chou, Laura Eva Faletti, Veronika Haunerdinger, Lennart Opitz, Pascal Joset, Christopher J. Fraser, Seraina Prader, Xianfei Gao, Luise A. Schuch, Matias Wagner, Julia Hoefele, Maria Elena Maccari, Ying Zhu, George Elakis, Michael T. Gabbett, Maria Forstner, Heymut Omran, Thomas Kaiser, Christina Kessler, Heike Olbrich, Patrick Frosk, Abduarahman Almutairi, Craig D. Platt, Megan Elkins, Sabrina Weeks, Tamar Rubin, Raquel Planas, Tommaso Marchetti, Danil Koovely, Verena Klämbt, Neveen A. Soliman, Sandra von Hardenberg, Christian Klemann, Ulrich Baumann, Dominic Lenz, Andreas Klein-Franke, Martin Schwemmle, Michael Huber, Ekkehard Sturm, Steffen Hartleif, Karsten Häffner, Charlotte Gimpel, Barbara Brotschi, Guido Laube, Tayfun Güngör, Michael F. Buckley, Raimund Kottke, Christian Staufner, Friedhelm Hildebrandt, Simone Reu-Hofer, Solange Moll, Achim Weber, Hundeep Kaur, Stephan Ehl, Sebastian Hiller, Raif Geha, Tony Roscioli, Matthias Griese, and Jana Pachlopnik Schmid. 2021. Multisystem inflammation and susceptibility to viral infections in human znfx1 deficiency. *Journal of Allergy and Clinical Immunology*, 148(2):381–393.

Thomas Wolf, Lysandre Debut, Victor Sanh, Julien Chaumond, Clement Delangue, Anthony Moi, Pierric Cistac, Tim Rault, Rémi Louf, Morgan Funtowicz, Joe Davison, Sam Shleifer, Patrick von Platen, Clara Ma, Yacine Jernite, Julien Plu, Canwen Xu, Teven Le Scao, Sylvain Gugger, Mariama Drame, Quentin Lhoest, and Alexander M. Rush. 2019. Huggingface's transformers: State-of-the-art natural language processing. *arXiv preprint*.

Jiaxin Wu, Mingxin Gan, and Rui Jiang. 2011. A genetic algorithm for optimizing subnetwork markers for the study of breast cancer metastasis. In *2011 Seventh International Conference on Natural Computation*. IEEE.

Zonghan Wu, Shirui Pan, Fengwen Chen, Guodong Long, Chengqi Zhang, and Philip S. Yu. 2021. A comprehensive survey on graph neural networks. *IEEE Transactions on Neural Networks and Learning Systems*, 32(1):4–24.

Rex Ying, Dylan Bourgeois, Jiaxuan You, Marinka Zitnik, and Jure Leskovec. 2019. Gnnexplainer: Generating explanations for graph neural networks. *Preprint*, arXiv:1903.03894.

Natacha Zanin, Christine Viaris de Lesegno, Christophe Lamaze, and Cedric M. Blouin. 2021. Interferon receptor trafficking and signaling: Journey to the cross roads. *Frontiers in Immunology*, 11.

Muhan Zhang, Zhicheng Cui, Marion Neumann, and Yixin Chen. 2018. An end-to-end deep learning architecture for graph classification. *Proceedings of the AAAI Conference on Artificial Intelligence*, 32(1).

Si Zhang, Hanghang Tong, Jiejun Xu, and Ross Maciejewski. 2019. Graph convolutional networks: a comprehensive review. *Computational Social Networks*, 6(1).

Chunyuan Zhao, Mutian Jia, Hui Song, Zhongxia Yu, Wenwen Wang, Qi Li, Lining Zhang, Wei Zhao, and Xuetao Cao. 2017. The e3 ubiquitin ligase trim40 attenuates antiviral immune responses by targeting mda5 and rig-i. *Cell Reports*, 21(6):1613–1623.

Wayne Xin Zhao, Kun Zhou, Junyi Li, Tianyi Tang, Xiaolei Wang, Yupeng Hou, Yingqian Min, Beichen Zhang, Junjie Zhang, Zican Dong, Yifan Du, Chen

Yang, Yushuo Chen, Zhipeng Chen, Jinhao Jiang, Ruiyang Ren, Yifan Li, Xinyu Tang, Zikang Liu, Peiyu Liu, Jian-Yun Nie, and Ji-Rong Wen. 2023. A survey of large language models. *arXiv preprint*.

Zhihan Zhou, Yanrong Ji, Weijian Li, Pratik Dutta, Ramana Davuluri, and Han Liu. 2023. Dnabert-2: Efficient foundation model and benchmark for multi-species genome. *arXiv preprint*.

A Appendix

We used ACMG/AMP guidelines (Richards et al., 2015) to classify the variant into putative pathogenicity groups, as described in our previous works (Saadat et al., 2023; Saadat and Fellay, 2024). In summary, we gather all the available evidences for a variant. Table 1 summarizes all the ACMG/AMP criteria that we used.

	Benign		Pathogenic			
	Strong	Supporting	Supporting	Moderate	Strong	Very strong
Population and controls	MAF is high in the population (BS1)		MAF is rare in the population and absent from the controls (PM2_supporting)			
Computational		Missense in a gene where mostly truncating variants cause disease (BP1) In-frame indel in a repeat region (BP3) Computational evidence suggest no impact on gene product (BP4)	Computational evidence supports a deleterious effect on the gene product (PP3)	Protein length changing variant (PM4) Novel missense change at an amino acid residue Where a different pathogenic missense change has been seen before (PM5)	Same amino acid change as an established pathogenic variant (PS1) Low confidence null variant (PVS1_strong)	High confidence null variant (PVS1)
Functional	Well-established functional studies show no deleterious effect (BS3)		Missense in a gene with low rate of benign missense variants and missense variants are common mechanism of disease (PP2)	Mutational hotspot or well-studied functional domain without benign variation (PM1)	Well-established functional studies show a deleterious effect (PS3)	

Table 1: the summary of ACMG/AMP criteria used for variant classification. MAF: minor allele frequency

To calculate the probability of pathogenicity (PoP), we use the Bayesian framework developed by Tavtigian et al. (2018). For a given variant, the PoP is calculated as follow:

$$P_x = \text{number of pathogenic criteria applied at the level of } x$$
$$x \in \{\text{Very strong, Strong, Moderate, Supporting}\}$$

$$B_y = \text{number of benign criteria applied at the level of } y$$
$$y \in \{\text{Strong, Supporting}\}$$

$$\text{odds of pathogenicity (OP)} = 350^{\left(\frac{P_{\text{Very strong}}}{1} + \frac{P_{\text{Strong}}}{2} + \frac{P_{\text{Moderate}}}{4} + \frac{P_{\text{Supporting}}}{8} - \frac{B_{\text{Strong}}}{2} - \frac{B_{\text{Supporting}}}{8}\right)}$$

$$\text{probability of pathogenicity (PoP)} = \frac{OP \times 0.1}{((OP-1) \times 0.1 + 1)}$$

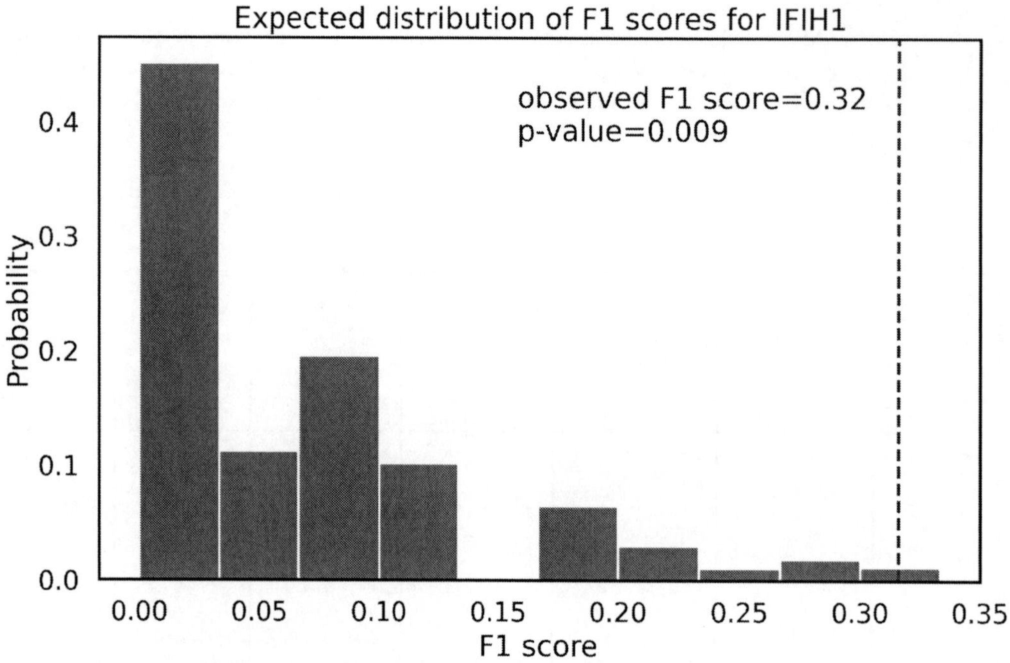

Supplementary Figure S1: Permutation test results for case-vs-control approach. Expected distribution of F_1 scores for *IFIH1* is shown in blue. The red line indicates the observed F_1 score.

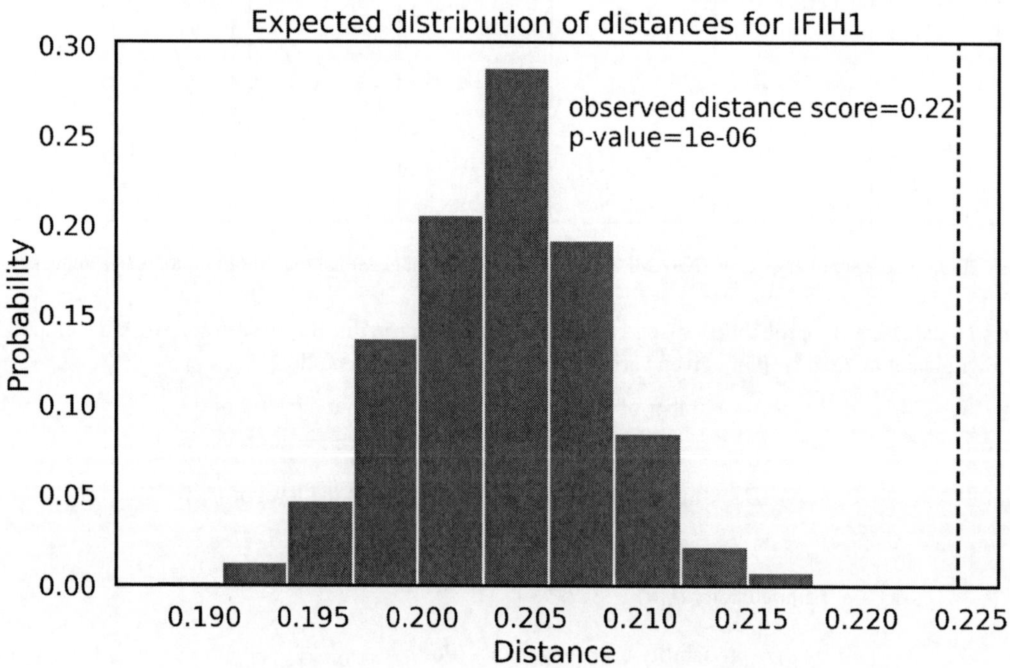

Supplementary Figure S2: Statistical test results for the case-only approach. Expected distribution of distance scores for *IFIH1* is shown in blue. The red line indicates the observed distance score.

Repurformer: Transformers for Repurposing-Aware Molecule Generation

Changhun Lee
UNIST
South Korea
changhun@unist.ac.kr

Gyumin Lee
Korea University
South Korea
optimizt@korea.ac.kr

Abstract

Generating as diverse molecules as possible with desired properties is crucial for drug discovery research, which invokes many approaches based on deep generative models today. Despite recent advancements in these models, particularly in variational autoencoders (VAEs), generative adversarial networks (GANs), Transformers, and diffusion models, a significant challenge known as *the sample bias problem* remains. This problem occurs when generated molecules targeting the same protein tend to be structurally similar, reducing the diversity of generation. To address this, we propose leveraging multi-hop relationships among proteins and compounds. Our model, Repurformer, integrates bi-directional pretraining with Fast Fourier Transform (FFT) and low-pass filtering (LPF) to capture complex interactions and generate diverse molecules. A series of experiments on BindingDB dataset confirm that Repurformer successfully creates substitutes for anchor compounds that resemble positive compounds, increasing diversity between the anchor and generated compounds.

1 Introduction

The design of valid and novel molecules with desired biological properties, known as *de novo* molecule generation, is vital to modern drug discovery. Recent advancements in deep generative models, particularly variational autoencoders (VAEs) (Kingma and Welling, 2022), generative adversarial networks (GANs) (Goodfellow et al., 2014), Transformers (Vaswani et al., 2017), and diffusion models (Ho et al., 2020), have significantly enhanced our ability to generate chemically valid and novel molecules. However, these models need to be further refined to generate molecules that interact with specific target proteins.

Target-specific molecule generation addresses this challenge by producing drug-like molecules that are more likely to bind with specific target proteins (Grechishnikova, 2021; Qian et al., 2022; Tan et al., 2022). Nonetheless, there remains a significant issue known as *the sample bias problem*, where reliance on existing protein-compound pairs results in the generation of structurally similar molecules. This phenomenon limits the diversity of generated molecules and hinders the discovery of novel compounds.

To address this, we propose leveraging multi-hop relationships among proteins and compounds to expand the generative space and increase the diversity of the generated molecules. Our method introduces the concept of repurposing-aware molecule generation, designed to identify and utilize latent multi-hop relations within the protein-compound interaction network.

In this paper, we present Repurformer, a novel model that integrates bi-directional pretraining and advanced signal processing techniques to overcome the limitations of existing models. Repurformer captures complex relationships between proteins and compounds by pretraining encoders in both protein-to-compound and compound-to-protein directions and applying Fast Fourier Transform (FFT) with low-pass filtering (LPF) to the latent space. This approach allows the model to distinguish the different scales of interactions. By focusing on low-frequency components, which correspond to the longer propagation through the multi-hop protein-compound interaction network, Repurformer generates as diverse compounds as possible with desired properties. In summary, the contributions of our work are threefold:

- We introduce a framework for repurposing-aware molecule generation to address the *sample bias problem* by leveraging multi-hop relations between proteins and compounds.

- We develop Repurformer, a model that integrates a bi-directional pretraining and an FFT-based approach to capture and utilize latent

Proceedings of the 1st Workshop on Language + Molecules (L+M 2024), pages 117–128
August 15, 2024 ©2024 Association for Computational Linguistics

multi-hop relations in an end-to-end manner.

- We demonstrate that Repurformer successfully generates valid and diverse molecules, creating substitutes for anchor compounds that resemble positive compounds.

2 Preliminaries

2.1 *De novo* Molecule Generation

De novo molecule generation is the process of exploring vast chemical space and producing novel molecules with desired biological properties. With the rapid advancement of artificial intelligence, recent deep generative models have been widely used in molecule generation tasks.

For example, several VAE variants have been introduced thanks to its manipulable latent space, such as charVAE (Gómez-Bombarelli et al., 2018), SD-VAE (Dai et al., 2018), and JT-VAE (Jin et al., 2018). GAN has been adopted due to their capability to generate new molecules that are highly similar in structure to existing ones, including ORGAN (Guimaraes et al., 2018), ORGANIC (Sanchez-Lengeling et al., 2017), and MolCycleGAN (Maziarka et al., 2020). More recently, Transformers and diffusion models have been utilized, based on their success in language modeling and image generation, respectively, such as MolGPT (Bagal et al., 2022), MDM (Huang et al., 2023), and GeoLDM (Xu et al., 2023).

2.2 Target-specific Molecule Generation

In drug discovery, identifying drug-target interactions (DTI) is crucial for understanding the bioactivity and therapeutic effects of drugs for specific diseases. Although the deep generative models have proved useful in generating novel and chemically valid molecules, further screening is necessary to evaluate their potential to bind with specific protein targets. Building on this notion, several researchers have developed target-specific molecule generation models to produce novel, drug-like molecules that are highly likely to interact with specific target proteins, including Transformer-based generation (Grechishnikova, 2021), AlphaDrug (Qian et al., 2022), SiamFlow (Tan et al., 2022) and POLYGON (Munson et al., 2024).

2.3 Repurposing-Aware Molecule Generation

Drug repurposing is a strategy that identifies new therapeutic uses for approved drugs beyond their original indications. This approach offers significant advantages over developing entirely new drug, such as lower failure risk and development costs. The concept of drug repurposing can be defined as multi-hop relationships in the protein-compound interaction network, which is not directly connected but can be accessed through intermediaries. In chemical spaces, proteins and compounds have many-to-many relationships based on their structural coordination. This leads to the assumption that if a compound can reach a specific protein through another compound that shares a common protein (*i.e.,* in the multi-hop relationship), there is potential for repurposing the focal compound.

The repurposability in chemical spaces can introduce a new paradigm for molecule generation, by serving as a key to expanding the generative space and increasing molecular diversity. Previous approaches for target-specific molecule generation tend to generate structurally similar molecules for a specific protein target due to their dependence on known protein-compound interactions. While incorporating randomness in the generation process can contribute to molecular diversity, it may neglect structural coordination with targets, possibly resulting in a trade-off between diversity and binding affinity. In this context, leveraging latent repurposability within the multi-hop relationships among proteins and compounds can provide a reasonable boundary for molecule generation, broadening the generative space and enhancing molecular diversity without sacrificing their drug potency.

3 Problem Statement

The discovery of new compounds often relies on existing protein-compound pairs. This results in that the compounds targeting the same protein exhibit similar structures. In other words, the generative space of models tends to be bounded in limited regions, reducing the diversity of the generation. We refer to this as a *sample bias problem*.

To address this problem, we leverage multi-hop relations among proteins and compounds. Specifically, given a pair of protein p and compound c that are known to interact, we assume that the compound relates to p within a 3-hop relation, *i.e.,* a positive compound c^+, has a potential interaction with p. Definitions from 3.1 to 3.3 describe the key concepts of our approach, and Figure 1 visually represents the rationale. Note that both protein and compound are represented by

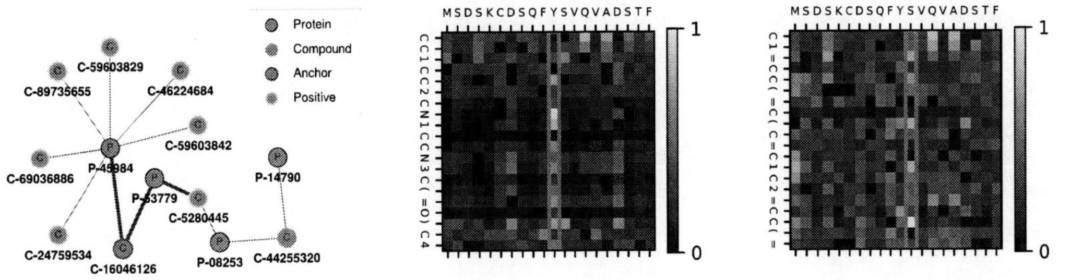

(a) Protein-Compound Graph (b) C-16046126 & P-45984 Attention (c) C-5280445 & P-45984 Attention

Figure 1: (a) illustrates a many-to-many relationship between proteins and compounds. The bold lines indicate potential repurposing flows by which, given an anchor compound's target protein p (P-45984), a positive compound c^+ (C-5280445) can be considered to replace the anchor compound $\acute{c}$ (C-16046126). Red boxes in (b) and (c) represent the parts of p (P-45984) to which $\acute{c}$ (C-16046126) and c^+ (C-5280445) attend, respectively. It is noteworthy that attending regions are right next to each other, implying c^+ may have a potential repurposability to p.

amino-acid and SMILES sequences, respectively: $p = [p_1, \cdots, p_{T_p}]$ and $c = [c_1, \cdots, c_{T_c}]$ with T_p and T_c being the fixed length of each sequence.

Definition 3.1 (Protein-Compound Graph). *The relations between proteins and compounds can be represented as a bipartite graph $\mathcal{G}(\mathcal{P} \cup \mathcal{C}, \mathcal{E})$, where $\mathcal{P}$ and $\mathcal{C}$ denote the sets of protein and compound nodes, respectively. Specifically, $p^{(i)} \in \mathcal{P}$ represents the i-th protein and $c^{(j)} \in \mathcal{C}$ represents the j-th compound, for $i = 1, \cdots, M$ and $j = 1, \cdots, N$.*

Definition 3.2 (Protein-Compound Pair). *A pair of nodes in $\mathcal{G}$ is represented by an edge $e_{ij} = \{(p^{(i)}, c^{(j)}) | p^{(i)} \in \mathcal{P}, c^{(j)} \in \mathcal{C}\} \in \mathcal{E}$. The presence of an edge e_{ij} indicates a link between the i-th protein and the j-th compound, such that $e_{ij} = 1$ if they are linked and $e_{ij} = 0$ otherwise.*

Definition 3.3 (Anchor/Positive Compounds). *Given a target protein $p^{(i)}$, a compound $c^{(j)}$ is defined as an anchor compound $\acute{c}$ if $e_{ij} = 1$. For another protein $p^{(k)}$ where $e_{kj} = 1$, any compound $c^{(l)}$ $(l \neq j)$ that satisfies $e_{kl} = 1$ is regarded as a positive compound c^+ for the target protein $p^{(i)}$.*

4 Repurformer

In this section, we propose Repurformer, a novel method designed to address the sample bias problem by leveraging multi-hop relations among proteins and compounds. Figure 2 illustrates how Repurformer seamlessly integrates the concepts of drug discovery and repurposing.

Bi-directional Pretraining To capture the many-to-many relationships between proteins and compounds, we employed bi-directional pretraining for the protein and compound encoders. Specifically, we built two Transformers with identical encoder-decoder structures but opposite training directions: one was trained in the protein-to-compound direction, and the other in the compound-to-protein direction (see Figure 2a). By doing so, we expect the protein encoder $f_p(c|p)$ and the compound encoder $f_c(p|c)$ to extract latent relations, z^p and z^c, that encompass both cases where proteins and compounds are the head and tail of an edge, and vice versa, *i.e.*, $f_p : c|p \to z^p$ and $f_c : p|c \to z^c$. For example, given a pair of $p^{(2)}$ and $c^{(1)}$ as shown in Figure 2b, z^p and z^c will represent the edges from $p^{(2)}$ to $c^{(1)}$ (*i.e.*, $p^{(2)} \to c^{(1)}$) and from $c^{(1)}$ to $p^{(1)}$ (*i.e.*, $c^{(1)} \to p^{(1)}$), respectively.

Transformer with Bi-directional Encoders The pretrained bi-encoders are then used as feature extractors; they are frozen and followed by a new compound decoder. The compound decoder $\pi(\cdot)$, parameterized by θ, receives a sum of the encoding vectors $h = z^p + z^c$ and a positive compound c^+ as inputs:

$$\hat{c}^+_{t+1} = \pi_\theta(\cdot | c^+_{1:t}, h_t) \quad \text{where} \quad h_t = z^p_t + z^c_t \,.$$

Here, $h_t \in \mathbb{R}^{|d|}$ represents a $|d|$-dimensional latent vector of 2-hop relation, *e.g.*, $p^{(2)} \overset{\text{1-hop}}{\to} c^{(1)}$ $(= \acute{c})$ $\overset{\text{2-hop}}{\to} p^{(1)}$ (see Figure 2b), from a t-th token perspective. Accordingly, feeding the compound decoder with a positive compound as a label enables it to learn potential repurposing relationships that emerge from an additional third-hop edge, *e.g.*, $\cdots \overset{\text{2-hop}}{\to} p^{(1)} \overset{\text{3-hop}}{\to} c^{(2)}$ $(= c^+)$. Putting it all to-

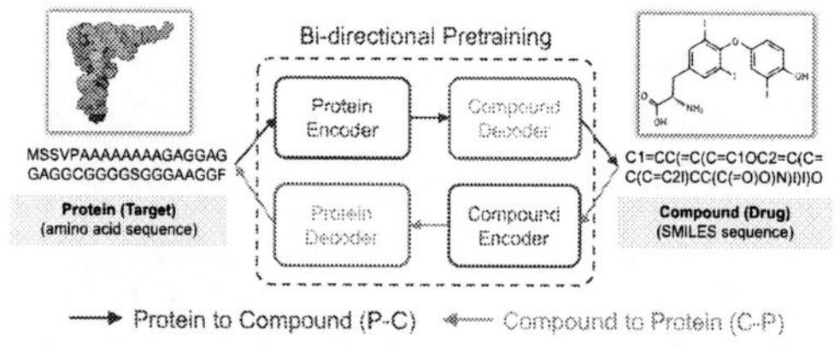

(a) Bi-directioanl Compound-Protein Relations Embedding

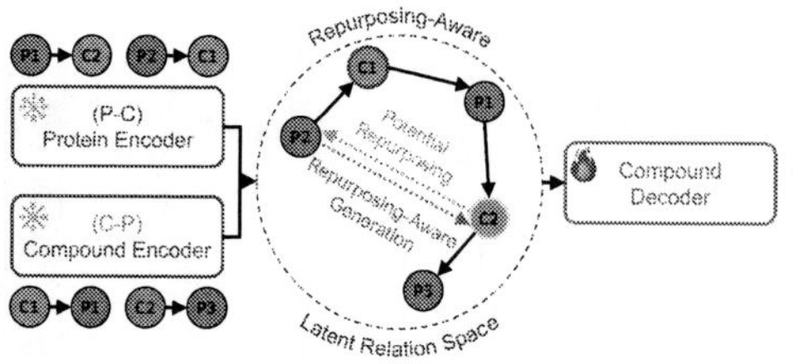

(b) Repurposing-Aware Molecule Generation

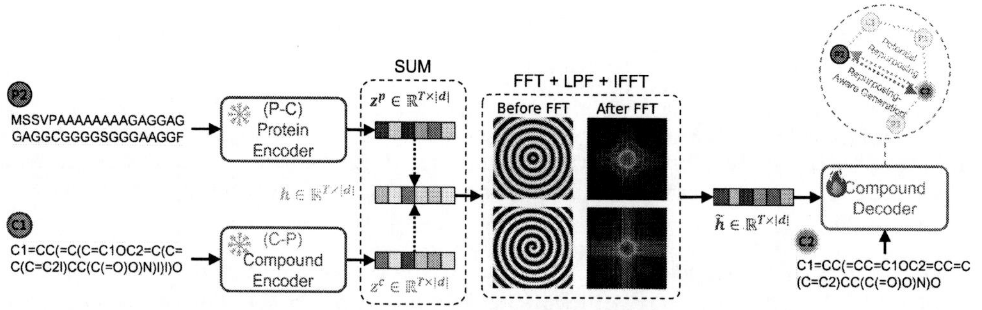

(c) Model Architecture

Figure 2: Overview of Repurformer

gether, the loss function is defined as follows:

$$\ln \pi_\theta(c^+|p, c) = \ln \prod_{t=1}^{T_c} \pi_\theta(c^+_{t+1}|c^+_{1:t}, p, \acute{c})$$
$$= \sum_{t=1}^{T_c} \ln \pi_\theta(c^+_{t+1}|c^+_{1:t}, p, \acute{c})$$

Fast Fourier Transform (FFT) The Fourier transform decomposes a function into its constituent frequencies using complex exponentials (sinusoids) as basis functions (Heckbert, 1995; Lee-Thorp et al., 2021). Given a sequence $\{x_1, \cdots, x_T\}$, the *discrete Fourier Transform* (DFT) is defined by the formula:

$$X_k = \sum_{t=0}^{T-1} x_t e^{-\frac{2\pi i}{T} tk}, \quad 0 \le k \le T-1$$

where X_k is the k-th frequency component, x_t is the t-th time-domain signal, and i is the imaginary unit. Calculating the DFT directly has a complexity of $O(T^2)$, which can be inefficient for large datasets. To address this, the *Fast Fourier Transform* (FFT) algorithm was proposed, reducing the complexity to $O(T \log T)$ (Cooley and Tukey, 1965; Brigham, 1988). In this study, we apply the FFT to $h \in \mathbb{R}^{T\times|d|}$ to construct eigenvectors along which the 2-hop propagation occurs. To be specific, the 2D DFT is utilized: one 1D DFT along the sequence dimension, $\mathcal{F}_{\text{seq}}$, and another 1D DFT along the feature dimension, $\mathcal{F}_{\text{dim}}$, keeping real-valued parts only as in Lee-Thorp et al. (2021):

$$H = \Re(\mathcal{F}_{\text{seq}}(\mathcal{F}_{\text{dim}}(h))) \in \mathbb{R}^{T\times|d|}.$$

Note that T is set to the length of a longer sequence; if $T_p > T_c$, then T is set as T_p and vice versa.

Low-Pass Filter (LPF) The Fourier-transformed features H comprise low frequencies that represent a globally smoothed signal and high frequencies that indicate a locally normalized signal. This separation of frequency components allows for distinct interpretations at different scales. For example, Tamkin et al. (2020) applied the discrete cosine transform (DCT) (Rao and Yip, 2014), which is closely related to the DFT, to separate latent information at different scales. They found that low frequencies capture topic-scale context while high frequencies capture word-scale context.

In our setting, a scale can be understood as the number of hops. Specifically, the lower frequency implies a longer propagation through multi-hop relations while the higher one implies a shorter propagation within a single-hop relation. From the repurposing perspective, we need to leverage the longer propagation so that only the multi-hop relations are considered. To achieve this, we can apply the *low-pass filtering* (Pollack, 1948; Costen et al., 1996), which removes the frequency components above a certain cutoff parameter α by setting

$H_{k,d} \leftarrow 0$ for all $k, d > \alpha$. This filtering can be easily implemented using a binary mask:

$$H_{\text{LPF}} = H \odot M$$

where $M = \{m_{t,d} | m_{t,d} \in \{0, 1\}, 1 \leq t \leq T, 1 \leq d \leq |d|\}$ is an one-hot matrix, with $m_{t,d} = 1$ for low-frequency components and $m_{t,d} = 0$ otherwise. Lastly, we transformed H_{LPF} back to the features of an original domain using the inverse FFT (IFFT), before passing it to the compound decoder:

$$\tilde{h} = \mathcal{F}_{\text{dim}}^{-1}(\mathcal{F}_{\text{seq}}^{-1}(H_{\text{LPF}})) \in \mathbb{R}^{T \times |d|} .$$

Implementation Details The structure of the Repurformer is essentially identical to that of pretrained transformers. It consists of encoder and decoder networks, each linearly stacked with 4 layers of 256 dimensions, with each layer divided into 4 heads of 64 dimensions. To tokenize the protein and compound sequences, we utilized existing vocabularies from previous works—the protein vocabulary from Rao et al. (2019) and the compound vocabulary from Honda et al. (2019). For training, we set the number of epochs, batch size, and learning rate to 20, 64, and 5e-05, respectively.

5 Experiments

Experiment Setup We collected data from BindingDB (Gilson et al., 2016) which contains over 2.8 million measured binding affinities of interactions between proteins and drug-like molecules. The collected dataset was then preprocessed to filter out missing values, duplicates, and proteins and compounds with excessively long or short sequences. In particular, given the many-to-many nature of protein-compound relationships, we selected compounds that interact with a reasonable number of individual proteins between 10 and 100, to enable our model to learn various compound structures reacting with different proteins. The resulting dataset comprised 60,719 protein-compound pairs derived from 3,006 proteins and 7,803 compounds. We split this dataset into train and test datasets with 8:2 ratio, ensuring that the proteins interacting with each compound did not overlap between the two sets. Our model was then trained on protein-compound pairs from the train set, representing proteins with amino acid sequences and compounds with canonicalized SMILES strings. We tokenized individual characters from amino acid sequences and SMILES strings, resulting in vocabularies containing 30 characters for proteins and 46 characters for compounds.

Evaluation Metrics To thoroughly assess the effectiveness and reliability of Repurformer, we employed several evaluation metrics, focusing on the generative performance of the model and physicochemical properties and drug-likeness of the molecules it generated. In terms of generative performance, we applied widely accepted metrics for sequence generation tasks: BLEU (Papineni et al., 2002), GLEU (Wu et al., 2016), and F1 score of ROUGE (Lin, 2004). In particular, we used 1- and 2-gram units as the evaluation basis for these generative metrics. We utilized physicochemical properties, specifically molecular weights and log of octanol-water partition coefficients (LogP) (Wildman and Crippen, 1999), to assess the feasibility of molecular structures as drugs. Furthermore, we used other widely used drug-likeness metrics, such as QED (Bickerton et al., 2012), SA (Ertl and Schuffenhauer, 2009), and NP (Ertl et al., 2008), to evaluate the potential effectiveness of the generated molecules as drug-like compounds.

Configurations This study aims to analyze whether the configuration of Repurformer is effective. Given that the distinguishing configuration of Repurformer is the application of FFT with LPF in the embedding space, we conducted comparative experiments with different configuration options:

- SUM Only: This is the baseline configuration. It directly passes h to the compound decoder.
- +FFT: This configuration transforms h to H but does not revert it to $\tilde{h}$.
- +MLP: This configuration adds a single fully-connected layer that mixes the values of h feature-wise.
- +FFT+MLP: This configuration mixes the frequencies of H.
- +FFT+MLP+IFFT w/ auxiliary losses: This configuration mixes the frequencies of H and reverts the mixed H to $\tilde{h}$. Note that L1, L2, and Frobenius norm are added as auxiliary losses to minimize the distance between the MLP output and $\tilde{h}$.

6 Results

Main Results To evaluate Repurformer, we conducted a comparative analysis of 11 configurations, focusing on generative performance, physicochemical properties, and drug-likeness.

		1-gram						2-gram					
		BLEU		GLEU		ROUGE		BLEU		GLEU		ROUGE	
		anc $\acute{c}$	pos c^+	anc $\acute{c}$	pos c^+	anc $\acute{c}$	pos c^+	anc $\acute{c}$	pos c^+	anc $\acute{c}$	pos c^+	anc $\acute{c}$	pos c^+
Baseline (SUM Only)		0.615	0.664	0.618	0.668	0.381	0.398	0.534	0.580	0.543	0.589	0.120	0.127
+FFT		0.155	0.164	0.179	0.188	0.060	0.054	0.098	0.104	0.126	0.132	0.024	0.016
+MLP		0.646	0.692	0.651	0.700	0.399	0.422	0.564	0.604	0.575	0.618	0.133	0.139
+FFT+MLP		0.281	0.289	0.306	0.318	0.011	0.012	0.144	0.156	0.198	0.209	0.004	0.004
+FFT+MLP+IFFT (w/ L1 Loss)		0.583	0.636	0.585	0.640	0.366	0.388	0.511	0.556	0.518	0.565	0.113	0.113
+FFT+MLP+IFFT (w/ L2 Loss)		0.623	0.672	0.627	0.679	0.382	0.398	0.543	0.588	0.553	0.600	0.118	0.123
+FFT+MLP+IFFT (w/ Frobenius Loss)		0.629	0.670	0.635	0.679	0.359	0.367	0.544	0.579	0.556	0.594	0.101	0.104
+FFT+LPF+IFFT (Ours)	α=2	0.620	0.660	0.626	0.670	0.331	0.348	0.512	0.548	0.528	0.567	0.102	0.112
	α=4	0.662	0.690	0.670	0.703	0.385	0.400	0.571	0.598	0.585	0.616	0.147	0.149
	α=6	0.583	0.630	0.587	0.635	0.386	0.406	0.513	0.553	0.521	0.563	0.142	0.150
	α=8	0.606	0.663	0.610	0.667	0.390	0.416	0.532	0.582	0.541	0.591	0.134	0.144

Table 1: Evaluation of Generative Performance. The numbers represent the average (n-gram-based) syntactic similarity of the generated compounds $\hat{c}^+$, which target specific proteins p, to both the anchor compounds $\acute{c}$ and the positive compounds c^+. Note that α is a cutoff parameter.

		MW	LogP
		$[0, \infty]$	$[-\infty, \infty]$
Baseline (SUM Only)		588.506	4.870
+FFT		*N/A*	*N/A*
+MLP		537.230	4.317
+FFT+MLP		533.193	11.559
+FFT+MLP+IFFT (w/ L1)		631.012	4.655
+FFT+MLP+IFFT (w/ L2)		554.490	4.892
+FFT+MLP+IFFT (w/ Frobenius)		572.882	6.092
+FFT+LPF+IFFT (Ours)	α=2	475.473	6.005
	α=4	479.357	3.888
	α=6	584.083	7.442
	α=8	566.942	5.529

Table 2: Evaluation of Physicochemical Properties. The numbers in the MW and LogP columns represent average molecular weights and octanol-water partition coefficients, respectively. By Lipinski's Rule of Five (Lipinski et al., 2012), compounds with MW $\leq$ 500 and LogP $\leq$ 5 have good absorption and permeation.

		QED	SA	NP
		$[0, 1]$	$[1, 10]$	$[-5, 5]$
Baseline (SUM Only)		0.320	4.033	-0.629
+FFT		*N/A*	*N/A*	*N/A*
+MLP		0.332	3.479	-0.796
+FFT+MLP		0.164	2.086	0.154
+FFT+MLP+IFFT (w/ L1)		0.227	4.209	-0.564
+FFT+MLP+IFFT (w/ L2)		0.355	3.696	-0.659
+FFT+MLP+IFFT (w/ Frobenius)		0.250	4.046	-0.368
+FFT+LPF+IFFT(Ours)	α=2	0.468	4.289	0.072
	α=4	0.598	2.696	-0.682
	α=6	0.254	3.067	-0.679
	α=8	0.352	3.404	-0.984

Table 3: Evaluation of Drug-Likeness. The numbers represent how likely the generated compounds are to be effective drugs. Note that QED, SA, and NP represent a compound's drug-likeness, synthetic accessibility, and natural product-likeness.

Table 1 shows the similarity of the generated compounds $\hat{c}^+$ to both the anchor $\acute{c}$ and positive c^+ compounds, calculated using BLEU, GLEU, and ROUGE scores. The results indicate that the "+MLP" and "Repurformer with $\alpha = 4$" exhibit remarkable performance compared to other configurations. Notably, the Repurformer ($\alpha = 4$) generated compounds with higher structural similarity to the anchor compounds than those generated by the +MLP configuration. This suggests that Repurformer successfully generates compounds that are potentially repurposable to the target proteins.

In Tables 2 and 3, we can compare the molecular properties of the generated compounds from different configurations. Table 2 shows that Repurformer with $\alpha = 4$ generates compounds that are the most physicochemically desirable. On the other hand, Table 3 shows that the Repurformer with $\alpha = 4$, with $\alpha = 2$, and "+FFT+MLP" configurations had comparative advantages in QED, SA, and NP, respectively. Given that QED is generally considered the most important metric for measuring drug similarity and efficacy, we can emphasize that Repurformer ($\alpha = 4$) excels in generating compounds with the highest potential for effective drug discovery. Figure 3 compares the generation results of the '+MLP' and 'Repurformer ($\alpha = 4$)' configurations.

Performance Comparison To assess the effectiveness of Repurformer as a target-specific molecule generation model, we compared its performance with the existing protein-specific generative approaches as external baseline models, including Transformer-based model (Grechishnikova, 2021) and AlphaDrug (Qian et al., 2022). Transformer-based model utilized the vanilla Transformer architecture (Vaswani et al., 2017) to generate compounds based on target proteins. This model viewed the target-specific molecule genera-

	1-gram				2-gram				Physicochemical Properties		Drug-Likeness		
	BLEU		GLEU		BLEU		GLEU						
	anc $\acute{c}$	pos c^+	anc $\acute{c}$	pos c^+	anc $\acute{c}$	pos c^+	anc $\acute{c}$	pos c^+	MW	LogP	QED	SA	NP
Repurformer (α=4)	0.662	0.690	0.670	0.703	0.571	0.598	0.585	0.616	479.357	3.888	0.598	2.696	-0.682
Transformer	0.541	0.495	0.599	0.572	0.476	0.440	0.533	0.513	9651.296	187.126	0.119	9.037	-0.128
AlphaDrug	0.638	0.652	0.665	0.685	0.555	0.567	0.585	0.603	389.616	2.947	0.507	2.685	-0.842

Table 4: Evaluation of Comparative Performance. Parts of evaluation metrics in terms of generative performance, physicochemical properties, and drug-likeness are used to compare the performance of Repurformer with the existing target-specific molecule generative models, such as Transformer and AlphaDrug.

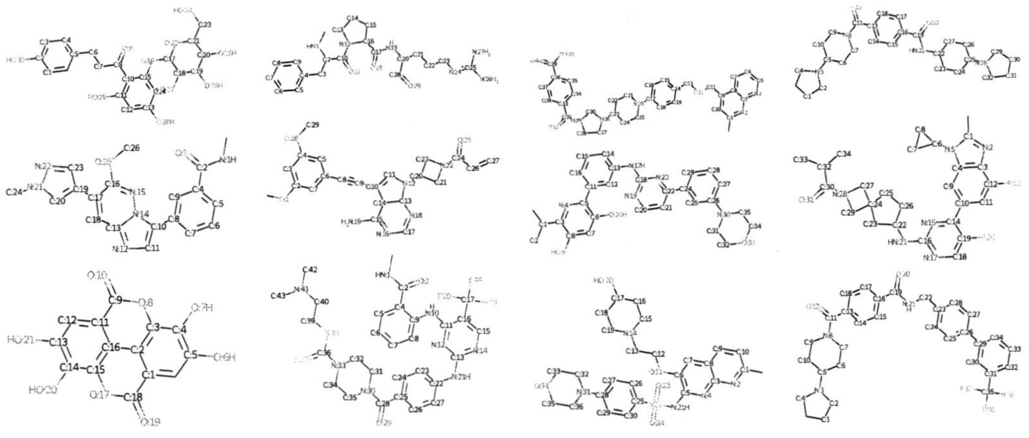

(a) Anchor $\acute{c}$ (b) Positive c^+ (c) Generated $\hat{c}^+$ (+MLP) (d) Generated $\hat{c}^+$ ($\alpha = 4$)

Figure 3: Comparison of 2D Molecule Drawings. From left to right, the drawings represent the anchor $\acute{c}$, positive c^+, and generated compounds $\hat{c}^+$, respectively. $\hat{c}^+$ is expected to interact with the target protein to which $\acute{c}$ interacts.

tion as a translational task, converting amino acid sequence into SMILES strings. AlphaDrug modified the vanilla Transformer by introducing skip-connections between its encoders and decoders, facilitating the joint embedding of target proteins and molecules. In addition, it employed a Monte Carlo tree search algorithm for the conditioned generation of novel molecules based on specific target proteins.

To ensure a fair comparison, we trained the external baseline models using our dataset using the same experiment setup and evaluation metrics as for Repurformer. Table 4 presents the performance comparison between our best configuration (Repurformer with α = 4) and the external baseline models. The comparison results demonstrate that the Repurformer (α = 4) outperformed the existing approaches on most evaluation metrics. In particular, our model generated compounds with high structural similarity to both the anchor and positive compounds than those generated by the external baseline models. This suggests that Repurformer can generate not only realistic but diverse compounds with methodological considerations for drug repurposability. Regarding drug-likeness, our model achieved the highest performance only on QED. Although the Transformer-based model excelled in SA and NP, the feasibility of its generated compounds is questionable due to its exceptionally high scores in physicochemical properties, which indicate the compounds might not be suitable as medicines. This is further validated by the evaluation of compound validity, as illustrated in Figure 8 in the Appendix. The compounds generated by the Transformer-based model were significantly less valid compared to those generated by Repurformer.

Mitigation of Sample Bias Figure 4a shows that the distance distribution of the generated compounds to the anchor compounds is similar to that of the positive compounds. We calculated the distance over the fingerprint domain to consider the patterns of molecular substructure. The result implies that the generated and positive compounds have different substructures from the anchor compounds to the same extent. However, Figure 4a compares *"the relative distances"* of the generated and positive compounds to the anchor compounds

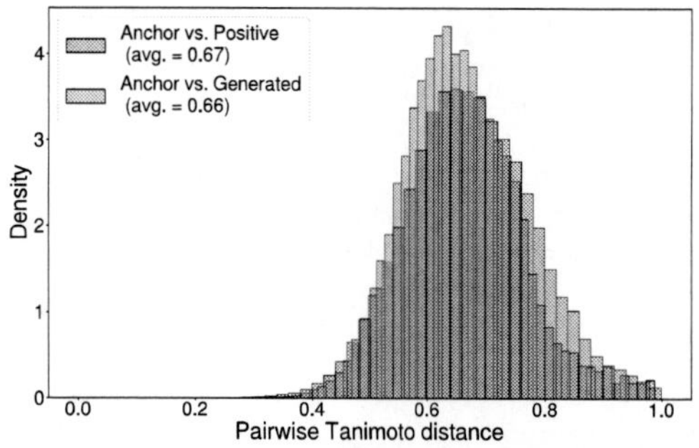

(a) Distribution of Pairwise Tanimoto Distances: Generated vs. Anchor and Positive vs. Anchor. The distance was defined over the molecular fingerprints domain.

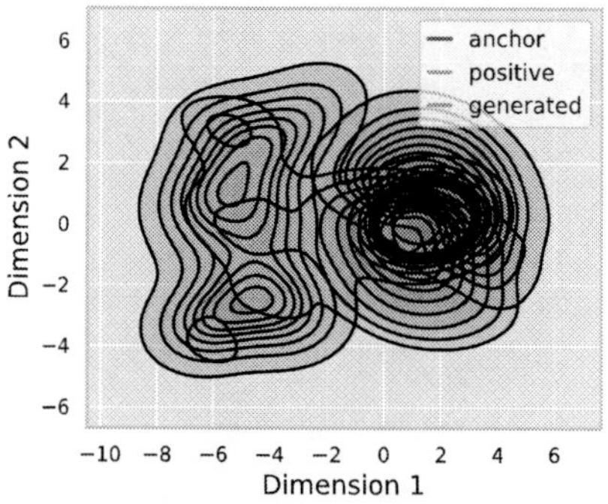

(b) 2D Gaussian KDE plots for the anchor, positive, and generated compounds. Before employing KDE, each compound was converted to an embedding vector using successive applications of Word2Vec and t-SNE embeddings.

Figure 4: (a) illustrates the distance distribution from the molecular fingerprint perspective. (b) describes the estimated two-dimensional Gaussian distribution of anchor, positive, and generated compounds.

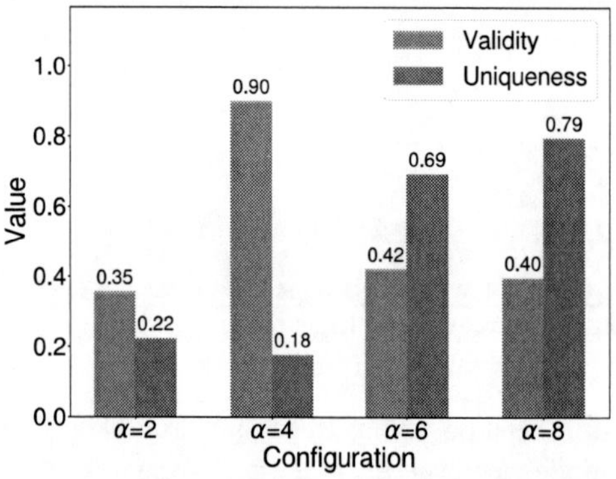

Figure 5: Validity-Uniqueness Trade-off at different values of α. Note that validity represents the quality of generated samples, while uniqueness represents the diversity of generated samples.

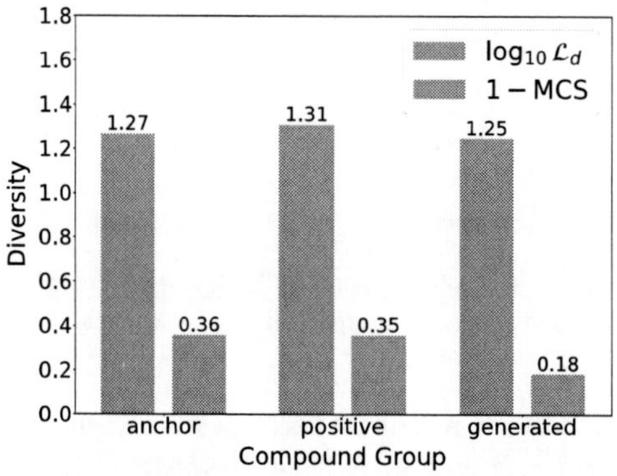

Figure 6: Internal Diversity per Compound Group. $\log_{10}\mathcal{L}_d$ measures the syntactic difference of SMILES strings, while MCS distance (1-MCS) measures the semantic dissimilarity at the atomic level.

"at the substructure level," making it difficult to directly compare the absolute distances to each other at the holistic level.

Figure 4b visualizes the overlapping representations among the anchor, positive, and generated compounds, *"directly comparing their absolute distances at the holistic level."* To do this, we extracted SMILES word embeddings (*e.g.,* C, N, F, =, +, [,], etc.) using Word2Vec (Mikolov et al., 2013) and defined the holistic representation of each molecule as the summation of these word embeddings. We then projected the holistic representation of each molecule into a 2-dimensional space by t-SNE (Van der Maaten and Hinton, 2008). Since t-SNE embeddings preserve pairwise similarities of high-dimensional data as neighboring points in a low-dimension, it allows for direct comparison of absolute distances between samples. Finally, we applied Gaussian kernel density estimation (KDE) to visualize the distribution of t-SNE embeddings.

The results from Figures 4a and 4b indicate that the generated compounds are more similar to the positive compounds than to the anchor compounds, both relatively and absolutely, and at substructural and holistic levels. This suggests that Repurformer successfully addressed the sample bias problem, creating substitutes for anchor compounds that resemble positive compounds.

Existence of Mode Collapse Mode collapse refers to a phenomenon where the generative model creates high-quality samples at the expense of in-distribution diversity (Adiga et al., 2018). In this section, we demonstrate that Repurformer suffers from mode collapse and thus the *"internal"* diversity of generated compounds is relatively lower than anchor and positive compounds.

Figure 5 illustrates the negative relationship between the validity and uniqueness of the generated compounds by different values of α. Validity represents the ratio of samples that can be depicted as 2D molecular drawings by RDKit (*i.e.,* the quality of generation), while uniqueness represents the ratio of non-duplicated samples (*i.e.,* the diversity of generation). As α increases, we observe that uniqueness increases but validity decreases. This is an expected outcome given that the low-frequency signals represent global structure whereas the high-frequency signals represent local structure. For example, low-frequency signals (*i.e.,* lower α) focus on the most fundamental structures, increasing the validity of generated compounds but reducing their uniqueness. Conversely, high-frequency signals (*i.e.,* higher α) focus on local details, increasing the uniqueness of generated compounds but reducing their structural validity. In short, Figure 5 demonstrates that Repurformer may be susceptible to the validity-uniqueness trade-off, *i.e.,* mode collapse, and thus α must be carefully selected.

Figure 6 describes the *"internal"* diversity of valid compounds generated by Repurformer with $\alpha = 4$, along with anchor and positive compounds that share the same target proteins with the generated ones. Following Pereira et al. (2021), we evaluated the internal diversity within each compound group using two metrics: Levenshtein distance ($\mathcal{L}_d$) and maximum common substructure (MCS). The Levenshtein distance (Levenshtein et al., 1966), also known as edit distance, measures the difference between two SMILES strings by calculating the minimum number of insertions, deletions, and replacements needed to make the strings identical. On the other hand, the MCS (Cao et al., 2008) measures the ratio of the number of atoms in the maximum common substructure of two compounds to their total number of atoms. Since the MCS represents a similarity score normalized between 0 and 1, the MCS distance can be obtained by 1-MCS, which captures the atom-level dissimilarities of compounds. The diversity of each compound group was computed by averaging the pairwise distances of all compounds. The result indicates that the internal diversity of the generated compounds is lower than that of the anchor and positive compounds, suggesting mode collapse in Repurformer.

Note that the existence of mode collapse does not contradict the mitigation of sample bias. Mode collapse refers to less internal diversity among generated compounds, while mitigating sample bias involves creating substitutes for anchor compounds that resemble positive ones, thus increasing diversity between the anchor and generated compounds.

7 Limitations

This study has some limitations. First, due to inconsistencies between the tokens in our dataset and those we borrowed from previous research, some generated outputs contained <UNK> tokens, which had to be excluded. Second, the study lacks experiments on binding affinity, which are necessary to evaluate how strongly the generated compounds bind to proteins. These limitations must be addressed in future research.

8 Concluding Remarks

In this study, we introduced Repurformer, a novel model designed to address the sample bias problem in *de novo* molecule generation by leveraging multi-hop relationships. Repurformer integrates bidirectional pretraining with Fast Fourier Transform and low-pass filtering, to capture complex interactions between proteins and compounds. This approach focuses on low-frequency components, corresponding to longer propagation through multi-hop protein-compound interactions. The results show that Repurformer successfully generates valid and diverse molecules.

Building on these positive results, there are several promising directions for future improvement. Enhancing the backbone architecture by incorporating advanced models like diffusion or graph neural networks and techniques such as contrastive learning could further improve Repurformer's ability to capture multi-hop protein-compound interactions. The results from Figures 5 and 6 also suggest promising directions to improve Repurformer such as leveraging reinforcement learning to maximize diversity rewards or introducing Wasserstein loss to address mode collapse. Additionally, while our current experiments have shown the potential of Repurformer, it is critical to validate its applicability in real-world scenarios. Therefore, we need to verify the performance of Repurformer on existing drug repurposing cases. Considering these aspects will strengthen the practical implications and utilities of Repurformer.

Acknowledgments

This research was supported by Basic Science Research Program through the National Research Foundation of Korea (NRF) funded by the Ministry of Education (RS-2023-00275796).

References

Sudarshan Adiga, Mohamed Adel Attia, Wei-Ting Chang, and Ravi Tandon. 2018. On the tradeoff between mode collapse and sample quality in generative adversarial networks. In *2018 IEEE global conference on signal and information processing (GlobalSIP)*, pages 1184–1188. IEEE.

Viraj Bagal, Rishal Aggarwal, P. K. Vinod, and U. Deva Priyakumar. 2022. MolGPT: Molecular generation using a transformer-decoder model. *Journal of Chemical Information and Modeling*, 62(9):2064–2076.

G. Richard Bickerton, Gaia V. Paolini, Jérémy Besnard, Sorel Muresan, and Andrew L. Hopkins. 2012. Quantifying the chemical beauty of drugs. *Nature Chemistry*, 4(2):90–98.

E Oran Brigham. 1988. *The fast Fourier transform and its applications*. Prentice-Hall, Inc.

Yiqun Cao, Tao Jiang, and Thomas Girke. 2008. A maximum common substructure-based algorithm for searching and predicting drug-like compounds. *Bioinformatics*, 24(13):i366–i374.

James W Cooley and John W Tukey. 1965. An algorithm for the machine calculation of complex fourier series. *Mathematics of computation*, 19(90):297–301.

Nicholas P Costen, Denis M Parker, and Ian Craw. 1996. Effects of high-pass and low-pass spatial filtering on face identification. *Perception & psychophysics*, 58:602–612.

Hanjun Dai, Yingtao Tian, Bo Dai, Steven Skiena, and Le Song. 2018. Syntax-directed variational autoencoder for molecule generation. In *31st Conference on Neural Information Processing Systems (NIPS 2017)*.

Peter Ertl, Silvio Roggo, and Ansgar Schuffenhauer. 2008. Natural Product-likeness Score and Its Application for Prioritization of Compound Libraries. *Journal of Chemical Information and Modeling*, 48(1):68–74.

Peter Ertl and Ansgar Schuffenhauer. 2009. Estimation of synthetic accessibility score of drug-like molecules based on molecular complexity and fragment contributions. *Journal of Cheminformatics*, 1(1):8.

Michael K. Gilson, Tiqing Liu, Michael Baitaluk, George Nicola, Linda Hwang, and Jenny Chong. 2016. BindingDB in 2015: A public database for medicinal chemistry, computational chemistry and systems pharmacology. *Nucleic Acids Research*, 44(D1):D1045–D1053.

Ian Goodfellow, Jean Pouget-Abadie, Mehdi Mirza, Bing Xu, David Warde-Farley, Sherjil Ozair, Aaron Courville, and Yoshua Bengio. 2014. Generative adversarial nets. In *Advances in Neural Information Processing Systems*, volume 27. Curran Associates, Inc.

Daria Grechishnikova. 2021. Transformer neural network for protein-specific de novo drug generation as a machine translation problem. *Scientific Reports*, 11(1):321.

Gabriel Lima Guimaraes, Benjamin Sanchez-Lengeling, Carlos Outeiral, Pedro Luis Cunha Farias, and Alán Aspuru-Guzik. 2018. Objective-reinforced generative adversarial networks (ORGAN) for sequence generation models. *arXiv preprint*. ArXiv:1705.10843 [cs, stat].

Rafael Gómez-Bombarelli, Jennifer N. Wei, David Duvenaud, José Miguel Hernández-Lobato, Benjamín Sánchez-Lengeling, Dennis Sheberla, Jorge Aguilera-Iparraguirre, Timothy D. Hirzel, Ryan P. Adams, and Alán Aspuru-Guzik. 2018. Automatic chemical design using a data-driven continuous representation of molecules. *ACS Central Science*, 4(2):268–276.

Paul Heckbert. 1995. Fourier transforms and the fast fourier transform (fft) algorithm. *Computer Graphics*, 2(1995):15–463.

Jonathan Ho, Ajay Jain, and Pieter Abbeel. 2020. Denoising diffusion probabilistic models. *Preprint*, arXiv:2006.11239.

Shion Honda, Shoi Shi, and Hiroki R Ueda. 2019. Smiles transformer: Pre-trained molecular fingerprint for low data drug discovery. *arXiv preprint arXiv:1911.04738*.

Lei Huang, Hengtong Zhang, Tingyang Xu, and Ka-Chun Wong. 2023. MDM: Molecular diffusion model for 3D molecule generation. *Proceedings of the AAAI Conference on Artificial Intelligence*, 37(4):5105–5112.

Wengong Jin, Regina Barzilay, and Tommi Jaakkola. 2018. Junction tree variational autoencoder for molecular graph generation. In *Proceedings of the 35th International Conference on Machine Learning*, pages 2323–2332. PMLR. ISSN: 2640-3498.

Diederik P. Kingma and Max Welling. 2022. Auto-encoding variational bayes. *Preprint*, arxiv:1312.6114.

James Lee-Thorp, Joshua Ainslie, Ilya Eckstein, and Santiago Ontanon. 2021. Fnet: Mixing tokens with fourier transforms. *arXiv preprint arXiv:2105.03824*.

Vladimir I Levenshtein et al. 1966. Binary codes capable of correcting deletions, insertions, and reversals. In *Soviet physics doklady*, volume 10, pages 707–710. Soviet Union.

Chin-Yew Lin. 2004. ROUGE: A package for automatic evaluation of summaries. In *Text Summarization Branches Out*, pages 74–81, Barcelona, Spain. Association for Computational Linguistics.

Christopher A Lipinski, Franco Lombardo, Beryl W Dominy, and Paul J Feeney. 2012. Experimental and computational approaches to estimate solubility and permeability in drug discovery and development settings. *Advanced drug delivery reviews*, 64:4–17.

Łukasz Maziarka, Agnieszka Pocha, Jan Kaczmarczyk, Krzysztof Rataj, Tomasz Danel, and Michał Warchoł. 2020. Mol-CycleGAN: a generative model for molecular optimization. *Journal of Cheminformatics*, 12(1):2.

Tomas Mikolov, Kai Chen, Greg Corrado, and Jeffrey Dean. 2013. Efficient estimation of word representations in vector space. *arXiv preprint arXiv:1301.3781*.

Brenton P. Munson, Michael Chen, Audrey Bogosian, Jason F. Kreisberg, Katherine Licon, Ruben Abagyan, Brent M. Kuenzi, and Trey Ideker. 2024. De novo generation of multi-target compounds using deep generative chemistry. *Nature Communications*, 15(1):3636.

Kishore Papineni, Salim Roukos, Todd Ward, and Wei-Jing Zhu. 2002. Bleu: A method for automatic evaluation of machine translation. In *Proceedings of the 40th Annual Meeting of the Association for Computational Linguistics*, pages 311–318, Philadelphia, Pennsylvania, USA. Association for Computational Linguistics.

Tiago Pereira, Maryam Abbasi, Bernardete Ribeiro, and Joel P Arrais. 2021. Diversity oriented deep reinforcement learning for targeted molecule generation. *Journal of cheminformatics*, 13(1):21.

Irwin Pollack. 1948. Effects of high pass and low pass filtering on the intelligibility of speech in noise. *The Journal of the Acoustical Society of America*, 20(3):259–266.

Hao Qian, Cheng Lin, Dengwei Zhao, Shikui Tu, and Lei Xu. 2022. AlphaDrug: Protein target specific de novo molecular generation. *PNAS Nexus*, 1(4):pgac227.

K Ramamohan Rao and Ping Yip. 2014. *Discrete cosine transform: algorithms, advantages, applications*. Academic press.

Roshan Rao, Nicholas Bhattacharya, Neil Thomas, Yan Duan, Peter Chen, John Canny, Pieter Abbeel, and Yun Song. 2019. Evaluating protein transfer learning with tape. *Advances in neural information processing systems*, 32.

Benjamin Sanchez-Lengeling, Carlos Outeiral, and Gabriel L Guimaraes. 2017. Optimizing distributions over molecular space. An objective-reinforced generative adversarial network for inverse-design chemistry (ORGANIC).

Alex Tamkin, Dan Jurafsky, and Noah Goodman. 2020. Language through a prism: A spectral approach for multiscale language representations. *Advances in Neural Information Processing Systems*, 33:5492–5504.

Cheng Tan, Zhangyang Gao, and Stan Z. Li. 2022. Target-aware molecular graph generation. *arXiv preprint*. ArXiv:2202.04829 [cs].

Laurens Van der Maaten and Geoffrey Hinton. 2008. Visualizing data using t-sne. *Journal of machine learning research*, 9(11).

Ashish Vaswani, Noam Shazeer, Niki Parmar, Jakob Uszkoreit, Llion Jones, Aidan N. Gomez, Lukasz Kaiser, and Illia Polosukhin. 2017. Attention is all you need. *Preprint*, arXiv:1706.03762.

Scott A. Wildman and Gordon M. Crippen. 1999. Prediction of physicochemical parameters by atomic contributions. *Journal of Chemical Information and Computer Sciences*, 39(5):868–873.

Yonghui Wu, Mike Schuster, Zhifeng Chen, Quoc V. Le, Mohammad Norouzi, Wolfgang Macherey, Maxim Krikun, Yuan Cao, Qin Gao, Klaus Macherey, Jeff Klingner, Apurva Shah, Melvin Johnson, Xiaobing Liu, Łukasz Kaiser, Stephan Gouws, Yoshikiyo Kato, Taku Kudo, Hideto Kazawa, Keith Stevens, George Kurian, Nishant Patil, Wei Wang, Cliff Young, Jason Smith, Jason Riesa, Alex Rudnick, Oriol Vinyals, Greg Corrado, Macduff Hughes, and Jeffrey Dean. 2016. Google's neural machine translation system: Bridging the gap between human and machine translation. *Preprint*, arxiv:1609.08144.

Minkai Xu, Alexander S. Powers, Ron O. Dror, Stefano Ermon, and Jure Leskovec. 2023. Geometric latent diffusion models for 3D molecule generation. In *Proceedings of the 40th International Conference on Machine Learning*, pages 38592–38610. PMLR. ISSN: 2640-3498.

A Supplementary Materials

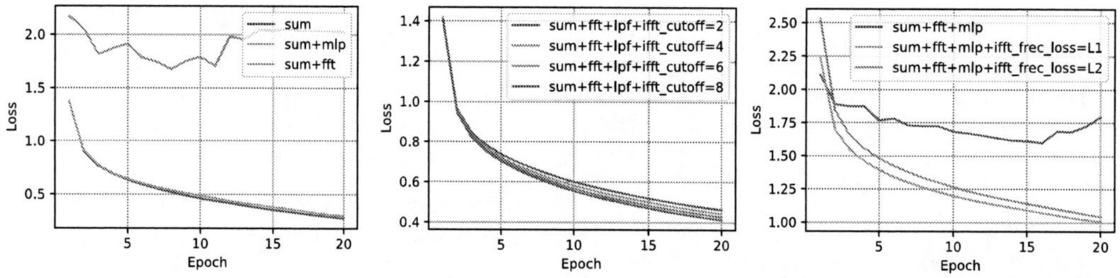

Figure 7: Comparison of Training Performance with Different Configurations. When embedding vectors from protein and compound encoders are mapped to the frequency domain using Fourier Transform (FFT), training performance does not improve unless they are transformed back to the original domain with an inverse Fourier Transform (iFFT). This indicates that applying FFT in the latent space leads to alignment issues between the encoders and the compound decoder.

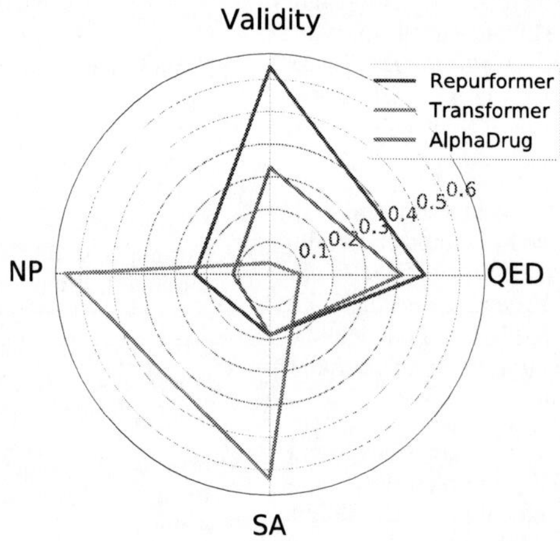

Figure 8: Comparison of Validity and Drug-Likeness Metrics. Validity, QED, SA, and NP scores were normalized to the same scale. Although the Transformer-based model (Grechishnikova, 2021) showed relatively higher SA and NP scores, its validity is extremely low. This indicates that the compounds generated by the Transformer-based model are not of sufficient quality to be considered as drug candidates.

Lang2Mol-Diff: A Diffusion-Based Generative Model for Language-to-Molecule Translation Leveraging SELFIES Molecular String Representation

Nguyen Doan Hieu Nguyen[†], **Nhat Truong Pham**[†], **Duong Thanh Tran**, **Balachandran Manavalan**[*]

Department of Integrative Biotechnology, Sungkyunkwan University, Republic of Korea
{ndhieunguyen, truongpham96, duongtt, bala2022}@skku.edu
[†]Equal contribution
[*]**Correspondence:** bala2022@skku.edu

Abstract

Generating *de novo* molecules from textual descriptions is challenging due to potential issues with molecule validity in SMILES representation and limitations of autoregressive models. This work introduces Lang2Mol-Diff, a diffusion-based language-to-molecule generative model using the SELFIES representation. Specifically, Lang2Mol-Diff leverages the strengths of two state-of-the-art molecular generative models: BioT5 and TGM-DLM. By employing BioT5 to tokenize the SELFIES representation, Lang2Mol-Diff addresses the validity issues associated with SMILES strings. Additionally, it incorporates a text diffusion mechanism from TGM-DLM to overcome the limitations of autoregressive models in this domain. To the best of our knowledge, this is the first study to leverage the diffusion mechanism for text-based *de novo* molecule generation using the SELFIES molecular string representation. Performance evaluation on the L+M-24 benchmark dataset shows that Lang2Mol-Diff outperforms all existing methods for molecule generation in terms of validity. Our code and pre-processed data are available at https://github.com/nhattruongpham/mol-lang-bridge/tree/lang2mol/.

1 Introduction

Molecules, the elementary constituents of all matter, play a pivotal role in dictating the properties and functionalities that govern our world. The immense scale of chemical space, estimated to encompass around 10^{33} molecules (Polishchuk et al., 2013), presents a significant challenge for traditional methods in finding new medicine, materials, and chemical processes. This has driven the exploration of artificial intelligence models for efficient molecule finding. A key advancement lies in the confluence of natural language and molecular representations such as SMILES (simplified molecular-input line-entry system) (Weininger, 1988) and SELFIES (SELF-referencIng Embedded Strings) (Krenn et al., 2020). These representations enable the seamless integration of natural language descriptions with corresponding molecular structures. By leveraging pre-trained language models and fine-tuning them on different benchmark datasets combining natural language and molecular string representations, researchers have successfully developed numerous downstream models capable of generating novel molecule structures based on textual descriptions outlining desired properties. Besides, the success of diffusion models in image generation has spurred their application to text generation, and more recently, to the domain of molecular representation.

In this research, we use the diffusion mechanism to address the limitations of autoregressive models, where errors from earlier predictions can propagate and magnify throughout the sequence and lead to inaccuracies, especially in long sequences. We also want to deal with validity issues in generating new molecules. The proposed method is a novel architecture that incorporates advancements in both the backbone model and the molecular representation. In essence, our key contributions are as follows:

- We employed SELFIES as the molecule presentation instead of SMILES for better validity in generating new molecules.
- This is the first study to leverage diffusion mechanism for text-based molecule generation using SELFIES molecular strings.

2 Related Work

2.1 Language Model-Based Approaches

The availability of molecular string representations like SMILES (Weininger, 1988) and SELFIES (Krenn et al., 2020) has transformed *de novo* molecule generation into a text-to-text task. Early approaches leveraged recurrent neural network

Proceedings of the 1st Workshop on Language + Molecules (L+M 2024), pages 129–135

(RNN) architectures, such as those described in (Segler et al., 2018; Grisoni et al., 2020), achieving some success. However, the recent emergence of the text-to-text transfer transformer (T5) model (Raffel et al., 2020) as a powerful text-to-text model compared to RNN has led to the development of several successful models for this task, including MolT5 (Edwards et al., 2022a), Text+Chem T5 (Christofidellis et al., 2023), BioT5 (Pei et al., 2023), and BioT5+ (Pei et al., 2024). Additionally, transformer-based models like generative pre-trained transformer (GPT) (Brown et al., 2020) have been fine-tuned for this purpose, with MolXPT (Liu et al., 2023) serving as an example. Despite their advancements, autoregressive models exhibited limitations when dealing with long-term dependencies within the data. These models processed information one element at a time, leading to an inherent accumulation of errors. Additionally, autoregressive models were restricted by a fixed-size context window, limiting their ability to capture crucial relationships between elements that may reside far apart in the sequence. Consequently, these limitations could hinder the effectiveness of autoregressive models in tasks that necessitate understanding long-range dependencies within the data.

2.2 Diffusion Model-Based Approaches

The recent breakthroughs in image generation using diffusion models have paved the way for their exploration of text generation tasks. Diffusion-LM (Li et al., 2022) exemplified this exciting trend, demonstrating the potential of diffusion models for achieving controllable text generation. To address the limitations of autoregressive models, TGM-DLM (Gong et al., 2024) pioneered the application of Diffusion-LM in SMILES-based molecule generation. This work introduced the first diffusion language model for SMILES-guided molecule generation. However, due to its reliance on SMILES strings, TGM-DLM required a two-phase approach: an initial molecule generation phase followed by a correction phase. The necessity of the latter phase was questionable, as experimental results suggested that the correction phase did not lead to significant improvements in molecule validity.

3 Methodology

3.1 Overview of Lang2Mol-Diff

As discussed in Section 2, most existing language model-based methods suffered from limitations imposed by autoregressive nature. Therefore, we adopt a diffusion-based approach to address this challenge, enabling iterative and holistic content generation. To eliminate the need for a correction phase, a shortcoming identified in TGM-DLM (Gong et al., 2024) when using SMILES strings (Weininger, 1988), we leverage SELFIES strings (Krenn et al., 2020) for molecule representation, ensuring the inherent validity of generated molecules due to their superior ability to capture molecular structure. To achieve this, we exploit a pre-trained BioT5 (Pei et al., 2023) base model, which was fine-tuned for text-to-molecule tasks. This pre-trained model serves as the encoder for both SELFIES molecular strings and natural language text. We further incorporate embedding layers to construct a model that predicts molecule embeddings corresponding to Gaussian noise, drawing inspiration from the core concept of Diffusion-LM (Li et al., 2022). The overall architecture of our proposed approach is illustrated in Figure 1, which includes three main steps in the diffusion process: forward (Figure 1a), reverse (Figure 1b), and sampling (Figure 1c).

3.2 SELFIES Tokenizer

This work addresses the limitations of SMILES strings (Weininger, 1988) in terms of syntactic and semantic robustness, which can hinder the validity of molecules generated by deep learning models. For this reason, we opt for SELFIES representations (Krenn et al., 2020) due to their superior ability to capture molecular structure accurately. We leverage the tokenizer employed in BioT5 (Pei et al., 2023) to tokenize the text before passing it into the model. SELFIES string representation leverages brackets to encapsulate chemically meaningful atom groups, which are then individually tokenized as distinct SELFIES tokens. For instance, the SELFIES string *[C][Branch2][Ring2]* would be tokenized into *[C]*, *[Branch2]*, and *[Ring2]*.

3.3 Language Model-Based Encoder

In contrast to TGM-DLM (Gong et al., 2024), which employed separate encoders for natural language texts and SMILES strings, namely SciBERT (Beltagy et al., 2019) for the first and uncased-

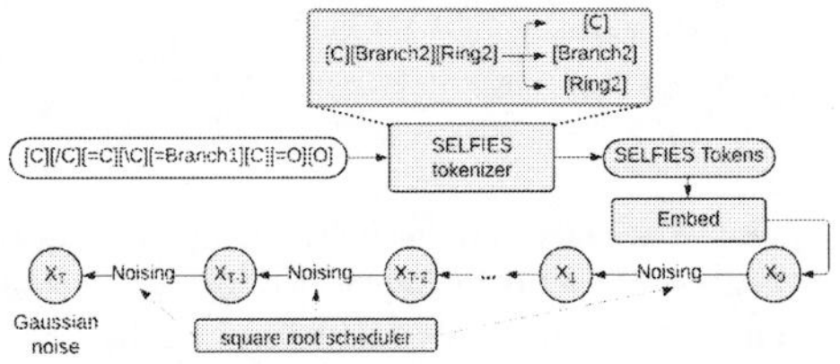

(a) Forward step in the diffusion process, noise is gradually added to the embed representation of molecular string (SELFIES) using a square root noise scheduler.

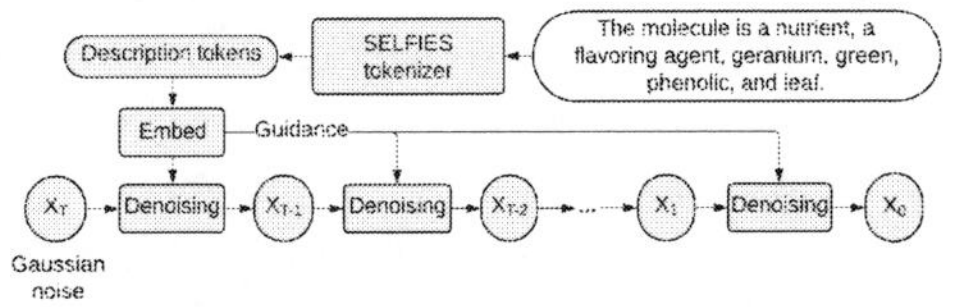

(b) Reverse step in the diffusion process, the model predicts the less noisy vector x_{t-1} from the noisier vector x_t.

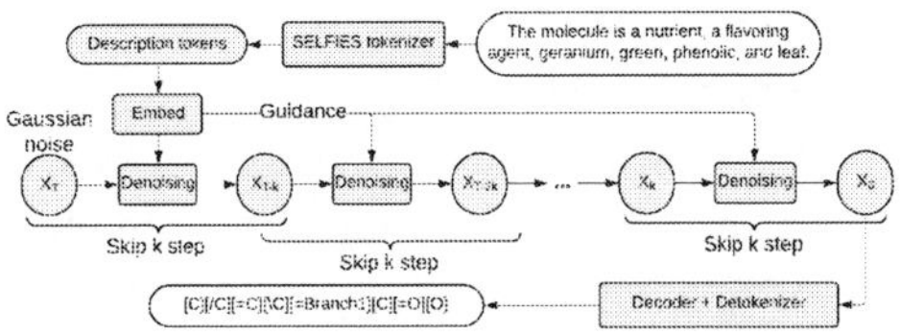

(c) Sampling step in the diffusion process, we skip some steps to reduce the Markov chain so that the inferencing will be faster.

Figure 1: Illustration of Lang2Mol-Diff's diffusion process. X_0 is the embeddings of molecules tokenized by BioT5's tokenizer in SELFIES format. T is the number of diffusion steps. (a) Forward step, (b) Reverse step, (c) Sampling step.

BERT (Devlin et al., 2018) for the latter, this work adopts a more efficient approach. As discussed in Subsection 3.1, we leverage a pre-trained BioT5 model's encoder (Pei et al., 2023) for encoding both tokenized SELFIES (Krenn et al., 2020) strings and natural language text. This unified encoder architecture offers several advantages. First, it allows us to finetune the pre-trained parameters of the BioT5 model, focusing training efforts on the latter layers specific to our task. This not only reduces computational cost but also potentially mitigates overfitting. Additionally, a single encoder streamlines the model architecture, enhancing overall efficiency.

3.4 Diffusion Process

3.4.1 Forward Step

This represents the initial stage of the diffusion process, which is shown in Figure 1a. Given a molecular string, denoted as M, the SELFIES tokenizer is utilized to perform tokenization, resulting in a list of tokens represented as $\{m_0, m_1, m_2, ..., m_{n-1}\}$ where n is the number of tokens. Subsequently, the BioT5 encoder is applied to convert these tokens into a vector representation, denoted as $Emb(M) \in R^{d_m \times n}$. Here, d_m signifies the embedding dimension, while n represents the length of the sequence. The initial matrix for the forward process, denoted as x_0, is generated by sampling from a Gaussian distribution with a mean centered at $Emb(M)$: $x_0 \sim \mathcal{N}(Emb(M), \sigma_0 I)$.

With the initial embedding of the molecular string x_0, the forward step in the diffusion process is initiated. This step involves the gradual introduction of noise to the embedding through the utilization of a noise scheduler, which uses the $squareroot$ function in our approach. The process continues until the embedding transforms entirely into pure Gaussian noise $x_T \sim \mathcal{N}(0, I)$, where T represents the number of diffusion steps. The diffusion step from x_{t-1} to x_t is defined:

$$q(x_t|x_{t-1}) = \mathcal{N}(x_t; \sqrt{1-\beta_t}x_{t-1}, \beta_t I) \quad (1)$$

where $\beta_t \in [0, 1]$ controls the amount of noise added to x_t at time step t.

3.4.2 Reverse Step

The objective of this step is to reverse the forward process, specifically by predicting the original vector x_0 from the Gaussian noise x_T. This involves continuously predicting the less noisy vector x_{t-1} from the comparatively noisier vector x_t. The proposed model is trained to perform this denoising step by calculating the loss between the original molecule embedding x_0 and the vector $\hat{x}_0$ predicted from x_t. Moreover, the denoising process refines the embedding vector under the guidance of the embedded description $Emb(D)$ extracted using pre-trained BioT5 (Pei et al., 2023) to create a relationship between the description and the generated molecular string at the last step in the reverse process. The loss function used in the training phase of the model is defined as:

$$\mathcal{L}(M, D) = \mathop{\mathbb{E}}_{q(x_{0:T}|M)} \left[\sum_{t=1}^{T} ||f_\theta(x_t, t, D) - x_0||^2 - log p_\theta(M|x_0) \right] \quad (2)$$

where f_θ is the proposed model with parameters θ; x_t, t and D are the molecule embedding vector at time t, the time embedding and the description embedding, respectively. $p_\theta(M|x_0)$ represents the rounding process, where the embedding matrix is reverted to the original molecular string.

3.4.3 Sampling Step

The aforementioned training methodology enables the construction of a model with the ability to generate a molecular string given a textual description. This is accomplished through an iterative denoising process involving T steps, wherein a complete Gaussian noise vector undergoes denoising to obtain an embedding representative of the molecular string. The denoising process is guided by the accompanying text description. Subsequently, the generated embedding is decoded by removing padding and start/end tokens, then rounding and transforming it into tokens, resulting in the final molecular string representation. This approach is also known as the Denoising Diffusion Probabilistic Model (DDPM) technique (Ho et al., 2020). However, it is important to note that this process involves a Markov chain, resulting in a significant computational time requirement to obtain the final result. To deal with this problem, instead of iterating through all steps in the diffusion process, we skip k steps in the sampling step. This means we predict the less noisy vector x_{t-k} based on the noisier vector x_t instead of x_{t-k+1}.

4 Experiments

4.1 Dataset

Our study employs the "split_train" split of the L+M-24 extra dataset (Edwards et al., 2022b, 2024) for training and the "split_valid" of the L+M-24 dataset (Edwards et al., 2022b, 2024) for evaluation. Each dataset comprises paired SMILES strings (Weininger, 1988) representing molecules and their corresponding descriptive captions. The training dataset was augmented from the original L+M-24 dataset by creating 4 additional captions for each existing molecule based on the randomly chosen available templates. Therefore, there are a lot of duplicated samples within the training split of the dataset. We first remove all of them to improve data efficiency. As a pre-processing step, we converted the SMILES strings to SELFIES representations (Krenn et al., 2020) using Python's *selfies* package [1]. It is important to note that a

[1]https://github.com/aspuru-guzik-group/selfies

Split	Original	After removing duplicated samples	After converting to SELFIES
train	634,320	533,953	533,949
valid	33,696	33,696	33,696

Table 1: Summary of train and validation splits of L+M-24 dataset. From the original dataset, we filtered out duplicated samples, then we converted the SMILES strings to SELFIES strings to get the final dataset.

small portion of the molecules could not be successfully converted to a SELFIES format. These inconvertible molecules were excluded due to their negligible impact on the overall dataset size. On the other hand, the evaluation dataset is kept as original. A summary of the final training dataset is provided in Table 1. Some molecules that cannot be converted from SMILES to SELFIES are displayed in Table 2.

4.2 Implementation Details

We choose the maximum length of the tokens for the tokenizer to be 256. Consistent with the pretrained BioT5 model (Pei et al., 2023), our approach leverages its established vocabulary. As detailed in the BioT5 paper, this vocabulary is segmented into distinct domains: molecules, proteins, and text. We specifically utilize BioT5's molecular vocabulary, encompassing 35,073 tokens, to ensure compatibility with the SELFIES string representation of molecules. This selection facilitates the efficient processing of molecule-related information within our model. The final Lang2Mol-Diff model architecture possesses approximately 218 million parameters. We opted for a diffusion schedule with T of 2,000 steps and a total training regime of 400,000 steps. The AdamW optimizer (Loshchilov and Hutter, 2017) was utilized with a learning rate of 0.5×10^{-5}. The training process ran for approximately 60 hours on a single NVIDIA GeForce RTX 4090 GPU with a batch size of 16. In the sampling step for inference, we set the step skipped k to be 10.

Because the L+M-24 dataset (Edwards et al., 2024) utilizes SMILES strings (Weininger, 1988) and established evaluation metrics are calculated based on this format, it is more precise for evaluation in this format of molecular string presentation. Moreover, to facilitate a fair comparison with existing research, we opt for SMILES over SELFIES representations (Krenn et al., 2020) for the evaluation phase. However, this decision is premised on the assumption that the SMILES molecules

SMILES	SELFIES	Caption	Image
N=IC=IF	Error	The molecule is a nutrient.	
F[P-](F)(F)(F)(F)F.[H+]	Error	When heated to decomp, it emits highly toxic fumes of hydrogen fluoride and phosphoxides.	
CC(C)COC(=O)CCc1ccco1	[C][C][Branch1][C][C][C][O][C][=Branch1][C][=O][C][C][C][=C][C][=C][O][Ring1][Branch1]	The molecule is a nutrient.	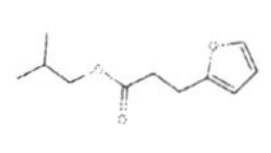
Cc1cc(N)c(C=O)cc1F	[C][C][=C][C][Branch1][C][N][=C][Branch1][Ring1][C][=O][C][=C][Ring1][=Branch2][F]	The molecule is a prmt5 inhibitor.	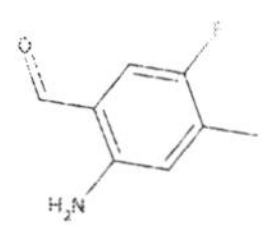

Table 2: Some samples in the L+M-24 dataset after being converted from SMILES strings to SELFIES strings, 2 of them cannot be converted and are removed from training and evaluation splits of the final dataset.

within the dataset are all valid and unique representations, which means a molecule corresponds to a unique SMILES molecular string. To verify this assumption, we leverage the RDKit cheminformatics toolkit [2] to confirm that all SMILES strings are canonicalized.

4.3 Results and Discussion

The evaluation results of our model compared to other approaches are displayed in Table 3. Notably, our proposed method achieves BLEU, Levenshtein, MACCS FTS, RDK FTS, Morgan FTS, FCD, and Validity scores of 54.28, 55.87, 60.64, 33.21, 32.78, 38.09, and 100.00, respectively. More specifically, our proposed method outperforms all state-of-the-art methods regarding validity. Compared to Meditron-7B, our proposed method improves Morgan FTS by 15.96%. Regarding the Levenshtein metric, our proposed method is better than MolT5-Small by 0.47%. The result statistics of the proposed model cannot yet outperform the existing methods. It might be because it was not pre-trained on a large enough dataset as other models before being fine-tuned on the L+M-24 dataset. Besides, the model was trained with the default model configuration used for TGM-DLM (Gong et al., 2024), which may be incompatible and not fully optimized.

Moreover, we also compare the molecules generated by our proposed method with MolT5-Based and MolT5-Large models. Some generated molecules of MolT5 (Edwards et al., 2022a), which has been fine-tuned on L+M-24 dataset (Edwards et al., 2022b, 2024), and Lang2Mol-Diff are shown in Table 4. The empirical findings demonstrate that our proposed method exhibits a higher level of novelty compared to MolT5 in the generation of molecules. Although the input description is different, they share some important keywords, which leads to the identical generation of molecules using MolT5. On the other hand, Lang2Mol-Diff generates differently for two distinct input descriptions.

5 Conclusion

This work presents Lang2Mol-Diff, a novel diffusion-based language-to-molecule generative model that addresses the challenges of *de novo* molecule generation from textual descriptions. By leveraging the strengths of BioT5 for accurate tokenization of the SELFIES representation and incorporating a text diffusion mechanism inspired by

[2]https://github.com/rdkit/rdkit

Model	BLEU↑	Exact↑	Levenshtein↓	MACCS FTS↑	RDK FTS↑	Morgan FTS↑	FCD↓	Validity↑
Ground Truth	100.00	100.00	0.00	100.00	100.00	100.00	0.0	100.00
MolT5-Small	56.56	0.00	56.34	64.22	58.10	37.44	NaN	80.52
MolT5-Base	68.38	0.00	44.79	76.03	65.23	47.46	NaN	100.00
MolT5-Large	56.42	0.00	55.40	75.70	65.01	39.51	17.52	99.44
Meditron-7B	69.40	0.00	46.49	77.16	69.34	16.82	2.46	99.63
Ours	54.28	0.00	55.87	60.64	33.21	32.78	38.09	100.00

Table 3: Text-guided molecule generation results on L+M-24 validation split. Data is taken from the report on the L+M-24 dataset (Edwards et al., 2024).

Input	MolT5-Base	MolT5-Large	Ours	Ground truth
The molecule is a nutrient and fat storage, and it impacts pancreatitis. The molecule is a thyroxine treatment that impacts cardiovascular disease, metabolic syndrome, and atherosclerosis.	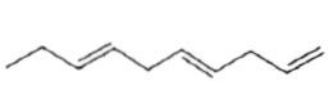	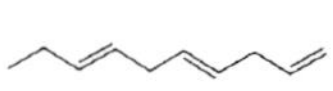	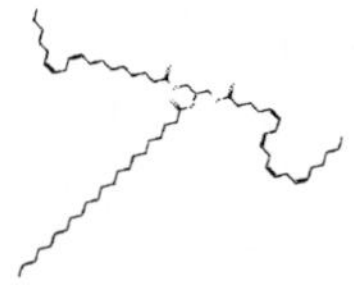	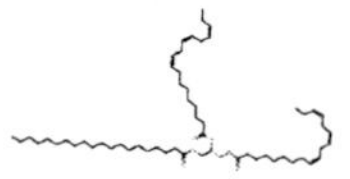
It impacts pancreatitis, cardiovascular disease, and metabolic syndrome. The molecule is a nutrient and a fat storage, it impacts atherosclerosis, and is thyroxine treatment.	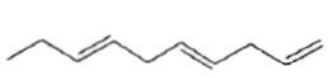	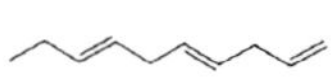	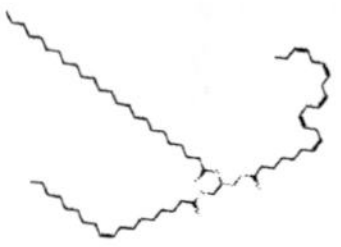	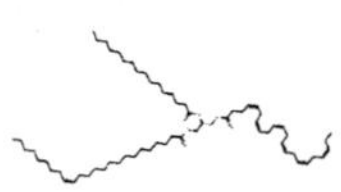

Table 4: Comparative visualization of *de novo* generated molecules across models. We use the Hugging Face's Inference API to collect the outputs of MolT5-Base and MolT5-Large.

TGM-DLM, Lang2Mol-Diff overcomes the limitations of SMILES-based approaches and autoregressive models. Extensive evaluation on the benchmark dataset confirms Lang2Mol-Diff's superior performance in generating valid molecules compared to the current state-of-the-art methods. This achievement paves the way for more reliable and robust methods for *de novo* molecule generation based on textual descriptions.

Our proposed model presents opportunities for future research and improvement. One promising direction for enhancement involves pre-training the model on a larger dataset, which would enable it to learn more meaningful representations and enhance its generalization capabilities. Furthermore, exploring alternative configurations such as adjusting the model's architecture and fine-tuning hyperparameters holds potential for optimizing performance and overcoming existing limitations. Pursuing these avenues is expected to refine the model and further optimize its ability to generate new molecules with improved outcomes.

Acknowledgements

This work was supported by the National Research Foundation of Korea (NRF) funded by the Ministry of Science and ICT (RS-2024-00344752). This research was supported by the Department of Integrative Biotechnology, Sungkyunkwan University (SKKU) and the BK21 FOUR Project. This work was supported by the Korea Bio Data Station (K-BDS) with computing resources including technical support.

References

Iz Beltagy, Kyle Lo, and Arman Cohan. 2019. Scibert: A pretrained language model for scientific text. In *EMNLP*. Association for Computational Linguistics.

Tom Brown, Benjamin Mann, Nick Ryder, Melanie Subbiah, Jared D Kaplan, Prafulla Dhariwal, Arvind Neelakantan, Pranav Shyam, Girish Sastry, Amanda Askell, et al. 2020. Language models are few-shot learners. *Advances in neural information processing systems*, 33:1877–1901.

Dimitrios Christofidellis, Giorgio Giannone, Jannis Born, Ole Winther, Teodoro Laino, and Matteo Manica. 2023. Unifying molecular and textual representations via multi-task language modelling. In *Inter-*

national Conference on Machine Learning, pages 6140–6157. PMLR.

Jacob Devlin, Ming-Wei Chang, Kenton Lee, and Kristina Toutanova. 2018. BERT: pre-training of deep bidirectional transformers for language understanding. *CoRR*, abs/1810.04805.

Carl Edwards, Tuan Lai, Kevin Ros, Garrett Honke, Kyunghyun Cho, and Heng Ji. 2022a. Translation between molecules and natural language. *arXiv preprint arXiv:2204.11817*.

Carl Edwards, Tuan Lai, Kevin Ros, Garrett Honke, Kyunghyun Cho, and Heng Ji. 2022b. Translation between molecules and natural language. In *Proceedings of the 2022 Conference on Empirical Methods in Natural Language Processing*, pages 375–413, Abu Dhabi, United Arab Emirates. Association for Computational Linguistics.

Carl Edwards, Qingyun Wang, Lawrence Zhao, and Heng Ji. 2024. L+M-24: Building a dataset for Language + Molecules @ ACL 2024. *arXiv preprint arXiv:2403.00791*.

Haisong Gong, Qiang Liu, Shu Wu, and Liang Wang. 2024. Text-guided molecule generation with diffusion language model. *Proceedings of the AAAI Conference on Artificial Intelligence*, 38(1):109–117.

Francesca Grisoni, Michael Moret, Robin Lingwood, and Gisbert Schneider. 2020. Bidirectional molecule generation with recurrent neural networks. *Journal of chemical information and modeling*, 60(3):1175–1183.

Jonathan Ho, Ajay Jain, and Pieter Abbeel. 2020. Denoising diffusion probabilistic models. *Advances in neural information processing systems*, 33:6840–6851.

Mario Krenn, Florian Häse, AkshatKumar Nigam, Pascal Friederich, and Alan Aspuru-Guzik. 2020. Self-referencing embedded strings (selfies): A 100% robust molecular string representation. *Machine Learning: Science and Technology*, 1(4):045024.

Xiang Li, John Thickstun, Ishaan Gulrajani, Percy S Liang, and Tatsunori B Hashimoto. 2022. Diffusion-lm improves controllable text generation. *Advances in Neural Information Processing Systems*, 35:4328–4343.

Zequn Liu, Wei Zhang, Yingce Xia, Lijun Wu, Shufang Xie, Tao Qin, Ming Zhang, and Tie-Yan Liu. 2023. Molxpt: Wrapping molecules with text for generative pre-training. *arXiv preprint arXiv:2305.10688*.

Ilya Loshchilov and Frank Hutter. 2017. Decoupled weight decay regularization. *arXiv preprint arXiv:1711.05101*.

Qizhi Pei, Lijun Wu, Kaiyuan Gao, Xiaozhuan Liang, Yin Fang, Jinhua Zhu, Shufang Xie, Tao Qin, and Rui Yan. 2024. Biot5+: Towards generalized biological understanding with iupac integration and multi-task tuning. *arXiv preprint arXiv:2402.17810*.

Qizhi Pei, Wei Zhang, Jinhua Zhu, Kehan Wu, Kaiyuan Gao, Lijun Wu, Yingce Xia, and Rui Yan. 2023. Biot5: Enriching cross-modal integration in biology with chemical knowledge and natural language associations. *arXiv preprint arXiv:2310.07276*.

Pavel G Polishchuk, Timur I Madzhidov, and Alexandre Varnek. 2013. Estimation of the size of drug-like chemical space based on gdb-17 data. *Journal of computer-aided molecular design*, 27:675–679.

Colin Raffel, Noam Shazeer, Adam Roberts, Katherine Lee, Sharan Narang, Michael Matena, Yanqi Zhou, Wei Li, and Peter J Liu. 2020. Exploring the limits of transfer learning with a unified text-to-text transformer. *Journal of machine learning research*, 21(140):1–67.

Marwin HS Segler, Thierry Kogej, Christian Tyrchan, and Mark P Waller. 2018. Generating focused molecule libraries for drug discovery with recurrent neural networks. *ACS central science*, 4(1):120–131.

David Weininger. 1988. Smiles, a chemical language and information system. 1. introduction to methodology and encoding rules. *Journal of chemical information and computer sciences*, 28(1):31–36.

Author Index

Association for Computational Linguistics
209 N. Eighth Street
Stroudsburg, Pennsylvania 18360

CURRAN ASSOCIATES INC.
proceedings.com

ISBN 979-8-3313-0167-5

9 798331 301675